THE IDEA OF THE THEATER
IN LATIN CHRISTIAN THOUGHT

The Idea of the Theater
in Latin Christian Thought

AUGUSTINE TO THE FOURTEENTH CENTURY

Donnalee Dox

THE UNIVERSITY OF MICHIGAN PRESS
Ann Arbor

2007   2006   2005   2004   4   3   2   1

A CIP catalog record for this book is available from the British Library.

Library of Congress Cataloging-in-Publication Data

Dox, Donnalee.
    The idea of the theater in Latin Christian thought : Augustine to
the fourteenth century / Donnalee Dox.
        p.   cm.
    Includes bibliographical references (p.   ) and index.
    ISBN 0-472-11423-9 (cloth : alk. paper)
    1. Theater—Rome—Historiography.   2. Theater—History—To 500—
Historiography.   3. Theater—History—Medieval, 500–1500—
Historiography.   4. Theater—Religious aspects—Christianity—
History of doctrines—Early church, ca. 30–600.   5. Theater—
Religious aspects—Christianity—History of doctrines—Middle Ages,
600–1500.   6. Christian literature, Early—Latin authors—History
and criticism.   7. Christian literature, Latin (Medieval and
modern)—History and criticism.   I. Title.
    PA6074.D695   2004
    792'0937'0902—dc22   2004003468

For Cary

Acknowledgments

I AM INDEBTED to numerous individuals and organizations. Stipendiary fellowships cosponsored by the Melbern G. Glasscock Center for Humanities Research and the Department of Performance Studies and Program in Religious Studies at Texas A&M University covered research expenses, which allowed for the timely completion of the manuscript. I thank Daniel Bornstein, Peter Lieuwen, and James Rosenheim for their support. Ideas and material that eventually became parts of chapters were accepted for publication as the larger project was taking shape. John Gronbeck-Tedesco (*Journal of Dramatic Theory and Criticism*), Blair Sullivan (*Viator*) and David Román (*Theatre Journal*) saw early explorations of this material into print. Nils Holger Petersen of the Centre for the Study of the Cultural Heritage of Medieval Rituals at the University of Copenhagen sponsored my attendance at the Centre's conference "Genre and Ritual: Traditions and Their Modifications" in 2002, which led to invaluable exchanges with several scholars. Mette Birkedal Bruun, Wim Verbaal, and Jeremy Llewellyn made connections between sources and writers I had overlooked. Their collegiality and scholarly generosity have been exceptional.

Several colleagues read and responded to parts of this manuscript in its formative months. I am deeply indebted to Pavel Blazek, then at Charles University, Prague, whose curiosity about the use of Bartholomew of Bruges in theater history set in motion the inquiry that became chapter 4. Comments from Bonnie Kent at the University of California at Irvine and John Christian Laursen at the University of California at Riverside were particularly helpful in the refinement of chapter 4. Constant Mews, of Monash University in Melbourne, prompted my more serious consideration of theological contexts for the texts considered here, during the conference "Culture and Belief" at Monash University in 2001. Constant's intellectual breadth is inspirational. The responses of John O. Ward at the Australia–New Zealand Association for Medieval and Early Modern Studies in 2001 and Nancy Struever at the joint conference of the Medieval Academy and the Arizona Center for Medieval and Renaissance Studies in 2000 helped give direction to chapter 3. Philipp Rosemann's enthusiastic response to my paper at the 2001 Texas Medieval Association meeting prompted me to continue working on Augustine. The interest of these collegial and rigorous scholars gave vitality to ideas that might otherwise have languished.

For their tireless attention to detail, Joy Richmond and Cathy Dineen deserve much credit for the initial preparation of the manuscript. Christina Francis and Neil Waldrop at the Arizona Center for Medieval and Renaissance Studies assisted in the final stages of its preparation, and I am grateful for their particular areas of expertise. Warren Smith at the University of New Mexico assisted directly with many of the Latin translations, though I take full responsibility for any errors in translation. My sincere gratitude goes to the anonymous readers for the University of Michigan Press. Their criticisms, suggestions, and queries strengthened the manuscript and saved me from many mistakes. From his immediate interest in this topic through the completion of the project, I could not have asked for a more thoughtful, careful, and efficient editor than Christopher Collins. Sarah Mann patiently answered my numerous questions, even when the answers should have been self-evident. Mary Hashman has my deep appreciation for her kindness and patience.

Two constants have sustained the construction of this book. Texas A&M's Department of Performance Studies, under the leadership of Peter Lieuwen, and the collegial environment of the Melbern G. Glasscock Center for Humanities Research provided excellent circumstances in which to work. The last words of appreciation—and they are woefully insufficient—go to Cary J. Nederman. The depth of Cary's commitment to medieval scholarship and intellectual history gave this project a context and, above all, meaning. Day in and day out, Cary has been a source of clarity. For his tolerance for tedium and well-placed provocations, I am grateful beyond measure.

Contents

Abbreviations

AL   Laurentius Minio-Paluello, ed. *Aristoteles Latina.* Vol. 33. Brussels: Desclée de Brouwer, 1968.

Baur   Ludwig Baur, ed. *De divisione philosophiae,* by Dominicus Gundisalvi. Beiträge zur Geschichte der Philosophie und Theologie des Mittelalters, vol. 4, nos. 2–3. Münster: Aschendorffschen Buchhandlung, 1903.

CCCM   *Corpus Christianorum Continuatio Medaevalis.* Turnhout: Brepols, 1967–.

CCSL   *Corpus Christianorum Series Latina.* Turnhout: Brepols, 1954–.

Hanssens   *Amalarii episcopie opera liturgica omnia.* Edited by Johannes Michael Hanssens. 3 vols. Vatican City: Biblioteca Apostolica Vaticana, 1950.

Keats-Rohan   John of Salisbury. *Ioannis Saresberiensis: Policraticus I–IV.* Edited by K. S. B. Keats-Rohan. *Corpus Christianorum Continuatio Mediaevalis.* vol. 118. Turnhout: Brepols, 1993.

Lutz   Remigius of Auxerre. *Remigii autissiodorensis commentum in Martianum Capellam Libri I and II.* 2 vols. Edited by Cora E. Lutz. Leiden: E. J. Brill, 1962–65.

Migne *PL*   Jacques-Paul Migne, ed. *Patrologia Latina.* 221 vols. Paris: Apud Garnier Fratres, 1844–64.

Sheridan   Alan of Lille. *Anticlaudianus; or the Good and Perfect Man.* Translated by James J. Sheridan. Toronto: Pontifical Institute of Mediaeval Studies, 1973.

Introduction

MUCH HAS BEEN DONE in the last two decades to assert the value of
medieval theater, performance, performing bodies (living and dead), modes
of representation, and texts independent of the consciously theatrical presentation of classical plays in the Renaissance.[1] Vibrant performance traditions
associated with medieval ceremonies, civic rituals, tournaments, festivals,
folk traditions, and religious rites, as well as *ludi,* have been explored for their
technical virtuosity and variations on mimesis. Recent scholarship in theater
history and historiography has looked outside the framework of "drama" and
"theater" defined by scripts, playhouses, performance rubrics, and records of
performances and beyond a developmental model that culminates in modern
realism. Interest in the material conditions in which medieval texts were produced, with particular interest in corporeality, has also opened new territory
for investigating medieval performance. Studies in the last two decades have
explored how documents of performance encode attitudes toward gender,
race, class, cultural alterity, cultural hegemony, religious beliefs, and power
relationships.[2]

The interest in popular, as opposed to literary, culture has drawn attention to a range of performative expressions that operated on the margins of or
in resistance to the official written culture of European institutions, especially
the church. New work on medieval performance has turned, for example, to
spectacles of torture (Jody Enders, *The Medieval Theater of Cruelty: Rhetoric,
Memory, Violence*) and the performative aspects of the human subject (Claire
Sponsler, *Drama and Resistance: Bodies, Goods, and Theatricality in Late
Medieval England*). Other studies have looked to variations on mimesis, con-

sidering the Host and relics as performative demonstrations (Caroline Walker Bynum, *The Resurrection of the Body in Western Christianity, 200–1336*), the corporeality of music (Bruce W. Holsinger, *Music, Body, and Desire in Medieval Culture: Hildegard of Bingen to Chaucer*), and distinct modes of representation (Michal Kobialka, *This Is My Body: Representational Practices in the Early Middle Ages*). The historiography of medieval theater, with its traditional trajectory into Renaissance humanism, has also been reassessed in relation to specific social transformations (Sarah Beckwith, *Signifying God: Social Relation and Symbolic Act in the York Corpus Christi Plays*) and local culture (Gail McMurray Gibson, *The Theater of Devotion: East Anglian Drama and Society in the Late Middle Ages*). Research in theatrical performance of medieval plays has continued in studies of the communicative power of physical gesture (Clifford Davidson, ed., *Gesture in Medieval Drama and Art*) and staging (Victor I. Scherb, *Staging Faith: East Anglian Drama in the Later Middle Ages*, and Dunbar H. Ogden, *The Staging of Drama in the Medieval Church*).[3]

The present study departs from current interests in the materiality of medieval theater practices and historiography to look at theater in medieval thought. Periods of intellectual renewal in the Western church were marked by reevaluations of classical learning and innovations in Christian thought, coincident with religious reform.[4] Collisions between classical knowledge and the authority of the Christian Scriptures, and the effort to integrate the two intellectual traditions, are in a sense the spine of the Christian intellectual tradition. Collisions in the late fifteenth century mark a more radical reevaluation of the classical tradition in the arts, literature, and sciences, a more severe challenge to the received knowledge of Catholic Christianity. Indeed, differences between the humanism of the twelfth century and that of the fifteenth are frequently attributed to interpretations of antiquity.[5] The dual impulse to dramatize (as well as read or write) plays on stages and to apply theories such as that offered by Aristotle's *Poetics* to the invention of new performance practices in the fifteenth century is thus well-traveled terrain; this new use of antiquity set in motion a theatrical tradition based on ancient models and distinct from the religious plays of the previous five centuries.

In a thorough essay on Hildegard von Bingen's *Ordo virtutum*, Nils Holger Petersen deals with the fine distinction between medieval drama and Christian ritual set out by Karl Young in 1933.[6] Petersen concludes, quite rightly, that records of medieval liturgical plays and performances show no signs of "a *consciousness of a concept of drama,* or any kind of departure from a liturgical thinking [italics added]."[7] It is precisely the consciousness of "drama" as "theater" in inquiries into human nature and culture that has traditionally separated the theatrical dramas of Renaissance humanism from the liturgical and secular *ludi* of the Middle Ages. Thinkers in the Western church were apparently far less interested in problems of representation than the meaning of representations (an issue that has suffered much under postmodernism and deconstruction).[8] The conscious reconstruction of Greco-Roman theater and drama has long been attributed to a change in intellectual orientation from a theocentric interpretation of the world to an anthropocentric worldview. As theories of mimesis, verisimilitude, and similitude and experiments in optics and architecture were put to use on the new proscenium stages of the Italian and French courts, the Greco-Roman past itself was dramatized for visual consumption in the retelling of pagan myths as dramas. Theater, now more easily distinguished from the improvisational performances of traveling players and spectacles at court or in church pageants by the attention to playwriting, also became a way of abstracting human behavior and setting it out for critical evaluation; fictional characters could reflect the spectators' world without referencing a transcendent authority.[9] With reinterpretations of Aristotle and Horace as guides to stage performance and application of the architectural treatises of Vitruvius to the development of perspective scenery, theater provided a method of inquiry into the past and a strategy for representing the present.

The effects of Renaissance humanism on the history of European theater and drama, and the use of the term *classical* to describe revived Greek or Roman plays by the eighteenth century, have been widely noted and debated.[10] As Ronald W. Vince noted in 1984, the national theaters of the Renaissance and modern drama itself have been regarded as a fusion of ancient Roman and medieval theatrical traditions since the late eighteenth century.[11] In practice, however, this fusion of traditions depended upon the reconception of Roman theater, itself an adaptation of the Greek, as a practice. Greco-Roman theater had to be taken from its place as a historical artifact and reconstituted as performance that was both an intellectual and literary activity. But the evidence is clear: a conscious desire to recoup the stages and dramas of ancient theater—now distinct from rhetoric and oratory— took hold in the sixteenth century. "Theater" and "drama" could thereafter be referred to Europe's Greco-Roman, rather than Christian, heritage. This is the crux of Petersen's observation that the Middle Ages did not construe theater in its own right as craft, artistry, or intellectual inquiry that was authored, authorized, and validated by human ingenuity.

The present study does not take issue with these historical narratives, but sets out to level the playing field, so to speak. It takes medieval discourses on theater out of their familiar frames (as records of Greco-Roman performance practices, evidence of medieval performance, points in the development of Western theater, and tensions between creative innovation and church authority) to explore the status of Greco-Roman theater in medieval thought. In other words, this book treats documents usually brought into play in the history of theater as moments in European intellectual history.

Certainly there was no shortage of information about Greco-Roman theater in the Middle Ages, and medieval scholars were well versed in ancient literature (including plays) as well as the affective power of oratory, rhetoric, and dialectic. Certainly, theologians adapted all manner of ancient treatises on rhetoric, grammar, dialectic, and natural philosophy to their understanding of a world redeemed by Christ. And certainly the Christian theology of the Incarnation lent itself extraordinarily well to various kinds of mimetic activity—symbolic impersonation in rituals, imitation of biblical figures in civic or church *ludi,* role-playing in mock combats, make-believe in mummings and folk plays, and later the stock characters of Roman comedy in the *commedia dell'arte.* But, despite these conditions, which would seem to make the Middle Ages ripe for adapting theatrical traditions from the ancient world, a link between theater and dramatic texts was not made in practice.[12] As Marcia Colish points out, ancient drama was treated as literature and was not appropriated as stage performance into medieval thought or practice.[13]

A pervasive "antitheatrical prejudice" in the church hierarchy is one explanation for this disconnect, but it is ultimately unsatisfactory. Mimetic activity (if not the demonstration of E. K. Chambers's now much-maligned "mimetic instinct") continued in and outside of religious institutions throughout the Middle Ages. Further, the church itself supported and encouraged effective preaching and visual reenactments as a way of engaging the laity and the less intellectually inclined of its own brethren as often as it railed against performative excesses. As Ronald Vince has quite rightly advised, "We should recognize not only that Churchmen distinguished between the 'regular' Roman theater and that represented by the *mimes* and *histriones* and *joculatores,* but that they made a similar distinction between popular, often sacrilegious and scurrilous, entertainment and the Christian drama performed as an act of worship or instruction to the faithful."[14]

Here, I suggest that a major reason medieval thinkers did not construe drama as theatrical performance lies in the ways thought was organized in the Middle Ages from the late classical transmitters through the Scholastics. Theater (as a performance practice and cultural institution) was initially distinguished from poetry, rhetoric, oratory, reading, and writing. At the height of the Scholastic period, early in the fourteenth century, this categorical distinction began to break down. This dissolution became one component in an array of changes that opened an intellectual space in which Petersen's "consciousness of a concept of drama" and theatrical representation was made. In yet another discursive frame, distinctions among medieval, early modern, and Renaissance blur.

With this basic thesis stated, several points must be made about the parameters of this study. First, this is an inquiry into Greco-Roman theater's status in Christian thought at specific historical points. Though medieval thinkers did not take up a systematic, ongoing, critical conversation about theater, theater came out in Christian writings as a function of other theological, epistemological, liturgical, or social concerns. My question goes to the function of theater in written discourse, rather than what medieval documents might tell us about medieval theatrical practice or Greco-Roman theater. Second is the issue of medieval representation. Past and present assumptions about mimesis have been central to contemporary discussions of medieval performance. In most cases, I will cite secondary literature in this rich and complex area of inquiry in order to keep the focus on the intellectual context in which the documents themselves operated. Third, the organization of this topic nuances the history of medieval theater in the West within the history of Latin Christian thought. This book does not offer a definitive explanation for a transition between medieval and early modern methods of knowing and analyzing, but sets out another pathway through the liminal territory between historical periods. The inquiry supplements rather than challenges recent studies that draw different conclusions from some of the same documents, for example, Enders's *Rhetoric and the Origins of Medieval Drama*, which presents strong connections between medieval drama and forensic oratory, and Kobialka's *This Is My Body*, which examines the specificity of representational strategies in a disparate array of early texts.[15]

One of the major problems in studies of medieval performance has been the distinction (if indeed there was one) between ritual and drama. Are we dealing, as David Bevington asks, with ritual drama or dramatic ritual?[16] Much of the discussion about medieval *ludi*—whether connected by scholarly inquiry to ritual, folk traditions, spectacles, or oratory—has relied upon modern criteria for drama: action, usually scripted first, presented through mimetic dialogue, gesture, and costume in a designated playing space via impersonation (role-playing).[17] Despite the prevalence of "performance" and "performativity" in poststructuralist analysis, here I will deliberately maintain a lexical distinction between "theater" (performance, building, institution, the process of putting on shows or plays) and "drama" (play script, playwriting conventions, narrative structure, genre, thematic organization). I will use "dramatization" to mean the process by which a script, scenario, or idea is re-presented (or realized) as a theatrical performance.

And finally, a note about method. Variations on the Latin *ludi* appear throughout the Middle Ages to describe what we now think of as "theatrical activity." Here, I turn to documents not as clues to medieval theatrical performances or ritual practices, but as indicators of particular understandings of Greco-Roman theater and drama in the Middle Ages. I am interested in how a given medieval document performs theater, so to speak, rather than what a document reveals about medieval theatrical performance. How does a document define or use the idea of Greco-Roman theater? Are judgments made? If so, on what grounds? What relationship does the idea of theater have to present social practices? Is theater construed as a past or present practice? If theater is used as a metaphor or analogy, how does the analogy work and what exactly does it signify? Why was Greco-Roman theater not adapted into Christian practice when other aspects of pagan learning and culture were?

Too often, medieval discussions of theater are divided into strands: those that can be culled for information about medieval performance (the liturgical allegories of Amalarius of Metz and Honorius Augustodunensis, for example), those that offer information about theatrical practice in the Greco-Roman world (the *Etymologiae* of Isidore of Seville, among others), and those that indicate an ecclesiastical "antitheatrical" bias, such as Gerhoh of Reichersberg's twelfth-century rant against liturgical histrionics or Augustine's polemics. But when these strands are taken chronologically rather than thematically, and are not bound into the search for a developing theatrical tradition, medieval discourses on theater and theatricality reveal significant variations in the relationship between ancient theater and Christian thought that (not surprisingly) follow major shifts in the Christian intellectual tradition (the patristic period, Carolingian reform, twelfth-century reform and renewal, Scholasticism). The juxtaposition of the familiar documents discussed here shows how answers to the questions posed above vary from writer to writer, context to context. As this study demonstrates, the performance of ancient theater in medieval thought is more nuanced than is acknowledged in studies of theater history.

Chapters 1 and 2 demonstrate that categories of Christian thought through the tenth century effectively separate theater (as understood through Greek and Roman sources) from Christian representation. Chapter 1, "The

Idea of a Theater in Late Antiquity," examines Augustine's response to theater as a material practice that produced a dangerous confusion of mind. But his analysis of Roman theater is multifaceted. Passages dealing with theater in *Confessions, The City of God against the Pagans, Concerning the Teacher,* and *On Christian Doctrine* show Augustine's personal antipathy toward heightened emotion and sexual feeling and the pagan roots of theater, but also theater's failure as a potential Christian sign system. By the seventh century, and in contrast to Augustine's personal response and Christian analysis, Isidore of Seville relegates theater to the status of a historical artifact. Based on classical authors and influenced by the Christian fathers, the *Etymologiae* defines, rather than judges, the ancient world (including its theater). The concern for representing truth (and for truthful representation) persists as a problem of perception in the encyclopedic tradition, but the emphasis is on categorizing theatrical practice with games, contests, athletic events, and debate. These two early treatments of theater—one experiential and theoretical, the other documentary and categorical—provide Christian thought with a concept of theater as a specifically Roman (as adapted from Greek) practice.

Chapter 2, "Transmission and Transformation," focuses on the ninth-century controversy over Amalarius of Metz's allegorical interpretations of the Mass. Modern theater history, especially when invested in finding ritual roots for theatrical practices, takes Amalarius's *Liber officialis* as a distinctly dramatic and theatrical interpretation of the Christian liturgy. Amalarius's critics, namely Agobard of Lyons and Deacon Florus of Lyons, condemned Amalarius's writings as heretical in part because of the theatricality—understood as pagan—they implied for the liturgy. The more pressing concern, however, was that Amalarius's allegories fragmented the imagery of the Mass, especially that of the body of Christ. Chapter 2 places Amalarius between the Christianized interpretations of theater in Remigius of Auxerre and Rabanus Maurus and examines the controversy as a representational issue.

Chapter 3, "Renaissance and Reorientation," shows that by the twelfth century, references to theater and theatricality are distributed more widely in Christian writings as a metaphor or illustration (some positive, some negative). Chapter 3 juxtaposes texts that are often treated independently in theater history and criticism. While different discursive contexts produced different ideas about theater and theatricality, the writings of Honorius Augustodunensis, John of Salisbury, and Hugh of St. Victor are marked by a consistent understanding of ancient theater as part of the material, human world rather than a theological or philosophical problem. Honorius is known to theater historians for comparing the Mass to a theatrical tragedy in the passage *De tragoediis* from the liturgical treatise *Gemma animae. De tragoediis* assumes that its readers have a working knowledge of ancient theater, and the chapter is consistent with other allegories in its explanation of parts of the Mass, the function of the celebrants, Christ's fight against opposition, and the gestures, objects, and rubrics of the Mass. Unlike Amalarius, however, Honorius uses ancient theater unapologetically as an analogy for the performance of the Mass, providing Benedictine priests with a model for communicative presentation of the Mass.

Among the seven mechanical arts listed in Hugh of St. Victor's *Didascalicon*, only theater is described as an archaic mechanical art. This is a distinctly different approach both to theatrical representation (entertainment itself as a cathartic endeavor for spectators) and to the application of the ancient past in the Christian present: Hugh gives no contemporary twelfth-century parallel to ancient theater, such as the Mass or liturgical drama. But, like *De tragoediis,* the *Didascalicon* comfortably integrates theater into Christian thought, though as an idea rather than a practice.

Augustine's problem with true and false representation returns in John of Salisbury's use of theater in the *Policraticus* as a metaphor for man's passage through earthly life. Based on Petronius's comparison of friendship to stage illusion in the *Satyricon,* John of Salisbury suggests that the thronging of the profane multitudes is more like a stage comedy than it is real life, and that life on earth is a comedy where one person forgets his own role and plays another's. John of Salisbury brings the knowledge of theater transmitted through ancient texts and the encyclopedic tradition to bear directly on the life of the Christian self. There is an underlying assumption of verisimilitude in John of Salisbury's references to theater. Ideal behavior and a precise moral compass are compromised by theatrical representation.

The thirteenth century saw the introduction of versions of Aristotle's *Poetics* into Latin discourse, where it had remarkably little impact. Chapter 4, "From Poetics to Performance," deals with the positioning in Scholastic discourse of Aristotle's description of Greek theater in the *Poetics.* Had the *Poetics* followed the transmission patterns of other Aristotelian texts in the twelfth and thirteenth centuries, a proliferation of translations, commentaries, *expositio,* and citations would testify to demand for the treatise. There are but twenty-four thirteenth-century copies of Hermannus Alemannus's translation of Averroës's *Middle Commentary on the Poetics* (1256) and two of William of Moerbeke's Latin translation of Aristotle's text from the Greek (1278). Hermannus Alemannus's translation of the Arabic commentary, though far removed from Aristotle's original, was certainly accessible (if not wildly popular) in the context of the medieval *Organon*. Moerbeke's translation of the *Poetics*, on the other hand, gave no indication that Aristotle had construed poetry as a discipline of logic. Nor did Moerbeke's translation of the *Poetics* fit the descriptions of ancient theater in the encyclopedias, the *artes poetica* tradition, the practice of rhetoric and oratory, or logic. Based on thirteenth-century translations of the *Poetics*, the Scholastic tradition creates a new and specific intellectual nuance for ancient theater as logic (distinct from popular performance, encyclopedic documentation, allegorical interpretations of ritual, the practice of the self in daily life, literary genres and rhetoric, and the mechanical arts), but fails to engage it.

Chapter 4 also looks at a little-known fourteenth-century transcription of the *Poetics* as a significant development in the treatment of ancient theater as the presentation of drama. Applications of Aristotle's *Poetics* to performance are frequently cited as a pivotal break between the religiously oriented drama of the Middle Ages and the consciously constructed and self-conscious theater of European secular courts and schools, and the idea that theatrical similitude and verisimilitude are ways of knowing truth. Bartholomew of Bruges's 1307 commentary on Hermannus's translation of Averroës's *Middle Commentary on the Poetics*, the *Brevis expositio supra poetriam*, I suggest, is part of an ongoing reorganization of thought in which theater can serve that purpose. Bartholomew's text, which is almost never mentioned in studies of theater history and dramatic criticism, is not a gloss on Averroës's commentary but on Aristotle's words.

Bartholomew begins an inquiry into theatrical mimesis as a distinctive form of artifice and, at the same time, places theatrical representation solidly in the context of the Aristotelian corpus, and thus as a method of philosophical inquiry. Through Bartholomew's gloss, the idea that dramatic poetry could actually be a method for distinguishing truth from falsehood, and good from evil, in practice entered medieval Scholastic thought. In Bartholomew's commentary, poetry becomes a form of logical argumentation when it produces an image of someone who is good and honest, or bad and dishonest. Thus, poetry is productive, rather than persuasive, and is both the art and science of the instrument that teaches knowledge of truth.

Chapter 4 demonstrates how the *Brevis expositio supra poetriam* marks a distinct shift in the position of ancient theater within the categories of medieval thought. The *Brevis expositio* itself was not widely read enough to be considered an influence on later interpretations of the *Poetics* as a guide to theatrical practice. It does, however, indicate a concept of theatrical representation that is corporeal and mimetic, but not connected to ritual or directly applicable to any number of medieval forms of performance. Bartholomew's commentary suggests a willingness to expand the domain of Scholastic logic to include theatrical representation as a kind of dialectic, on the order of rhetoric. In its emphasis on the productive and imagistic, the *Brevis expositio supra poetriam* marks a reorientation from deductive reasoning to verification by contingent experience that has heretofore gone unnoticed. The Middle Ages, until the early fourteenth century, thus perpetuated a far greater range of interpretations of Greco-Roman theatrical representation than is generally recognized.

Three criteria have generally distinguished the humanistic theater of the sixteenth century from that of the Middle Ages: playwriting on an Aristotelian model, reconception of verisimilitude as *veritas* rather than probability, and mimesis. The conclusion of the present study shows how each of these criteria surfaces in medieval writings within a larger discourse on discerning truth from falsehood rather than the reconstruction of theater as a material practice. The emergence of mimetic dramas in the early modern period appears, in light of this study, as a reconfiguration, not a rediscovery, of European understandings of its classical heritage.[18]

CHAPTER ONE

The Idea of a Theater in Late Antiquity

Augustine's Critique and Isidore's History

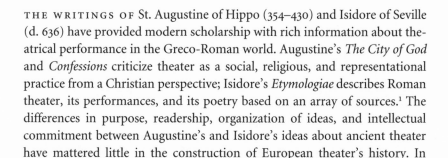

THE WRITINGS OF St. Augustine of Hippo (354–430) and Isidore of Seville (d. 636) have provided modern scholarship with rich information about theatrical performance in the Greco-Roman world. Augustine's *The City of God* and *Confessions* criticize theater as a social, religious, and representational practice from a Christian perspective; Isidore's *Etymologiae* describes Roman theater, its performances, and its poetry based on an array of sources.[1] The differences in purpose, readership, organization of ideas, and intellectual commitment between Augustine's and Isidore's ideas about ancient theater have mattered little in the construction of European theater's history. In Christianity's intellectual tradition, however, the differences between Augustine's and Isidore's writings on theater are pronounced.

Augustine's zealous condemnation of theater as a debauched social activity rooted in Roman polytheism was grounded in his experience of the behavior (on and off the stage) that theatrical shows encouraged. Generations away from the plays and pantomimes of Augustine's Carthage and Rome, Isidore documented theater and theatrical practice as a Christian historian. Theater had become an artifact of the old world, an idea that could be transmitted along with other Christian assessments of pagan learning. Unlike rhetoric, oratory, and literary genres (including drama), Latin Christian thought would not find theater—as a performance practice—of significant concern or interest in and of itself. But whether or not Augustine and Isidore had their facts right about how theater was done in the Greco-Roman world, they created a space for ancient theater in Christian thought.[2] Chapter 1 and the subsequent chapters of this study take medieval discourses on ancient theater out of their familiar place in the history of Western European theater and drama in order to trace the transmission of ideas about theater in the context of a developing intellectual tradition. This first chapter identifies how two writers of late antiquity, Augustine and Isidore, present theater differently in relation to their own intellectual projects.[3]

Augustine, the Christian Person, and Theatrical Representation

Augustine discusses theater in four of his major texts—*Confessions, The City of God, Concerning the Teacher,* and *On Christian Doctrine*—as well as in occasional sermons and soliloquies. He is responding to the *ludi* performed in permanent or (more often) temporary theater structures that were built throughout the Roman Empire (with raised stages, *scaenae frons* replacing the Greek *skene* building, and a semicircular orchestra), as well as to the spectacles of the circuses and amphitheaters. Though the religious aspects of Roman theater, especially their associations with festivals, diminished during the empire, the statues, effigies, and altars that kept the gods in full view in the theaters clearly marked theater as the domain of the pagan gods.[4] Theater figures prominently in Augustine's *Confessions* as a site of moral and physical debauchery, and *The City of God* construes theater as a social practice inappropriate for Christian participation on the grounds of its close ties with pagan religion. *Concerning the Teacher* and *On Christian Doctrine,* documents cited much less frequently in theater history, briefly suggest theater as a sign system inadequate for representing Christian things *(res)*.[5] Together, these four texts outline the logical reasons why Christianity cannot tolerate theater or theatrical representation (as Augustine experienced and understood it).

Augustine's attitude toward theater has often been tied to his rejection of the lust and passions that, as he writes in *Confessions,* dominated his life prior to his embrace of Christian chastity.[6] Augustine's reasoning, however, goes further than his second- and third-century predecessors—namely, Tertullian—in demonstrating exactly how and why theater and theatrical representation were fundamentally incompatible with a Christian view of the world. Three themes run through his arguments against theater (as distinct from dramatic poetry, rhetoric, oratory, or music): theatrical shows encourage bad behavior (solipsism, lust, devotion to actors, and uncharitable acts); theater is so rooted in pagan religion that a Christian city could not sustain it as an institution; and theatrical representation interferes with Christians' ability to know God.

Augustine understood theater as a social reality in a way later Christians could not. Theater was as much a part of the social fabric of the empire as was the status of Christians in imperial North Africa.[7] Theaters were physical places, and performances were regular events. Actors were visible presences in Roman cities, and their affective power on the stages appealed to Christians as well as to pagans.[8] Theater was thus one of the most visible demonstrations of pagan culture at which a zealous Christian might launch a critique.[9]

Perhaps no single passage from Augustine's writings better encapsulates the three dimensions of Augustine's thinking about theater than the following:

> The actors do not fail to portray even the most ignoble acts of the gods by means of their comic art; but, clearly, the priests fail when, in their purportedly sacred rites, they endeavour to portray the gods as having an honour which does not exist.[10]

By this definition, theater is a misguided human craft in which performers impersonate gods as if they were human, ignoring completely the Christian mystery of a single God made flesh and represented in the communal meal of the Eucharist. The craft of acting is thus an overtly false mode of signification: actors deliberately impersonate a false pantheon and present it as real, then undercut the sanctity of the reality by lampooning their gods. Theater is distinguishable from pagan rituals only because priests, as opposed to actors, take the gods seriously and try to represent them with dignity. Yet the priests are ultimately no better than stage actors; they represent religious and social forces opposed to Christianity. If, as Ramsay MacMullen points out, fourth-century Christian monotheism had no place for the superhuman beings of the Roman pantheon, how much less could a Christian tolerate their impersonation by obviously human actors?[11]

The son of a Christian mother and a pagan father, Augustine was baptized a Christian in 387 after three years of tutelage under St. Ambrose of Milan. A decade later, as bishop of Hippo and actively engaged in an ongoing battle against heresies and enemies of Christianity, he wrote the autobiographical *Confessions* (397), which analyzes his path to conversion in his early thirties. Book 3 chronicles Augustine's late teenage years in Carthage, where he had sharpened his skills in rhetoric and legal oratory, found Manichaeism, and attended the theaters with enthusiasm.

Marcia L. Colish notes Augustine as the only one of the Latin fathers who applied a truly philosophical mind to the search for Christian truth in pagan sources. His confessed passion for Christian monotheism was no exception, and his memory reconstructed events that could be manipulated for rhetorical effect in service of demonstrating Christianity's truth against the problem of evil. Augustine's intellectual positions, as Colish notes, were tightly bound to his lived experience.[12] What was represented on the theatrical stages of North Africa in the mid–fourth century apparently resonated all too well with Augustine's life experience, without offering the intellectual challenges he found in Greco-Roman rhetoric, law, and philosophy. The matter-spirit dichotomy prevalent in Manichaeism and Neoplatonism is evident in Augustine's criticism of theater—from the feelings the performances inspire to the indulgent materiality of the performances themselves; from the desire to see the immortal soul as the image of God to the soul's culpability in its fall from God; from the belief in Christ as the universal way to Christian truth to reconciling Christian truth with the truth proposed by Plotinus.[13] In the tradition of Tertullian and Ambrose, Augustine sees beyond the mendacity of the material world and, through reason derived from belief, perceives God's truth in the words of the Scripture and worldly signs.[14] Augustine admits that mere reason shows him the illusion of truth. "How could I have seen this," he asks, "for my vision was limited with my eyes, to material bodies; with my mind, to phantasms?"[15]

Confessions, unlike *The City of God* and *On Christian Doctrine,* makes autobiography and self-revelation authoritative testaments to the great divide between pagan theater and Christian representation. Book 3 focuses immediately on Augustine's lusts for sex and comfort in late adolescence, which left him sick in his soul, blind to God, and unable to respond to the suffering of others. In this context, he describes his desire for the theater as a lust for emotional intensity, a sin—along with pride and sensual pleasure—on a Plotinian triangle of iniquities.[16] The attraction of theater and the emotional affect it produced were as powerful and dangerous as his sexual appetites. Augustine condemns theater because his desire of it in his youth had clouded his spiritual sight.

The emotional intensity of the theater played out in ways that, in Augustine's retrospective, seemed only to simulate true feeling. He confesses that the theater, "filled with depictions of my miseries and with tinder for my own fire, completely carried me away."[17] The superficial, vicarious emotions encouraged by the theater impeded his Christian consciousness and kept him from perceiving God's truth. In *Confessions,* he recoils from the memory of living a false life without God, in which reason failed when confronted with the lies of the stage. He had enjoyed the vicarious pangs of sorrow he saw on the stages in Carthage—the more intense the feeling is, the better the experience is. With an equally powerful desire to confess, he rehearses the memory of a perverse and shallow pleasure offered by the stage.

> Hence arose my love of suffering, not of the kind that would affect me deeply (for I had no desire to be afflicted with the things which I saw), but such as would supply, as it were, a superficial scratching as I listened to those fictions. Yet, an inflamed sore, and putrefaction, and blood poisoning followed, as if from the scratches of finger nails. Such was my life—or was it life, O my God?[18]

Not only had Augustine enjoyed watching love stories and tragedies performed before his eyes (troubling enough in itself), but he had also relished the sexual feelings they produced—the very proclivities his postconfession mind found repugnant.[19] Those fictional scenarios, structured in narratives and set out for display with living bodies, showed him only too clearly that human behavior untouched by Christian revelation was inherently flawed. The stage showed Augustine his own, deeply flawed behavior.

When the Augustine of *Confessions* measures himself against stage imagery and measures stage imagery against his now Christian soul, he is forced to confess that his soul suffered far more damage than pleasure in the theater. Augustine, the Christian, realizes that the world mirrored from the shiny surface of the proscenium was an unnatural world, a world without the Christian God, seen through the godless eyes of his youth.

Augustine's self-critique is itself a kind of performance of self-criticism. The temporal pleasures of the theater had lulled him into unchristian solipsism, fascination with his own sexuality, and a passion for fiction. Theater had perverted both his logic and his emotions. He pities his degraded self, as well as those who remain in the seductive hold of the theater and those who share joy and grief with lovers on the stage. Far from the now familiar Aristotelian idea that watching dramatic performances purges a person of negative emotions through a healthy catharsis,[20] Augustine concludes that the audience's emotions are as contrived as the shows themselves. Just as he genuinely pities theater audiences, he realizes that pity for theatrical characters is merely contrived emotion. To his Christian mind, the false emotions theater elicits (including pity) are misdirected; the desire for meretricious pity is nothing less than unchristian. Christian reason reveals that theater abuses the human capacity for pity, because "though he who sorrows for the unfortunate is commended for a work of charity, he who is sincere in his compassions would much prefer to have no reason for feeling sorrow."[21]

With his days in Carthage at a safe distance and in the security of his appointment as bishop of Hippo, Augustine makes the Roman theaters a site from which he can perform his confession. If God alone gives life joy, Augustine's Christian reason leads to the conclusion that if he (like so many others) had enjoyed going to the theaters, he had done so in a state of godless misery. Only in such a state could he have found pleasure there. His youthful self becomes the character to be pitied, his memory the stage, and Christianity the agent that transforms the lie of his youth to the truth of his Christian maturity. As a rhetorical device, the Roman theater—well-known to his readers as a social institution, a mode of representation, and a common form of entertainment—allows him to make sharp distinctions between spirit and matter, truth and falsehood, body and soul, Christian monotheism and pagan polytheism.

Part of Augustine's problem is that theater—whether judged as a social practice, as a mode of representation, or by its entertainment value—is indistinguishable from the culture that produces it.[22] From Augustine's descriptions, theater offers representations of the pagan world. But it is also—and perhaps this is more dangerous from Augustine's point of view—a product of that world. As both representation and product of Roman culture, theater is inextricable from a world Augustine had rejected as illusory, sensual, and seductively anti-Christian. Thus, theater had to be distinguished from other, more useful products of classical thought. Unlike rhetoric, with its performative extension in oratory, narrative poetry, and music, all of which offered intellectual resources for Christian thought, Augustine could not (or saw no reason to) synthesize pagan theater with Christian learning.[23] For Augustine, theater's inherently deceptive nature could only confirm and reify a world inhabited by pagan souls to whom the truth of the Scriptures had not been revealed. Whereas Augustine could adapt classical rhetoric by investing its mechanics of persuasion with a transcendent knowledge of God's word incarnate,[24] theater offered no such useful mechanism. He could not tease theater out of its cultural function as popular entertainment and let it serve Christian ends.[25] Thus, any soul who could enjoy watching imaginary lovers on stage remained, by definition, unchristian.[26]

Augustine claims knowledge of commiseration in the carnal acts, amorous misery, and brutal revenge plots shown in the theaters and sets that knowledge against the truer satisfactions of a Christian soul. But his problem

goes beyond theater's unhealthy appeal to bodily functions and base emotions—to theater's challenge to reason. In *Confessions,* Augustine's pity for
the sinful lovers who appeared on stage and his unwitting identification with
the scripted scenarios of love created a serious intellectual conundrum.[27]
Prior to his conversion, Augustine claims he could not distinguish between
what he saw on the stage and his own experience. His conversion gave him a
kind of critical distance from which to evaluate both theatrical representation
and personal experience. He thus found himself caught in Aristotle's
dilemma, taking pleasure in admiring representations of pain and sorrow.[28]
The result, for a Christian, is an ethical problem and a perversion of logic:
stage plays allow people to remain impassive to sufferings and misfortunes
that should otherwise incite them to action. Theater establishes a dynamic
between an observer and a sufferer precisely opposite to that demanded by
Christianity. The more convincing the suffering is, the greater are an audience member's enjoyment and praise for the author and performers. Augustine explains that a member of the theater audience "is not incited to give
help; rather, he is simply enticed to feel sorrow: the more sorrowful he
becomes, the more highly does he regard the author of those presentations."
Augustine continues:

> Thus, if these calamitous events of the men of old, or of fiction, are so
> presented that the spectator is not moved to sorrow, he goes away
> scornful and critical; but, if he does become sorrowful, he remains,
> giving full attention and enjoying it.[29]

Augustine finds that the counterfeit emotions of the theater fail to provoke
proper Christian compassion. How authentic or legitimate, then, is the pity
aroused for fictional characters who suffer in imaginary scenes, when there is
no opportunity for action? Pity remains lodged in the soul of the observer,
with no outlet other than the enjoyment of the emotion itself and with no
reinforcement of Christianity's ethical demand for compassion. Augustine
sees not just the sinfulness of the lusts represented on the stage but the more
severe sin produced by watching that lust: self-involvement. Theatrical
tragedies turned the mind inward, rather than outward in compassion for
others.[30] For Augustine, there is no Brechtian form of or use for theater to
give spectators a critical distance and allow them to judge their own short-
comings as compassionate Christians (Augustine himself is the exception,
and he presents his self-awareness as coming from God, not from any quality
of the theater itself).

Theater failed to make the Romans, blind to the Christian Scriptures, aware of their sins. But Augustine also argues for theater's uncanny ability to represent human failures accurately. His attraction to the theater was precisely the anticipation of watching his own unhappiness (especially in love) reflected empathetically. The critical distance of Christian knowledge allows him to see that if one responded to the suffering presented on the stage by actors and turned one's mind inward as plays (unlike rhetoric) encouraged, one could not hope to respond to real suffering with genuine Christian feeling. Any pleasure derived from the illusions produced by the theater was as unacceptable to Christians as the illusion of the pagan pantheon.[31] Again, theatrical representation is judged inherently false and dismissed on that ground.

Augustine also reveals theater—and with it the rest of pagan culture—to be a mock reality, an earthly obsession that substitutes for the spiritual joy of knowing God through Scripture. The cultish devotion audiences paid to performers, who made their living on the margins of Roman society, cast theater further away from proper Christian activities. Without the critical distance of Christianity, theater could only show an illusory, godless world and could only produce the shallowest of pleasures.

The moral judgments Augustine directed at the content of Roman theatrical shows were exactly those for which his mature Christian self disparages his uncommitted youth—sensuality, depravity, lasciviousness, lewdness, lust, desire for material things, and veneration of performers. These are the characteristics usually invoked in discussions of Augustine's "antitheatrical" stance and usually associated with the form of Christian chastity Augustine certainly embraced. But in a subtler and more intellectually substantial way, theater presented Augustine with a perfect diagram for distinguishing between truth and falsehood as well as a metaphor for contrasting the true life of Christian faith with the deceptions of Roman religion. The language with which Augustine describes theater as illusory and deceptive parallels that with which he thinks through similitude in *Soliloquies.*

> Food in dreams is very much like food when one is awake, but sleepers are not nourished by it, for they are asleep. But, those viands were not in any way like Thee, as Thou has spoken to me now, for they were bodily phantasms, false bodies. Those true bodies, which we see with bodily vision either in the sky or on earth, are more certain than they. We see these things as the beasts and birds do, and they are more certain than when we imagine them. Again, we picture these in imagination more certainly than when we form from them conceptions of

other things, greater and unlimited, which are completely non-existent. On such empty things was I then nourished, and I was not nourished.[32]

Could manufactured stage characters ever make the image of the immaterial God Augustine now says was his true desire? Augustine's problem in *Confessions* is in part that the stage satisfied his emotions only temporarily and always falsely. Watching love stories acted out threw his sexuality into relief and exposed his libidinal excesses to the scrutiny of his consciousness. But more profoundly, he is disturbed not by what is represented on the stages but by what is not. Ultimately, actors on a stage could not satisfy his desire for a single God any more than prostitutes could satisfy his body or Plotinus his mind. Long after the events he describes, he comes to understand that his desire for God was far more powerful than anything the stages could evoke. Man might be made in God's image, but theater cannot make an image of the Christian God.

Confessions uses theater in part as a rhetorical device, a reference to popular culture with which Augustine can contrast his preconversion blindness with an enlightened, Christian worldview. This familiar, if not ubiquitous, entertainment allowed Augustine to confront the personal difficulties posed by conversion: lust and sexual depravity, solipsism, the danger of misreading pagan signs as truth, the fake quality of life outside Christianity, and how Christian truth can (or cannot) be represented by human craft. A Christian mind, he finds, cannot accommodate what the theater represents. Moreover, because (for Augustine) theatrical plays by definition present lascivious humans and Roman gods in an overtly deceptive way, theater could be of no use to Christian proselytizing.[33] *The City of God* (413–27) undertakes the problem of theater not as a personal memory but as a temporal institution.[34]

"Who of sound mind," Augustine asks in book 4 of *The City of God*, "does not see that, in this case, in submission to the will of malignant demons from whose dominion nothing releases us save the grace of God through Jesus Christ, men were compelled by force to exhibit to the gods plays which right judgment should have declared shameful?"[35] If *Confessions* set up theater as a cipher for Augustine's psyche, the idea of theater's incompatibility with God's heavenly city is the theological heart of his arguments in *The City of God*. Theater, in *The City of God*, is a barometer for the decay of a culture whose laws and customs serve a cancerous pantheon.[36] Rome is a city consumed by love of wealth, whose people neither see nor love the true God.[37]

In response to accusations that Christianity was to blame for the invasion of Rome by the Goths in 406, Augustine set out to reverse the charges against Christians (a project that took fourteen years). Clearly, theater was one of the more accessible and visible expressions of Greco-Roman polytheism when Augustine wrote *The City of God;* he frequently cites theater as evidence in his case that an unruly crowd of hybrid demon-gods is rotting Rome from the inside out.[38] His critique of theater is directed at ingrates who fail to see the truth of Christianity, blame Christ for their suffering, and do not realize that they owe their very survival of the wars to the protection of Christian basilicas.[39]

Roman blindness to the malignant effects of the gods and failure to see Christ are almost mantras for Augustine. The dualistic thinking that pitted God's divine plan against Satan's competing power made the gods a tangible reality as destructive demons who themselves stage battles on earth.[40] Indeed, as Ramsay MacMullen argues, Christianity may very well have been the intellectual force that gave demons legitimacy as agents of malevolence in the everyday world of human survival.[41] Augustine's problems with the pantheon are numerous: the gods cannot help people live better lives,[42] they themselves are morally bankrupt, they have no investment in human affairs, and they have offered humanity no doctrines of faith. Moreover, no one should expect to gain eternal life from gods who allow their own criminal acts to be celebrated in stage shows.[43] Augustine goes to great lengths to dismantle the pantheon, especially the claim that Jupiter's rule constitutes a kind of competing monotheism.[44] The Romans can improve their situation only by abandoning the gods (who have demanded stage plays in their honor) and turning to Christianity.[45]

The problem with theater, according to *The City of God,* is in large part typological. As far as Augustine is concerned, theater is virtually indistinguishable from religious rituals, games, and other spectacles instigated by the gods. "Do not the actors and priests alike represent Priapus as having enormous private parts?" Augustine asks; "When [Priapus] stands still to be adored in the sacred places, is he different from when he runs about in the theatre to be laughed at?"[46] Though they differ in venue, social purpose, and conventions of performance, all such activities are devoted to and inspired by the gods and, therefore, equally anathema to Christianity. Theater comes under Augustine's fire because, unlike combat games and other spectacles, the shows represent the gods directly: "In these games, the vilest actors would sing and act out the part of Jupiter as the corruptor of modesty—and thus please him!"[47] Also, unlike rituals, the theater holds up the gods to jocular ridicule, which, since they take pleasure in seeing their own exploits lampooned by actors, proves to Augustine that the gods themselves are as depraved as the actors who portray them. Varro's descriptions of the myths honored in rituals fuels Augustine's critique that rituals and shows are equally immoral: "The mythical theology, then—that of the theatrical performances, full of unworthiness and vileness—is referred back to the civil: the whole of the mythical theology, rightly judged worthy of condemnation and rejection, is a part of the civil theology, which is deemed worthy to be cultivated and observed!"[48] Augustine gives actors some credit, if perhaps sarcastically, for not revealing on the stage the entire content of the rituals.

Whereas *Confessions* sets theaters as a site from which Augustine can describe his own debauchery, the defense of Christianity in *The City of God* requires a wider range of references. Augustine draws on his experience, on Roman history, and on pagan authors—most prominently Plato, Cicero, and Varro. He has sympathies with Plato's ban on theater and with Cicero's disapproval of Homeric fictions. But to Augustine, any person in his or her right mind (i.e., a mind freed by Christ) would recognize that demons controlled the performers in theatrical shows. Thus, as in the case of the Roman Senate's vote to dismantle the *cavea* of a Greek theater in 155 B.C.,[49] Augustine faults both pagan writers for stopping short of an outright ban on theater. While he observes that Roman laws are close to Plato's dialogues in that Plato rejected poetic fictions and the Romans restrict slanderous poetry, Augustine can only encourage the next logical step.

> Plato excludes poets from dwelling in the city; the Romans at least exclude the actors of poetic fables from membership of the city. Presumably, indeed, if the actors had dared to do anything contrary to the will of those gods who demanded their theatrical performances, the Romans would have banished them altogether.[50]

Augustine would have Cicero's disapproval of Homer extended from poetry to theatrical presentations.

> Why, then, are the theatrical displays in which these crimes are portrayed, sung and enacted, exhibited in honour of the gods and reckoned, by the most learned men, to be among things divine? Cicero should here protest not against the fictions of the poets, but against the institutions of our forebears. But would not they exclaim in reply: "What have we done? It was the gods themselves who commanded that these performances be exhibited in their honour."[51]

Varro's classification of theater gives Augustine's conflation of theater and religion its authority. In the division of the world into things divine and things human, Varro, himself a Roman raised in Rome, classified theater as a divine service. (Augustine cannot resist the opportunity to observe that had the state been composed of upstanding men, theater would have had no place even if Varro had classified it with human endeavors.)[52] Christian monotheism, however, cannot accommodate Varro's dispersal of gods across the phenomenal world. Even if Varro had proposed that natural gods were for the universe, civil gods for cities, and mythical gods for the theaters, Augustine can only respond that the universe is a divine creation, whereas theaters are made by man.

> You say, indeed, that the mythical gods are adapted to the theatre, the natural ones to the world, and the civil to the city. But the world is a divine work, whereas cities and theatres are works of men; and the gods laughed at in the theatres are none other than those who are adored in the temples; and those to whom you exhibit games are none other than those to whom you sacrifice victims. How much more honestly and perceptively would you have classified them if you had said that some gods are natural whereas others are instituted by men, and that, of those so instituted, the writings of the poets give one account and that of the priests another. But both poets and priests are so united with one another in a fellowship of falsehood that both are pleasing to the demons, to whom true doctrine is hateful.[53]

But these deceiving gods who represent themselves in obscene spectacles[54] are palpable forces of malevolence for Augustine, despite Varro's acceptance of them. Augustine traces Roman history to find evidence that the gods routinely coerce Romans into imitating their own destructive behavior. He cites a battle on the plains of Campania (also the site of a gladiator school),[55] which licensed the worst of human behavior.

> In order, therefore, to reduce as far as possible the loathing occasioned by such great evils, and instead to inspire more and more delight in the weapons of war, the hurtful demons—the demons whom the Romans supposed to be gods and considered worthy of worship—chose to appear to men as fighting among themselves. They did this so that civic affection should not shrink from initiating such strife: they desired that human crimes should be excused by divine example.[56]

This same impulse motivates the gods to demand theater, with an intent to deceive and to promote conflicts.

> Thus [the gods] confirmed the songs of the poets in order to deceive mankind: that is, by displaying their clashes to human eyes not only through actors in the theatre, but also in their own persons on the battlefield.[57]

These are the gods who, as far as Augustine is concerned, may have cured the great plague but in the process deliberately infected Roman morality, which weakened the civilization far more effectively than imported Hellenistic stage traditions could have done. These are the gods who, for Augustine, gleefully authorized stage plays as a medium for spreading knowledge of their own nefarious deeds (whether true or invented by poets). The Romans, he concludes, were addicted to the cure at the peril of their souls and culture.[58]

The certainty of Christian truth driving the hermeneutics of *The City of God* to its condemnation of theater is not without its own rigorous logic. Inconsistencies in the practice of Roman law trouble Augustine. That actors are denied citizenship, honors, and kinship communities seems appropriate. Augustine demands proof of the consistent principle that both stigmatizes the players who serve the gods and continues to honor the gods with plays. Similarly, he applies the same critique to the Greeks, whose theater the conquering Romans had adapted.[59]

Three other aspects of this paradoxical relationship between actors, poets, priests, and the gods trouble Augustine: poets are free to disparage the gods but not to slander men; actors are stigmatized, but poets are honored;[60] and censorship laws value men above the gods.[61] Augustine's logic gets around the truth status of the gods in the following way: if the gods and their exploits are indeed true and real, then the theaters explicitly reinforce the gods' inherent evil. If the depiction of the gods in the theaters is the fancy of poetic imagination, then the performances themselves mock religious devotion. What decent gods would choose to be (or allow themselves to be) venerated with debauched entertainments? If the stage representations of the gods' crimes, which delight so many Romans, are actually the work of demon trickery, this is the worst condition of all.[62] The theaters that captured Augustine's emotions in Carthage and the fake lovers who seduced him away from Christian truth are of a different order than shows linked directly to the gods he attacks in *The City of God*. Without the supernatural dimension, theater is a base activity without merit, which endangers the potentially Christian soul by distracting it from God. The danger to a society, a culture, and a city, as described in *The City of God,* is theater's very origins in and dependency on pagan belief.

Far outweighing Augustine's concerns for the nature of theatrical mimesis are his numerous passages on the gods and their representations in shows; on Roman laws protecting men, but not gods, from ridicule; on the origins of theater in the commands of the gods; on theater as a social problem and a spiritual travesty; on the complicity of actors and poets and spectators in moral corruption; on theater as a mode of worship; and on theater as a sign of an entire culture's decay.[63] Augustine's reason is grounded in Christian belief: the gods instituted theater, which proves it is an inherently evil institution; men then devised indecent spectacles that ridicule the gods in the name of worship, thus demonstrating a serious human failure; the gods do nothing to stop these shows, which in turn demonstrates a failure of the gods to be truly divine; finally, Roman civic laws are established to protect men from slander but do not protect the gods from mistreatment, which proves that the Roman state is itself corrupt beyond repair. God's city cannot sustain or tolerate such an institution.

On a more theoretical level, *On Christian Doctrine* invokes theater in its systematic treatment of Scripture. Here, Augustine considers the relationship between the soul (the subject) and the world (the signifier) in the effort to know God's truth.[64] Early Christians, as Ramsay MacMullen points out, may have revealed Scripture through exegesis, but unlike their pagan neighbors, fourth-century Christians had no coherent symbolic system—in visual arts, performance, or ritual—through which to express their beliefs.[65] *On Christian Doctrine,* however, briefly notes the power of theater as a representational practice. God's medium was specific; the Scriptures provided the signs that revealed God. If biblical *verba* offered access to divine *res* (with classical rhetoric as an exegetical tool), there was no corresponding mode of analysis for the conventions of words and gestures in the theater.[66]

As always for Augustine, signs are necessary to express the nondiscursive reality of God. In an often cited passage from book 1 of *On Christian Doctrine,* he distinguishes "things" from "signs," always with the awareness that interpretation is a matter of discerning the message of the Bible. In service of understanding *signa,* he is concerned with *res,* the existence of "things."

> All teaching is teaching of either things or signs, but things are learnt through signs. What I now call things in the strict sense are things such as logs, stones, sheep, and so on, which are not employed to signify something; but I do not include the log which we read that Moses

threw into the bitter waters to make them lose their bitter taste, or the stone which Jacob placed under his head, or the sheep which Abraham sacrificed in place of his son. These are things, but they are at the same time signs of other things. There are other signs whose whole function consists in signifying. Words for example . . .[67]

But for their meaning to be understood, signs must be accompanied by agreement. Theater is suspect because its signs may be unknown *(ignota signa)* and must be explained in or by the performance.[68] The reciprocity between actors' gestures and what they represent is simply too great and, like language itself, is dependent on cultural conventions. Theater thus cannot be trusted as *propria signa*.

[I]f the signs made by actors while dancing were naturally meaningful, rather than meaningful as a result of human institution and agreement, an announcer would not have indicated to the Carthaginians, as each actor danced, what the dance meant, as he did in earlier days. . . . It is quite credible, for even now if a person unfamiliar with these frivolities goes to the theatre his rapt attention to them is pointless unless someone tells him what the movements mean.[69]

This disconnect between signs and their meanings was not an issue in *Confessions,* in which the theatrical representation of love and sex was all too painfully transparent to Augustine. As a sign system, a means of communication that might be useful to Christianity, theatrical representation falls short of signifying God on purely formalistic grounds. Its mimed gestures required verbal explanation and, being invented rather than naturally occurring, could not appropriately carry meaning *(signa data)*.[70] So Augustine concludes that for Christians, theater is a human, not divine, institution that may be connected to gods but not to the one true God.

Another reason theatrical representations cannot signify truth is because they are, by definition, grounded in false knowledge, like the lies of "thousands of fictional stories and romances, which through their falsehoods give people great pleasure."[71] In this context, "falsehood" describes something not "in the state in which it is asserted to be true."[72] Theater has signifying power but, by definition, signifies untruths in a consciously false mode of representation. Theater led people to take theatrical signs (e.g., sinful lovers) as the things themselves (the characteristic of theater Augustine found so troubling in *Confessions*).

Mistaking signs for the things themselves is a serious problem for Augustine, because discrepancies between signs and the things they represent prevented both spiritual interpretation and divine revelation. Augustine considers, for example, the distinction between pagan and Jewish interpretation of sign systems. Though Jews were in servitude to signs, Augustine considers Jews closer to spiritual understanding than the Roman pagans, because Jews were at least dealing with the right set of signs. Though they erred in their collective ability to read biblical signs, Jews, according to Augustine, rightly directed their worship to the true eternal God.[73] But even when Augustine considers the potential for pagan signs to encode Christian truths, he singles out theater as being beyond the limits of acceptable signification. Though theater remains firmly rooted in pagan culture, an exception can be made for music's value.

> [Christians] should not avoid music because of the associated pagan superstitions if there is a possibility of gleaning from it something of value for understanding holy scripture. Nor, on the other hand, should we be captivated by the vanities of the theatre if we are discussing something to do with lyres or other instruments that may help us appreciate spiritual truths.[74]

A similar issue surfaces in *Concerning the Teacher*, Augustine's dialogue on Christian pedagogy. The third chapter addresses the problem of how to actually show things "of which these [words] are signs."[75] Given the polemics of *Confessions* and *The City of God*, *Concerning the Teacher* analyzes theatrical representation in a surprisingly neutral way. This is essentially a more sophisticated version of Augustine's earlier dialogue with Reason in *Soliloquies*. Though Augustine accounts for voice and gesture as "symptoms" of feeling, *Concerning the Teacher* acknowledges the signifying potential of theatrical representation, quite apart from condemnations of its lascivious content and paganism.

Augustine points out that "actors in the theater present and exhibit entire dramas for the most part by means of pantomime without using words," and he considers theatrical gestures to be relational, as are words (i.e., a sign will stand for an object, and a subject will interpret). But he concludes that "whatever bodily movement the pantomimic actor may use in order to show me the thing signified by the word, the motion will not be the thing itself but a sign."[76] Here, theater is presented as an example of physical signification, like walking, a step toward Augustine's central concern:[77] theatrical performance—an illustration of the limitations of physical gestures, such as point-ing—can never show Christian truth.

Jonas Barish has argued that Augustine clarifies "the nature of theatrical imitation" in *Soliloquies*.[78] But Augustine's dialogue with Reason in *Soliloquies* 2.9–12 presents theater within orders of similitude and investigates the roles that the soul, the senses, and sight play in distinguishing falsity from truth (a crucial skill for Christians invested in setting their version of Jewish monotheism apart from pagan polytheism). In dialogue with Reason, Augustine reconciles four conditions of false perception: things can appear to the senses other than they actually are; there can be a subject of sense other than the soul; an object, such as a stone, might exist but still not be true; and truth itself might be otherwise defined. Reason's four options set Augustine to thinking through similitude—resemblance between equal things or comparison of inferior to superior things—in dreams, delusions, reflections in mirrors and water, optical and aural illusions, twins, eggs, and document seals, and he reaches the conclusion that "the resemblance of things which pertains to the eyes is the mother of falsity."[79] Augustine's fear, of course, is always that the soul, the senses, or sight will fail to distinguish God's truth from false (man-made) likenesses: "we call that false which tends to be something and is not."[80]

Theater is a tangential example of this problem, not a target as it was in *Confessions* and *The City of God*. Augustine wants a method for discerning truth from the phenomenal world, including human-made representations. An image may be false, but it will tend toward the thing it represents, with the intent either to deceive the perceiver or to provide an imitation of human behavior for enjoyment. Mimes, comedies, and poems fall into this less problematic category.[81] On this basis, Reason separates jests, poetry, and other imitations from the category of things that tend toward false representation but are not themselves false. Inconsequential imitations (sculpture, painting) are works of humans; such a work tends toward a likeness of the thing it imitates, but the mode of imitation demonstrates that the work is a copy, not the thing itself.[82]

Stage acting is an example of this kind of imitation. A stage actor (Augustine's example is Roscius) is truly a man and truly a professional tragedian even if his portrayal of a character (Hecuba or Priam) is, by definition, false. Similarly, a picture is true to itself, though it is not truly what it represents. The theatrical example demonstrates the ultimate Christian task—to seek what is uniformly true, not true in one aspect and false in another.[83] So, while trivial imitations, such as stage shows, are not ontologically suspect, as they were for Plato, they also do not reveal Christian truth. Acting (though Augustine does not explore the entire theatrical medium) is one example of the bifurcation of human artifice and behavior, part true and part false.[84]

Barish, focusing on an "antitheatrical" bias in Christianity, mourns that faith overrides reason in Augustine's meditations on truth. With their secular emphasis on reason, Barish finds the arguments in *Confessions* and *The City of God* (which deal more explicitly with theater as a social practice and cultural expression than as mimesis) "less rigorous," at best, than those of *Soliloquies*. At worst, he finds them prejudicial.[85] Our interest here is not the formation of a persecuting tradition but how a foundation in Christian faith combined with classical dialectic construes theater. Augustine's arguments against theater in *The City of God* have far more to do with Christian-pagan dualism than with theater itself or, for that matter, theatrical mimesis. Augustine's analysis is no less rigorous for its steadfast adherence to the transcendent truth revealed by Christ. When put in the only social and cultural context Augustine knows, theater, while not evil in theory, is quite so in practice. The intellectual grounds follow a logic that exceeds a personal resistance to moral and sexual license.[86]

Augustine's reference point in Christianity will, of course, be replaced by an idealization of Greco-Roman culture and a desire to imitate its expressive forms—theater, sculpture, art, architecture—as a deliberate, recuperative intellectual move in the Renaissance. It is hardly surprising that this impulse went hand in hand with a serious investigation of mimesis, verisimilitude, and similitude and with a "preoccupation with representation."[87] But the idea of remaking the world in the image of humans, which will become the ideal of theatrical verisimilitude twelve centuries later, remains for Augustine a representational travesty.

While Christian truths might find inadvertent expression in the writings and music of pagan cultures, theater had no such potential value for Augustine. Not only did theater put immoral acts on visual display, but it also presented them as fictions, which set the entire effort against the revelation of Christian truth. Theater led to distorted perceptions of truth and provoked emotional responses to human-made artifice rather than encouraging judgment based on Christian principles of compassion and community.[88] Though numerous studies have investigated the relationship between Christian rituals and what might properly be called "theater" or "drama," Augustine effectively distinguishes between theater and any Christian practice of worship or pursuit of knowledge.

Theater becomes the site at which Augustine distinguishes those things of the world that have their origins in the Christian God from those that do not. In a sense, the Roman theater becomes a casualty of Augustine's arguments for Christian truth: theater is a false mode of representation; the content of the shows (love stories and pagan myths) falls short of conveying Christian beliefs and values; and theater originated with edicts of the gods with which men in weakness complied. But most important for a Christian consciousness, theater is part of the world of artifice, of signs that point not to God but to the material world of human creation. This cycle of reference—artifice pointing to artifice—cannot reference the immortality of the soul, the eternality of God, or Christ's transcendence. Nor, as is clear from Augustine's discussions, is theater a sufficiently discursive medium to offer a method for argumentation or reasoning. Theater simply falls short of Christian expectations for social behavior, institutional order, signification, and moral content.

Augustine's influence on later Christian thought was pervasive and far-reaching. A bias against Roman entertainments persists in the subsequent writings of Isidore of Seville, Remigius of Auxerre, Agobard of Lyons, and Florus of Lyons, though with far less critical nuance and with more concern for Christian practices. But the precision of Augustine's analysis of theater's pagan affiliations, potential for Christian signification, and paradoxical presentation of truth and falsity does not appear again in the medieval Christian intellectual tradition. When this kind of attention is paid to theater in the Renaissance, it is with the desire to recoup the very theater Augustine condemned.

Isidore of Seville, without the Pagan Gods

Classification, rather than analysis, marks the next significant body of medieval writings to deal with theatricality, theater, and entertainments. These writings relegate theater to the status of cultural artifact in the effort to preserve remnants of Christianity's Greco-Roman heritage. They detail the logistics of theatrical performances; the architecture of arenas and amphitheaters; other kinds of games, sports, and contests done for entertainment; and the physical characteristics of the theater (e.g., the *thymele* and placement of performers). But though plays and playwrights are mentioned, theater itself is distinguished from discussions of poetry, literary genres, and rhetoric. The process of formal categorization required that theater's characteristics be defined and distinguished from other buildings and activities of the ancient world.

Two centuries after Augustine, with Roman polytheism no longer in competition with Christianity, Augustine's analysis of theater as a social practice became but one strand of information from which Christians distinguished the pagan past from the Christian present. When it came to ordering that past in definitive categories based on written information, Christian "encyclopedias" reconstituted theater as an artifact of Roman culture, rather than a site of resistance.

The *Etymologiae* of Isidore of Seville marks an epitome in the effort to synthesize knowledge of Christianity's Greco-Roman heritage.[89] The scope and accessibility of the *Etymologiae*'s systematic arrangement of information made it an essential reference work in its time, with widespread influence as a historical document throughout the Middle Ages.[90] It remains one of the most important links between the intellectual culture of the Roman Empire and that of European Christianity, and Isidore's descriptions of ancient theater in particular persisted until the sixteenth century.[91] But in the process of synthesizing information, Isidore lifted those bits from pagan and patristic texts that fit his topical and etymological entries.[92] He takes sources out of context, conflates information, comments without analyzing, and ignores inconsistencies.[93] For these reasons, his composite image of Greco-Roman theater is wildly inaccurate (and Isidore's erroneous information has prompted lively debate for centuries).[94]

As a development in Christian thought, however, the *Etymologiae*'s presentation of theater and theatricality moves into the new intellectual territory won by Augustine's philosophical battles with polytheism. The organization of entries on Roman theatrical practice in the *Etymologiae* (books 8, 10, and 18), with their cryptic and erroneous descriptions, puts Greco-Roman theater into a system of Christian knowledge.[95] That system would not be radically altered until the reassessment of secular thought in the Renaissance conceived ancient theater as performative, experiential, and immediate; as a legitimate intellectual activity; and as the appropriate mode of representation for ancient and new dramas.

The categorical structure of the *Etymologiae*, as Ernest Brehaut pointed out in 1912, responded to a view of the phenomenal world that saw patterns of likeness and difference.[96] Augustine's condemnation of theater as anathema to Christianity and his analysis of theatrical signification is grounded in what George Lakoff would call experiential realism, firsthand knowledge of Roman theater and theatrical practices.[97] Augustine's treatment of theater changes according to context and takes the form of metaphors, metonymies, and images. In contrast, Isidore constructs categories as objective frames for information outside his immediate experience. Ancient theater becomes part of a larger codification project, one part of the whole of Greco-Roman culture. Through categorical descriptions arranged with reference to other like things, any Christian could understand the information, whether or not the categories themselves were appropriate to the material.

If Christian words were thought to cleanse the pagan past by rendering it knowable and subject to Christian judgment, Isidore could order the material world by constructing categories based on etymological relationships.[98] The origin and meanings of words could be assumed to yield knowledge of the reality designated by those words.[99] In effect, however, the arrangement of topics in the *Etymologiae* effectively sets theater apart from daily practices by framing it as historical data (an option not available to Augustine). Isidore's documentation of theater thus exists in the strong tension between the impulse to present the pagan past as historical record and, at the same time, to scrutinize it from the Christian present.[100] Though Augustine had clearly stated that theater had no place in Christian culture, such a comprehensive set of notes on Roman culture as the *Etymologiae* had to include theater; it was better to order historical information in the language of Christian truth and make its pagan origins plain than to risk ignorance or misinterpretation of ancient texts.[101] The *Etymologiae* thus became a legitimate source for knowledge of the pagan legacy, as well as part of the effort to reconcile secular knowledge with Christian belief. The design of the *Etymologiae* provided a foundation for a new and developing intellectual tradition by assessing and ordering that legacy to distance, rather than replicate, its practices. From the structure of this broader effort emerge ideas of theater as a distinct kind of entertainment.

Isidore describes theater and theatricality most specifically in books 15 and 18. Book 15, *De aedificiis et agris*, is devoted to kinds of ancient architecture, of which theater buildings are one example.[102] Within the broad category of architecture, theaters are described in *De aedificiis publicis*, which groups public buildings by function, architectural design, and origin. To readers of the *Etymologiae*, then, theaters would have appeared as one type of permanent municipal structure, categorically distinct from homes, tombs, munitions works, farm buildings, or places of worship.[103] At the next level of specificity, theaters belong with municipal buildings intended for entertainment and refreshment, including gymnasia,[104] equestrian arenas,[105] amphitheaters,[106] and mythical labyrinths (described as horrific places full of terrifying sounds, monstrous statues, and dark passageways).[107] Isidore's categories also separate theater from ritual by putting theaters and temples into different categories based on their location and function. Temples, or sacred buildings *(De aedificiis sacris)*, for example, were places where priests made blood sacrifices, songs were sung, and demons could be heard.[108] Theaters were places for viewing spectacles, where people could watch as scenes were played out for amusement.[109] Other than his classification of the buildings as public, Augustine's concern for theater's associations with the gods is not important to the documentary value of book 15.[110]

Book 18, *De bello et ludis*, defines theatrical entertainment itself—what went on inside the buildings. Isidore presents Greco-Roman theater as the performance of comedies and tragedies in mime, dance, and narration on raised platforms in purpose-built spaces.[111] Their purpose is recreation. But theater's defining characteristic is that it presents a spectacle of combat or contest, a characteristic shared by other performances of war and games— legal debates (chap. 15, *De foro*), athletic competitions (chap. 17, *De ludo gymnico*), wrestling matches (chap. 24, *De palaestra*), gladiatorial contests (chap. 27, *De ludis circensibus*) and chariot races (chap. 35, *De curru;* chap. 36, *De equis quibus currimus*).

Conflict (between individuals, an individual and a higher authority, or an individual and himself or herself) has long been considered an organic, structural element of Western dramatic narratives, the force that drives dramatic structure to a crisis and its resolution. Seventh-century Christianity was much more likely to conceive conflict not as a narrative structure or performance of a mock combat but as a very real battle between Christ (or Christians) and the devil (evil personified as pagans, heretics, or demons). This idea seems inherent in Isidore's categorization of theater with athletic contests and games.[112] Later strands of the European intellectual tradition would separate the body from the mind and set competitive sports (as a less intellectually sophisticated, more popular entertainment) apart from visual, performing, and linguistic arts. But the connection between theater and physical sport is assumed throughout the *Etymologiae*. Christianity can now easily conflate theatrical conflicts (considering theater a form of public contest) with Christianity's struggles against its enemies (be they the devil and demons or heretics and pagans). Thus, book 8 puts combat games in a Christian context.

> [Satan] himself is surely the adversary, who is truly hostile, and he is always against the virtue of sacred men or things. [Satan] is also a transgressor, because he did not stand firm, he is a double dealer who was created in truth, on which side he was established. He is also a

tempter, who demands that the innocence of the righteous must be tried, as was written in Job.[113]

But the *Etymologiae* does not make a direct link between this eschatological Christian conflict and pagan narrative poetry or ancient theatrical performances. The Christian struggle between good and evil has no direct parallel in the moral dilemmas of Greco-Roman plays, such as *Medea,* or in the combat games of the arenas.

In the *Etymologiae,* theatrical performances belong unequivocally with the games of men *(ludi),* and the lexical overlap between theater and sports will continue through the Middle Ages.[114] But the *Etymologiae* also draws a categorical distinction between theater as a spectacle and social activity and drama as a narrative form. Isidore does not define tragedies and comedies themselves as narratives of conflict or debate. It is performance in a theater building that categorizes theater with sport, forensic oratory, contests, and games rather than with poetry, music, dance, or scripted drama.[115] As Joseph Jones notes, Isidore is an exception among Christian writers in that he does not outrightly condemn comedic performances as blasphemous and obscene, though he holds onto theater's idolatrous origins.[116]

Chapter 18, *De theatro,* for example, gives no indication that theater, construed as a kind of physical sport or display, shares any characteristics with poetry, oratory, or even dramatic poetry. The theater is, rather, associated with physical bodies, sex and prostitution, and vulgar public display.[117] Dramatic genres appear separately in the descriptions of performers who sing poetry, dancers, and mimes who perform while a poet recites.[118] Still, the defining characteristic of theater, along with sports and legal debate, was the presentation of an agon. Was Isidore thinking of theater itself as a contest with prizes and winners for poetry and performance; or that the performances represented contests; or that the physical demands theatrical shows made on performers constituted a kind of athletic event; or that performances were judged?

The criterion for the general category of war and games (even in debate) seems to be stamina, particularly of the body.

Contests produced: immensity of strength/virility, swiftness of races, skill in shooting arrows, physical endurance, the carriage of the body while marching to the lyre or pipe, also the manner and form of singing to rhythmic accompaniment, fights on earth and in sea battles, and the endurance of extended supplication in debate contests.[119]

Contests may be competitions of skill, speed, or endurance, with a clear winner, or, as in the case of mock battles, representations of conflict in which one side eventually emerges victorious. It is not always clear from Isidore's definitions whether he thinks songs, instrumental music, and choreography were judged or whether the performances represented narratives of conflict, that is, whether the content or the form of a theatrical presentation is a contest. Depending on the translation of *De orchestra,* theatrical performances either were judged or were themselves engaged in combative dialogue.

> Moreover, the orchestra was the raised platform of the scene, where a dancer could perform or two [performers] could debate with each other. Here, also, poets of comedy and tragedy ascended to settle debates, and while they were singing, others provided gestures.[120]

Isidore is clear in book 8 that some classical poetry was meant to be performed.[121] But he does not refer to the desultory plays that obsessed Augustine. Isidore's reference points are the plays and poems of classical Latin rhetoric, which Augustine had judged inappropriate but not obscene. This dramatic poetry was characterized by the evidence that performers, rather than poets, took on speaking roles, as indicated by Isidore's well-known sources.

> Of poets, moreover, three characteristics are spoken of: one in which only a poet speaks, as in the book of Virgil's *Georgics;* another is dramatic, in which the poet at no time speaks, as in comedies and tragedies; the third is mixed, as in the *Aeneid.* For there the poet and presented characters speak.[122]

Nevertheless, the categorical structure of the *Etymologiae* makes difficult a conceptual overlap between drama or poetry and theater. Isidore follows well-established literary definitions of the content of the two poetic genres in book 8 (e.g., tragedy is mournful; comedy is joyful).[123] Book 18, however, describes comedy and tragedy only as discrete parts of theatrical performance. There is no conceptual integration of the forms of language described in book 8 or the *ludi* described in book 18. The *Etymologiae* is not specifically concerned with the performance of dramas, though it acknowledges that plays were performed.

In addition, one effect of Isidore's categories was a distinction between ancient entertainments and performance practices of southern Europe in the seventh century. These would have certainly included rhetoric, oratory, and Christian pageants, as well as performances of mimes, scops, joculatores, and singers. Isidore's categories marked theater as a kind of entertainment defined by specific physical features: a theater building, a raised platform, and space for musicians. Performers are defined by their functions. *Histriones* represented historical narratives, as well as fictions, whereas mimes imitated human things *(rerum humaniarum).*[124] Mimed actions were coordinated to a story told by a narrator[125] and were performed on a raised stage resembling a house.[126] Performers' accessories included shoes, masks, makeup, and costumes.[127] Isidore's project demanded descriptions of the mechanics of theater, not a judgment about its significance to seventh-century Christianity. A contemporary seventh-century performance could, by Isidore's definition, be theatrical but not necessarily thought of as theater, given the working descriptions Isidore lays out. For a seventh-century Christian reader, the *Etymologiae* reinforced theater's historical place as a pagan practice linked to polytheism.

Isidore's criteria for judging theater, however, differ from Augustine's regarding theater's incompatibility with Christianity.[128] The entry *De theatro* follows a series of entries describing kinds of spectacle entertainments: equestrian acrobats,[129] their horses,[130] and footraces.[131] *De theatro* comes immediately after *De coloribus equorum,* which describes the color of horses in Roman circuses and asserts that the Romans consecrated horses, like the circus games in general, to the gods (here Mars, Jupiter, and Neptune).[132] But Isidore makes it clear that the horse arenas were inhabited by the spirits of Satan and possessed the power of unclean pagan deities.[133] The circus was also a place for performances instituted by the gods for the celebration of the gods, performances in which could be seen the demons of the cult.[134]

Theaters, however, were defiled not by demons but by human bodies. Theaters exposed people to sexual license, which made theaters unfit places for Christians. In Isidore's categories, theatergoers themselves—not the content of the performances or demons (Augustine's main concerns)—fouled the space. A theater is defined as a semicircular edifice, derived from the circular structure of an amphitheater, in which people stand to watch performances *(ludos contemplaretur).* Theater is also defined as synonymous with brothel *(prostibulum, lupanar),* because harlots prostitute themselves at theaters immediately after performances. Theaters are unclean places less because they possess unclean spirits (as do the equestrian arenas) or originated in pagan cultures than because they are places associated with bodily (sexual) pollution.[135]

The problem that theater is firmly rooted in the social, human world rather than the transcendent world of Christian spirit carries over from Augustine.[136] Similarly, following Varro, Isidore says that plays derive from the entertainments by which young men amused people during festivals of the gods and at temples during religious rites, which gave great pleasure.

> Spectacles, it is supposed, are generally given the name not because they themselves defile pleasure, but by those things themselves being done there. They are also called spectacles because they set men out for public scrutiny. These are also called plays because plays are done as entertainment during meals.[137]

Jones, tracing medieval performance traditions, proposes further study of "how Isidore's views, together with the distorted interpretations of them, affected the poets, playwrights, and actors of the Middle Ages and early Renaissance."[138] His concern, like that of many theater scholars, is how the composite description of Greco-Roman theater provided by Isidore, with all its inconsistencies and (what are now recognized as) errors, might have been used by medieval performers or patrons of entertainment.

This proposal, shared by many historians interested in the development of medieval performance toward the theatrical conventions of realistic mimesis, secular subject matter, and artistic goals, carries prejudices of its own. Those prejudices in some ways obscure a clear view both of the intellectual goals of a project like the *Etymologiae* and of the reason it includes theater at all. The expectation that medieval thinkers would take the information of the *Etymologiae* as a blueprint for reconstructing ancient theaters, as did early modern architects and poets, obscures the effort of medieval Christians to incorporate, but not imitate, the social (as opposed to intellectual) practices of the classical past.

The project of the *Etymologiae* works against this expectation. Late classical writings did not present Greco-Roman theater or dramatic performances as a site for inquiry, analysis, or direct application. If medieval documents like the *Etymologiae* are expected to prompt direct application to performance— as the Aristotle's *Poetics,* and Vitruvius's *De architectura* did in the fifteenth century—its transmission will remain a tantalizing puzzle compared to the "explosion of accurate knowledge in the fifteenth and sixteenth centuries" and the interest in theatrical representation in the Renaissance.[139] By shifting the focus away from Isidore's relevance to theatrical practice and to the development of a European dramatic tradition, we can take his categorical notes on theater as a marker in the transformation of Christian thought about the social practices of the pagan past. The issue is not teasing a dramatic tradition out of Isidore but understanding how Isidore's presentation of theater marks changes in Christian thinking about the social world of the Roman Empire.

Seventh-century Christianity sought to continue ancient traditions (e.g., grammar, rhetoric, and dialectic) insofar as Christian faith could reconcile and use those traditions productively. Nothing known of ancient theater warranted integration into Christian practice. If Isidore presents ancient theater with suspicion, he does so without Augustine's vitriol. If theater was associated with prostitution, false representation, bawdy behavior, idolatry, purpose-built architecture, and a network of professional performers supported by pagan institutions, seventh-century Christians could salvage little for their own edification. But more important, beyond documentation for Christian judgment, Isidore is not concerned with what the Romans did for entertainment. Isidore has no need for Augustine's detailed analyses of pagan culture to prove its opposition to true Christian monotheism or to show theater as a symptom of a disintegrating state. Isidore's descriptions of Greco-Roman performance as gesture accompanied by singing or recitation do not present theater or theatrical representation as the theological problem it was for Augustine. Isidore's concerns are for the practical and material technicalities of theatrical production. Even when he describes actors disguised as women or theaters as places for prostitution, he is recording a receding past, which he has no need to recoup.

Between the middle of the fourth century and the middle of the seventh century, Christian thought had transformed theater (as an institution and a cultural practice) from a site of analysis and resistance to a historical category temporally and culturally distinct from the contemporary Christian world. Isidore is not immune to issues of signification, however. He can assume, like Augustine, that products of human artifice, such as theater, bear likeness to the things they represent. He does so in the following passage from De diis gentium.

> Images are named after likeness because by the hand of the craftsman, out of stone or some other material, are imitated the faces of those in whose honor they are devised. Therefore because images are similar, or because they are imitated and made up, they are also false.[140]

But the difference between Augustine and Isidore's presentation of theater shifts as the classical past begins to recede; theater is no longer a problem for Christian signification, because the intervening centuries have transformed theater from a site of inquiry to a relic of the past.

For Augustine, the existence of theater (its performers, stages, and plays) demonstrates the hopeless inadequacy of pagan culture. Debauchery and sexual license, as well as theater's ability to seduce unsuspecting Christians into empathizing with fictions, are his immediate concerns. *The City of God* makes a hearty case for condemning Roman theater on the grounds of its pagan origins. *Confessions* lays out the danger of theatrical representation to Christian morality. The stages show the worst of human behavior and misdirect proper Christian sympathies. Theater is anathema to Christianity not only as a practice but also, in these two texts, as an institution. But in *Soliloquies, Sermons, On Christian Doctrine,* and *Concerning the Teacher,* Augustine uses theater much more neutrally, to investigate the problem of truth and falsity writ large. Theater functions in these texts as an illustration or example within a broader theological concern for how Christian truths can be read in the signs of the material world (and for determining which signs can point to those truths).

Isidore's task is different: reconstituting ancient culture in the context of Christian knowledge (rather than affirming Christianity in a hostile culture).[141] Isidore transmits, rather than creates, knowledge. Framed in the categories of the *Etymologiae,* Isidore's picture of theater is seen at a distance from seventh-century Christian experience. Augustine provides analysis without description, whereas Isidore gives description without analysis. To present factual descriptions of theater, Isidore slices away the possibility that theater, like rhetoric and dialectic, could be a site, if not a method, of intellectual inquiry (as it would become in the sixteenth century).

Two comparisons illustrate the change that the concept of theater underwent in Christian thought between the fourth and the seventh centuries. The first is Isidore's distinction between fallacious and mendacious falsehoods in the *Differentiarum,* in which he uses Augustine's soliloquies. The second is Isidore's definition of *hypocrita* in book 10 of the *Etymologiae,* which reproduces pseudo-Augustine sermon 62 on Matthew 6:1–6.

In *Soliloquies* 2.10, Augustine reasons his way through two kinds of falsehood: that which deliberately deceives (fallacious) and that which overtly presents harmless falsehoods for enjoyment (mendacious). Comedies, tragedies, jests, mimicry, and some poetry are mendacious. Augustine does not specifically indicate the broader practice of theater here but implies performance. Reason tells Augustine that nothing can be false except that which pretends to be what it is not or tends toward a likeness of something else. Of those things that pretend, some are intentionally deceptive, which is an attitude of the soul and should be judged harshly. But mimes, jokes, comedies, and poems can present innocent lies that, by accepted convention, feign likeness of something else. These can be legitimately fun.

With its passing reference to performance, this passage sorts out the relationship of man-made imagery to Christian truth. But Augustine takes the problem of fallacious and mendacious representation a step further by using it to illustrate conditions in which a thing (here a person) might be intentionally true and not true at the same time.

> Because it is one thing to want to be false; it is quite different to be unable to be true. So, we can group the works of men, like comedies, tragedies, farces, and other things of that type with the words of painters and sculptors. A man in a painting cannot be as true, even though it tends toward the appearance of a man, as those things which are written in the works of the comic authors. Such things do not choose to be false nor are they false, through their own desire to be so, but they are compelled by a kind of necessity to conform as much as they are able to the artist's will. On the other hand, the actor Roscius was by choice a false Hecuba on the stage, though, by nature, a true man; he was by choice a true tragedian in that he fulfilled his purpose, and a false Priam because he played the part of Priam though he was not Priam.[142]

The example of theater (construed specifically as a human craft of representing likenesses, on the order of painting and sculpture) here leads Augustine to a definition of truth in relation to the inherent (if harmless) lie of representation. Augustine's familiarity with theater—the immediacy of stage plays and performers—make acting an easy reference for illustrating a notion of truth that is not compromised by representation.

> To the end that we may be true to our nature, we should not become false by copying and likening ourselves to the nature of another as do the actors and the reflections in a mirror and the brass cows of [the Greek sculptor] Myron. We should, instead, seek that truth which is not self-contradictory and two-faced so that it is true on one side, false on another.[143]

Augustine's use of Greek sculpture and first-century Roman theater in exploring the larger philosophical problem of how representation compromises truth is completely absent when Isidore uses theater to illustrate the conceptual difference between willful deception and delightful lies. In the *Differentiarum*, he gives the following definition.

> Between "fallax" and "mendax." A fallacious person deceives people by his behavior; but not everyone who presents a lie intends to deceive; so there are mimes, comedies, and many poems where delightful lies are written to amuse rather than with a desire to deceive. And almost everyone who jokes, lies.[144]

The result of Isidore's differentiation between "fallacious" and "mendacious" is a sanction of lies in comic representation, but not in human behavior. Without Augustine's syllogism for discerning truth (and the graphic illustration of Roman tragic acting as the paradox of a soul's essence and a person's behavior), truth falls away as the ultimate referent for falsehood. A definition of performed humor, useful and unproblematic, remains as a truth-claim.

A more pronounced transformation from theater's use as an illustration in an argument into a record of past theatrical practice comes from pseudo-Augustine sermon 62[145] and Isidore's entry on *hypocrita* in the *Etymologiae*.[146] Isidore's task is to provide an etymology for *hypocrita,* which he does by way of Greek and Latin, following the biblical sense of "pretender."[147] Isidore's definition of *hypocrita* traces the word's Greek origins and gives the Latin translation as *simulator interpretatur,* "one who simulates by interpretation." A hypocrite is a person who is bad on the inside but outwardly presents himself as good; that is, he allows himself to be judged *(krises)* as what he is not *(hypo)*. This name for a deceptive person comes, Isidore says, from the Greek word for those who took part in spectacles with their faces covered or painted, as a disguise to deceive people who went to see the shows *(ludi)*.[148] By altering their faces and hair, Greek actors could simulate what they were not; they could appear to be men or women, young or old. Isidore defines the Greek word for "actor," in its generic Latin usage, to mean a person who misrepresents himself, a person whose physical appearance (self-presentation) does not match his inner or true self—as opposed to *histrio,* which Isidore uses to describe actors. The end result is a description of Greek acting as representation, which has come through the centuries as a document of ancient theatrical practice, however accurate it may or may not be.

Isidore's description of Greek actors and their masks or face painting reproduces pseudo-Augustine sermon 62. But the sermon's purpose is to encourage private prayer (as opposed to the ostentatious display of religious faith), as well as rigorous honesty. It draws primarily from Matthew 6:1–6:

"When you pray, do not be like the hypocrites! They love to stand up and pray in the houses of worship and on the street corners so that everyone will see them. I assure you, they have already been paid in full." The warning against hypocrisy in perception and behavior is drawn from Luke 6:42: "How can you say to your brother, 'Please brother let me take that speck out of your eye,' yet cannot even see the log in your own eye? You hypocrite! First take the log out of your own eye, then you will be able to see clearly."[149] Greek spectacles (here *spectacula,* not *theatrum*) are the filter through which the author arrives at the revealed truth of the Scriptures.

But it is not a small or insignificant thing to wear the stain of hypocrisy. For whoever wishes to be seen for what he is not is a hypocrite. Whoever says his prayers like a singing trumpet is a hypocrite. Whoever speaks out [prayers] in synagogues and on street corners, and so he might be seen by men, is a hypocrite. He who destroys his own form to display in his countenance his belly's emptiness, he is also a hypocrite. By all these things the hypocrite—those who do whatever they please so they might be glorified by men—is known to all.[150]

As these two examples indicate, the discursive contexts in which theater appears in Augustine (or pseudo-Augustine) and Isidore are two distinct variations on early Christian understandings of theater and theatricality. Augustine positioned theater in a discourse on the religion and the decadence of Roman culture, and his critique of theater extended from Christian morality to Christian signification. Theater is, for Augustine, a function of pagan culture and definitively a pagan practice (though not all of his references to theater harp on this theme). Augustine's critique of theater as a mode of representation assumes Christianity's resistance to non-Christian religions and the governments that support them.

By the seventh century, theater could be put safely into a Christian frame and judged, but it demanded no analysis. Augustine's suspicions of theater as a false mode of representation are evident in the encyclopedic tradition, and its roots in pagan idolatry are acknowledged. But the categorical arrangement of topics separates textual traditions (e.g., poetry, tragedy, rhetoric, and philosophy) from theater, which is classified with athletic contests and debate. Theater was defined in part by the spaces constructed for it, the social conditions of that space, and conventions of performance, rather than by the content of the shows. So by the end of the seventh century, theater and theatricality had been established in two distinct ways: as a mode of representation in Augustine's theology and as a material practice in the encyclopedists' categories of pagan activities. In either discourse, theater and theatricality are anathema to Christian belief and Christian practices. But in Augustine, the threat is real and tangible; for Isidore, it is theoretical.

From these two distinct discursive strands, it would have been difficult to connect Greco-Roman theater with the mimes, joculatores, scopes, and bards who entertained during the early centuries of Latin Christian culture. Augustine's critique makes theater's pagan affiliations too dangerous for Christian practice. Isidore's schematic summaries reduce theater to technical descriptions without providing either a cohesive manual for duplicating past theatrical practices or, perhaps more important, a reason to do so. The theater of the ancients remained ensconced in the curio cabinet of Isidore's categories and in the shadow of Augustine's multifaceted critique of Roman culture.

CHAPTER TWO

Transmission and Transformation
Liturgical Allegory and the Idea of Theater

AS CHRISTIANITY TOOK institutional hold in Western Europe, churches, monasteries, ceremonies, iconography, and texts began to create distinctly Christian modes of representation. Elaborations on the liturgies of the Mass and offices yielded what twentieth-century scholars have come to recognize as the emergence of a dramatic tradition in the *Quem quaeritis* trope and *Visitatio sepulchri* ceremonies of the tenth- and eleventh-century liturgies.[1] Also by the late tenth century, the plays of Terence (conceived as literature or poetry) were adapted without the masks, cothurni, stage buildings, professional actors, or prostitutes associated with the ancient pagan stages. Hrotswitha of Gandersheim (ca. 935–1002) depicted virtuous Christian women in literary dramas for which she used Terence's plays as her model, and an anonymous poet produced a Latin verse prologue in which Terence is a character.[2] But while performers entertained in what many scholars consider the continuation of the Roman theatrical tradition,[3] the idea of theater as a distinctive mode of representation, a cultural practice, and a social institution remained bound to the ancient world. Even as knowledge from that distant culture was transmitted and integrated into Christian intellectual practice, the characteristics of *theatrum* were evoked but not replicated.[4]

This chapter looks at adaptations of the idea of pagan theater in Christian texts. For Rabanus Maurus (ca. 780–856) and Remigius of Auxerre (ca. 841–908), ancient theater becomes part of the typology of the pre-Christian world. Each interprets ancient theater through Christianity's triumph over the pagan past, wrapping their information with Christian analogies, metaphors, and interpretations, but not changing theater's fundamental alterity to Christianity.[5] The liturgical allegories of Amalarius of Metz

43

(775/80–850), however, raised the specter of theatricality amid concerns for ongoing paganism, Christian materialism or worldliness, and the limits of human interpretation.[6] Writing in a tradition of liturgical commentary that can easily be traced to Isidore's *De ecclesiasticis officiis,* Amalarius was part of an entire genre of learned reflection on the Mass and its meanings. In this case, however, comparisons with ancient theater provided Amalarius's critics with a cipher for accusations of theological transgressions.[7] The set of texts discussed in this chapter demonstrates the distinction made in Christian thought between the idea of ancient theater and Christian intellectual or ritual practices.[8]

In a sense, the writings of Rabanus Maurus and Remigius moved the medieval discussion of theater in the opposite direction from that of Amalarius and his critics. Rabanus Maurus and Remigius actively tried to find analogues for pagan history in Christian experience. The suggestion of experiential symbolism in Amalarius's liturgical allegories, however, brought to light differences between Christian hermeneutic strategies and the entertainments of the pagan past, as well as an uncomfortable relationship between scriptural exegesis and its sensual representation.

Rabanus Maurus: Theater as Metaphor

The Carolingian interest in the liberal arts—their use in inquiries into Christian faith and history as well as their value in speculation—shifted the interpretation of ancient theater in relationship to Christian thought and practice. John Marenbon recognizes the Carolingian emphasis on the liberal arts and education in general as an ongoing Neoplatonic inquiry into knowledge, its methods and objects.[9] In this intellectual climate, Rabanus Maurus produced what Marcia L. Colish refers to as a "user-friendly" version of Isidore's *Etymologiae,* including its descriptions of the ancient theaters.[10] As a pedagogical supplement to liberal arts studies, Maurus's *De universo* guided a student through edited entries modeled on those of the *Etymologiae* but reorganized. Working in a missionary context, Rabanus Maurus also cast Isidore's factual documentation of pagan theater in a language of Christian mysticism. The pagan past, as Isidore had laid it out, became a lens through which Christianity could be understood and taught as an evolutionary process moving from Christ's birth to his redemption of the physical world. Without suggesting that Christian representation might actually use ancient theatrical techniques, Rabanus Maurus mined records of Greco-Roman entertainments for

their latent Christian symbolism and meaning in the broader effort to promote Christian faith over the beliefs of barbarian paganism.

Following book 18 of the *Etymologiae, De universo*'s book 21 continued the
classification of theater with competitions and sports—rather than with language, literary forms, dialectic or rhetoric, as would be the case in the Renaissance. In that book, theater was still joined categorically to athletic contests,
footraces and horse races, gymnastic exhibitions (dancing, throwing contests,
deeds of bravery, wrestling), public debates in the forum (chap. 15, *De foro*),
and war games with their paraphernalia (chap. 1, *De bellis;* chap. 5, *De armis;*
chap. 13, *De loricis;* chap. 14, *De galeis*).[11] So classified, theater again fell under
entertainments and social activities associated with bravado, physical
strength, combat (including debate), and masculine virility, expressed
through the performance of competitive games.

In *De universo,* ancient theater was still closely associated with the agon,
which gives modern literary drama its conflict-centered narrative structure.[12]
Rabanus Maurus did not, however, put such conflicts on the same plane as the
spectacular combats, public debates, or scripted *ludi* that Augustine described
and Isidore later cataloged as contests. Instead, he found in the historical
record an analogy for the ongoing Christian struggle against evil. Theater
became a metaphor for the fundamental struggle of Christian experience, not
merely the site at which dramas, narrative poems, and contests were played
out for pleasure in the ancient world. Rabanus Maurus's *De generibus
agonum,* for example, took Isidore's description of contests verbatim as the
base for an exegetical shift in Christian ideas about theater.[13] Rabanus Maurus
revised the documentary quality of the original with a wholly Christian reference to 1 Corinthians 9:25. In *De universo,* ancient contests (of which theater
was one genre) thus became evidence of Christian eschatology, the historical
transformation of pagan to Christian culture, and the triumph of Christianity.

> Moreover, from earthly contests, the Apostle took the example for
> spiritual conflict saying: but everyone who competes in public games
> abstains from everything else, and indeed those men receive a corrupt-
> ible crown: but we receive an incorruptible crown.[14]

The conflict Rabanus Maurus extracted from Isidore's description of contests was not physical, nor was he concerned primarily with the desultory
nature of Roman entertainments or the structure of scripted *ludi*. In a
demonstration of the tenacity of Christian spirituality, *De generis agonum*
moved from describing contests of strength, endurance, and beauty per-

formed in the Roman amphitheaters to the strength of the Christian spirit. The narrative move, as well as the analogy itself, demonstrated the triumph of Christian faith over the pagan world, in keeping with scriptural metaphors.[15] Without actually suggesting that such contests might be useful as a Christian practice, Rabanus Maurus made ancient athletic contests a metaphor for Christians' spiritual stamina and the promise of heavenly rewards due to Christians who persevere—the "winners" of the ongoing contest against evil. Thus, as the pagan competitors perfected their skills and their bodies, so Christians should strive continually for purity of body, spirit, and heart. The analogy effectively gave pagan performance practices new meaning in the language of Christian experience. Christianity, like performance, required appropriate discipline—abstaining from laziness, restraining food or drink, and taking up serious contemplation. Only with the discipline of athletes might a Christian be freed from anxiety, sadness, and secular concerns (even those of marriage). Moreover, Christians' reward would come not from the earthly judge of a contest, as in the pagan past, but from God, who would judge what no one could see—an uncorrupted heart and mind.[16]

But Rabanus Maurus did follow Augustine and Isidore in the assumption that imperfect men acting on the order of demons had established the vain spectacles of cruelty performed in the Roman arenas. In Rabanus Maurus's interpretation of Isidore's information, spectacles functioned only within a specific historical context to illustrate Christians' ongoing struggle against evil. Roman audiences, he proposed, unlike his own audience of reading Christians, had missed the eschatological significance of performed contests because they had failed to see them through the revealed truth of Christianity.[17] Christian participation in Roman entertainments thus constituted a misunderstanding tantamount to a betrayal of Christian faith. Documentation of ancient spectacles did not—indeed could not—offer a model for Christian representational practices or performance. Passages from *De universo* deliver a warning to ninth-century Christians against the dangers of vain spectacles, instituted by demons, in the past as well as in the present.

> There ought to be nothing for a Christian in the insanity of the circus, the lewdness of the theater, the cruelty of the amphitheaters, the atrocity of the arenas, and the excessive luxury of the games. He who goes to such things denies God and is made a double-dealer of Christian faith; he seeks again that which he had renounced in baptism, the devil with his pomp and works.[18]

Categorizing by etymological likeness, which had been essential to Isidore, gave way in *De universo* to the authority of Christian interpretations of the categories' contents. In his thematic reorganization of the *Etymologiae*, Rabanus Maurus advanced the idea of framing the pagan world in a Christian order by investing Isidore's historical data with Christian meaning. He gave the information value (though not practical application) in Christian thought. Isidore, for example, had been concerned with warning Christians that Roman circuses were possessed by the unclean spirits of Satan.[19] Rabanus Maurus took this concern out of its descriptive context in the *Etymologiae* to make it relevant for a contemporary Christian. In Rabanus Maurus's *De coloribus equorum* (which immediately precedes the entry on theater), the colors of the horses became signs of Christians' struggles against the devil.

> But the red horse on which he who had taken peace from the earth sat signifies the perverse people, bloody from their rider, the devil, who always takes pleasure in discord. . . . For the devil and his ministers, by metonymy, are named death and hell, for the reason that they are the cause of death and hell for many.[20]

This intellectual move, which made Isidore's information on equestrian shows a starting point for Christian symbolism, then extended more generally to theater and theatricality. Since Rabanus Maurus had no other referent for theater than the entertainments of Greek and Roman culture, he conceived of theater as part of a social world in which Christians had been identified as a cultural and religious alterity. Thus, chapter 16 of *De universo* calls "spectacles" *(spectacula)* "vices" *(generaliter nominantur voluptates)*, precisely because people were looked at or watched *(quod hominibus publica ibi praebeatur inspectio)*. Christian martyrs and prophets were mocked, injured, or killed for sport *(ludicra)* or entertainment *(ita et apostoli spectaculum facti sunt: quia publice irridebantur positi ad injuriam et mortem, quam passi sunt)* in the theaters and arenas. For Rabanus Maurus, the reciprocity between a game and a theatrical play implied by variations on the word *ludi* was clear: game, sport, and theater involved Christians being made visible as objects of ridicule to pagan spectators.

Theater's inextricability from the social world, as well as its institution by the gods, kept it in the same category as the systematic violence of the Roman arenas. Following the schematic arrangement of the *Etymologiae*, *De universo* (chaps. 36 and 16) also put theater after entries on chariot races, horse races, and footraces, assuming theater's association with both prostitution and pagan gods.[21] But in *De universo*, theater did not prompt warnings against moral depravity, sexual license, or the lure of paganism; it became the site of persecution. Theater could not be assumed to be neutral about Christians or Christianity; it had been invented in a world that held Christians in contempt and put them on display for entertainment. Thus, if theaters did exist in the present day, their presentations would, by definition, disparage Christians and Christianity.[22]

As presented in *De universo*, theater has become an abstract symbol for the harshness of Christian experience under imperial Roman rule. Drawing on 1 Corinthians 4 for his metaphor, Rabanus Maurus concluded in *De theatro:*

> In a mystic sense, the theatre can mean the present world, in which those who follow the luxury of this age hold the servants of God in mockery, and rejoice in looking on their punishment. Hence the Apostle says, "For God's sake we are made a spectacle in this world for [bad] angels and men."[23]

Unlike Isidore, who had documented the past, Rabanus Maurus was vitally concerned with the Christian present. If theater had ridiculed Christians in the ancient world, Christians could not adopt theater as a practice, but the *idea* of theater could serve as an illustration of Christian struggle. Maurus's text brought theater into Christian thought without proposing theatrical representation as a method for inquiry or a mode of representation for ritual and without expanding the idea of theater to include the jongleurs, mimes, scopes, singers, and other performers who provided entertainment. *De universo* legitimized theater as a symbol for Christian struggle with (and in) the material world and gave ancient theater a place in Christian knowledge of the ancient world.

Ancient theater had held the material world up for view in overtly contrived settings. Theater could thus serve Christian thought as an example of the infidelity to spiritual truths that had characterized the church's formative century. With five centuries and countless documentary texts to distance him from Augustine's outrage at the form, content, and social setting of Roman plays, Rabanus Maurus could extend the Augustinian notion that constructions of human artifice were inadequate for representing Christian truth. The world that theaters represented in the first century had been hostile to Christians and Christianity; therefore, theater as a practice was best left to decay along with the ruins of the buildings themselves. But the textual memory of that theater now provided a metaphor for the method by which Christians should view and judge the material, earthly world, as if that world were itself a kind of false performance.

But if Augustine's concern had been that theater would mislead unsuspecting Christians by its false mode of representation, this was nowhere an issue in *De universo*, in large part because Rabanus Maurus's knowledge of theater as a cultural practice was conceived from texts rather than experience. In the absence of an ongoing tradition of scripted plays performed in purpose-built structures, the idea of theater became, in the language of modern semiotics, an empty sign, an idea rendered in texts but decoupled from a physical referent. Rabanus Maurus and his readership need not encounter an active continuation of Roman theater to understand its significance to immediate Christian experience. Still, while Rabanus Maurus could find positive Christian symbolism in other forms of Roman entertainment (even the filth of the equestrian fields), theater remained a conceptual impasse in Christian thought. That impasse surfaced in the controversy over the *Liber officialis* and *Eclogae de ordine Romano* of Amalarius of Metz.

Liturgical Allegory and Pagan Theater

The organization of Christian monasteries and worship went hand in hand with the translation of theological truths into rituals, hymns, and iconography. The ceremonies taking shape as Gregorian reform accommodated local folk rituals and challenged ceremonialists to find appropriate means of representing scriptural narratives—most important, Christ's Last Supper, crucifixion, and resurrection—and their spiritual truths.[24] Standardizing Christian ritual at the institutional level demanded symbolic systems that could give the ceremonial performance of the Mass immediate meaning for learned and unlearned worshipers. For Amalarius of Metz, the emerging genre of liturgical allegory proved an effective way of constructing correspondences between the objects and rubrics of the Mass, Christian history, and belief.[25]

Amalarius remains one of the earliest and certainly the most prominent proponents of applying classical allegorical methods to the liturgy. His service to church and state as Bishop of Treves, envoy to Constantinople, ambassador to Rome, and temporary governor of the Lyons diocese, in addition to his loyalty to Louis the Pious, gave his creative efforts the widespread influence that comes from solid political backing. But from his early studies in logic with Alcuin, Amalarius invested his intellectual energy in the development of Catholic ceremony.[26] In the context of the Carolingian courts, Amalarius was perhaps less concerned with the immediate threat of barbarian paganism than were many of his contemporaries. Amalarius pressed into the service of Christian pedagogy a wide range of classical and oriental sources, shifting them from rhetoric and dialectic to ceremony.[27] As noted by Allen Cabaniss, Amalarius made a conceptual link between ancient theater and the Mass in service of recouping and justifying his allegorical method: if the ancient *ludi* were understood as allegories, then Christians could likewise interpret their ceremonies allegorically.[28] With Isidore's *Etymologiae* at hand, as well as the writings of Augustine and Bede, Amalarius constructed elaborate matrices of meaning to explain the liturgy of the Western church.[29]

The allegorical method, as well as the use of classical sources in allegories, became for Amalarius a way of describing correspondences between the physical components of the Mass and their spiritual referents. Amalarius extended rememorative allegory from words to action so that the Mass itself became a kind of hermeneutic process.[30] In defense of the allegorical method, he held that allegory served Christian exegesis better than it had served any purpose in the ancient world, precisely because it was being applied to God's revealed truth. Drawing on Isidore's description of ancient dice playing, for example, he outlined the value inherent in seeking the Christian meaning in all natural and man-made things.

> If the gentiles argue that some games of theirs emerge allegorically, like dice players, who claim that three time-periods are meant by their dice—present, past, and future—and who distinguish their paths by the number six because of the six ages of men, how much more has it befallen to Christian industry, and to prayer granted them by God, by no means in vain to establish something.[31]

Though Amalarius did not specifically invoke theater as a symbol, analogy, or metaphor or compare the Mass directly with ancient theater, modern scholarship has long regarded his allegories as indications of a theatrical sensibility in early liturgy. So extensive is the scholarship on this topic that it is now almost impossible to decouple liturgical allegory from modern notions of theater and theatricality.[32] In light of Rabanus Maurus's effort to give the ancient world, including its theater, significance in Christian thought, it would seem that Amalarius was giving that conceptual effort a practical application. But the controversy over Amalarius's allegories calls into question the idea of theater in Christian thought. The controversy also reveals significant differences in the modern Western concept of theater (which since the Renaissance has drawn heavily on the ritual theater of the ancient Greeks for its understanding of mimetic representation) and the concepts of ancient theater operating when Amalarius set his allegories on parchment.

The *Prooemium* of the *Liber officialis,* much discussed by theater historians, describes a visual likeness between the Eucharistic celebrant and Christ. The relationship between the celebrant and Christ was the same, Amalarius suggested, as that between the Communion bread and the historical body of Christ.[33]

> What things are brought about by the celebration of the Mass, in the sacrament of God's passion are brought about, as he himself took them before, saying: "As many times as you do this, do this in memory of me." For that reason, the celebrant sacrifices the bread and wine and water, which is the sacrament of Christ; bread, wine and water is the sacrament of Christ's body and his blood. Sacraments should have a likeness to the things of which they are the representation. Therefore the priest is like Christ, as the bread and liquid are like the body of Christ. So is the sacrifice of the priest at the altar therefore like the sacrifice of Christ on the cross. Because man is the likeness of Christ resurrected in that manner, he eats his flesh and drinks his blood.[34]

Amalarius's implication that likeness is a visual and participatory commemoration of the historical event is, as noted by Rainer Warning, precisely what allowed Amalarius to construe the Mass as a return of the original event to the present time. This idea departed from the more orthodox understanding of the Mass as part of a progression toward the salvation of the world.[35] In *Christian Rite and Christian Drama* (1965), O. B. Hardison, Jr., suggests that Amalarius's description of the Stational Mass inadvertently revealed the essential characteristics of theatrical drama.[36] Hardison's widely accepted thesis, grounded in a concept of modern dramatic narrative, holds that Amalarius understood the Mass as a drama, with a plot and character roles, but was unable to bridge the conceptual gap between Catholic ritual and theater or drama proper.[37]

> [Amalarius] could only express his insight [into the dramatic nature of the Mass] by speaking of a "plot" and assigning to the participants the roles which they played in the history from which the "plot" is derived.

The medieval writer, unable to say that the Mass was a ritual drama, was forced to say simply that it was a drama.[38]

Amalarius seems to present the Mass as a rememorative drama showing Christ's life, work on earth, death, and resurrection. The Mass could thus be described in modern terms as a hero-narrative performed with the stylized gestures of classical theater and with a cathartic release at its narrative end. But the task of making Amalarius's allegorical explanations describe a theatrical drama also requires, as Hardison points out, rationalizing inconsistencies and reconciling differences between Amalarius's description of the Mass and ninth-century worship.[39]

Modern concepts of drama and theater, shaped by humanist traditions in which theater is the embodied form of drama, posit theater as an artistic endeavor requiring impersonating fictional characters in the events of a scripted plot. As Hardison shows, the overall scheme of Amalarius's explanations corresponded remarkably well to modern expectations for dramatic structure (central conflict, rising anticipation, climax and resolution, a central protagonist). Consistent with mid-twentieth-century literary theory, Amalarius's description of the Introit can be read as a "frame drama," which foreshadowed the historical events commemorated in the service, in a kind of holographic microcosm of the entire Mass.[40] The physical performance of a Mass has been seen by modern scholars as a consciously symbolic staging of Christian history, with the basilica as a theatrical space where Christian history and eternity are represented simultaneously on two intersecting "stages." The altar, like the role-playing priest, must lose its identity as an altar to become a "stage for the events of the Passion and Resurrection"; the participants in the Eucharist must likewise submerge their own identities as they become part of the imitation of Christ speaking to his apostles.[41] For Hardison, Amalarius crossed a conceptual line between allegorical interpretation and dramatic mimesis, thus reinforcing the familiar idea that sacred ritual develops by increments into secular theater.

> The interpretation devised by [Amalarius] fuses setting, characters, and action into a visible expression of the unseen realities of the Mass. The remainder of the Mass is focused on the sacrifice, but the sacrifice is firmly held *sub specie aeternitatis* by the symbolic drama extending from Introit to Gloria. Christ emerges from the timeless, dies, and ascends in the figure of the bishop. He re-emerges in the figure of the

celebrant. At the end of the Mass, when the bishop rises to give his blessing, the celebrant is again enfolded in the world beyond time.[42]

Since Hardison's study of medieval ritual drama, the strategies of post-modern historiography have challenged (in some cases, dismantled) the idea of theater as framed, text-based, mimetic performance. Late-twentieth-century attention to performing bodies as signifiers, identity construction, representational strategies within historical documents, cultural difference, deferred (rather than hidden) meaning, performativity as a cultural practice and, above all, the critique of presence has in some cases dismantled traditional notions of medieval theater.[43] Such revisions have made the ritual-to-theater model less tenable without qualification, by focusing on the discursive contexts of the documents themselves or on the corporeality of the performances to which the documents point. Still, in the context of Western intellectual and theater history, Hardison's recognition of role-playing and dramatic structure in Amalarius's allegories resembling staged theater remains strong, if not pervasive. But as Hardison points out, it was not likely that Amalarius himself actually conceived of the Mass as a drama in any modern sense. Nor did Amalarius himself lay out a direct analogy between classical theater and the Mass, as Honorius Augustodunensis would do in the twelfth century. Given the status of classical theater in Christian thought, what was the relationship between liturgical allegory and ninth-century concepts of theater?

The kind of imaginative embodiment of biblical events and sensual participation Amalarius joins to scriptural exegesis certainly resonates with modern, Western notions of theatrical mimesis (which are frequently grounded in Aristotle's *Poetics*). But classical theater did not function as an allegory in Amalarius's interpretations and suggestions of mimetic embodiment, which were pedagogical as well as exegetical. Nevertheless, he was accused of making the Mass theatrical. Both Deacon Florus of Lyons, whose antipathy toward allegorical interpretation was already well known, and Archbishop Agobard of Lyons, who had reasons for wanting to curtail Amalarius's influence in the Lyons diocese, took issue with the effects of allegorical interpretation on Christian belief.[44] Given the importance of expressing political unity in ritual, Louis the Pious delivered no punishment beyond censure after the Council of Kierzy pronounced Amalarius in error in 838.[45] As Rainer Warning has highlighted, the theological issues at stake were no less than the figuration of Christ's sacrifice, the status of Christian history in the present, and the way in which Christ's suffering was understood and presented as a guarantee of salvation. In Warning's words, "[F]or Florus and the tradition he represents, the ritual repeats and structures an event (the Last Supper), whereas for Amalarius it repeats and structures a history."[46]

Despite the modern assertion that Amalarius had inadvertently found dramatic potential in ritual in his effort to make the Mass accessible, the ecclesiastical contingent opposing Amalarius found that allegorical interpretation failed precisely because it relied on symbolism and embodiment, rather than language, to represent Christianity's "eternal truths."[47] But for Amalarius, the materiality of the Mass as an event, together with the corporeality of Christ, could indeed offer access to the spiritual dimension of salvation history, by reconstructing that history as immediate experience. Christ's body could be both human and divine (*Ut similis sit homo Christi resurrectioni, aliquo modo manducat carnem et bibit sanguinem eius*).[48] Amalarius implied that human ingenuity could create the conditions of the Crucifixion from the altar, paten, chalice, or cross, by establishing perceptible likenesses, which gave Christian spirituality a dangerously material and visible component. That Amalarius's interpretive strategy led to a description of the body of Christ as represented in the discrete parts of the Eucharist drew fire from his detractors in Lyons. Theater, understood as a pagan practice, provided a frame for this criticism.

Two charges brought against Amalarius addressed his liberal invention of liturgical allegories and his use of pagan allusions.[49] Both charges were indirectly associated with theater in their distrust of man-made craft as a conduit to God and of any unqualified acceptance of non-Christian forms of knowledge. Further, even if Amalarius's allegories gave Christian theology material form for the benefit of illiterate laypeople and potential converts, the process of constructing allegories put power in the mind of the interpreter rather than in the Scriptures. Making allegorical relationships thus proved potentially dangerous because it threatened to replace the scriptural foundation of the Mass with symbolic meanings for objects, rubrics, garments, and the priests themselves. Allegory taxed the relationship between the ephemeral performance of a Mass or liturgical office and eternal Christian truths. If performing the Mass was given more importance than the truths it was thought to represent, the next logical analogies for Amalarius's detractors were to the debauched theatrical shows of the empire and then to pagan idolatry, on Augustine's authority.

Florus's concern that Amalarius's allegories implied a triform body of Christ prefigured one of the early debates over the relationship between

Christ's body and the Eucharistic bread, centering on whether Christ is present or symbolized in the Eucharistic elements. For Paschasius Radbertus, the ceremonial bread became Christ's body in the ritual reenactment of the Last Supper.[50] Ratramnus proposed that the ritual evoked Christ's body figuratively but that Christ's body was not physically present.[51] Paschasius's inquiry into the relationship between *figura* and *veritas* and Ratramnus's effort to preserve the interplay between sacramental signs and Christian faith may have been prompted by the controversy over Amalarius's *Liber officialis.*[52]

Precisely an emphasis on materiality, figuration, and "visible expression" (qualities valued in modern theatrical performance and suspect in early Christianity) distorted the theology of Christ's body. In *De correctione antiphonarii* 12, Agobard complained of *theatralibus sonis et scenicis modulationibus.*[53] Indeed, the tension between the impulse to embody faith in service of pedagogy and the ecclesiastical impulse to repress liturgical excesses is one of the stranger paradoxes in the Christian tradition.[54] But Agobard's criticism of liturgical practice, grounded in prevailing concepts of ancient theater, evoked *theatralibus sonis et scenicis modulationibus* as a comment not on theater but on theology. Such a complaint carried with it an a priori knowledge of theater's pagan roots, its representational perfidy, and its hostile use against Christians. Theater remained, in concept, a site that separated Roman Christians from their heretical neighbors.[55]

The problem of ecclesiastical control over pagan beliefs still active in supposedly Christianized Frankish regions was quite real, and there was ecclesiastical concern about pagan practices continuing in the Germanic and Frankish territories. This concern was deeply embedded in the critique of Amalarius's allegories.[56] Part of the problem with liturgical allegory was precisely that by referring the spiritual transcendence of the Mass to material things and by his frequent references to classical mythology, Amalarius was encouraging pagan, rather than Christian, beliefs.[57] That Amalarius's efforts on behalf of spiritual instruction could indeed bring non-Christians closer to understanding the Mass put the Lyons contingent in the awkward position of curtailing an effective proselytizing tool. Fear of the reverse effect—that the popularity of Amalarius's allegories would spark unauthorized beliefs and rituals—proved an equally powerful motivation for restraining the spread of his teaching. An implication that the Mass was like theater, with the accompanying shadow of pagan idolatry and false representation, thus evoked more than a preference for solemnity and reverence; it struck at the core of ecclesiastical control over the beliefs and practices of the laity.

Amalarius did not call on available sources on ancient theater to draw parallels with Christian ritual, as Honorius Augustodunensis would do three centuries later. He did not, for example, compare priests' robes to the masks and cothurni of ancient costume, the altar to the raised platform of the ancient stages, antiphonal singing to theatrical dialogue, or celebrants' gestures and Scripture reading to theatrical recitation. Amalarius's correspondences are strictly between a celebrant and his figurative resemblance to Christ, the sacramental elements and their symbolic resemblance to Christ's body and blood, and the act of sacrifice performed at the altar and Christ's historical sacrifice. These correspondences were grounded in a Neoplatonic understanding of the Mass rather than in an Aristotelian concept of mimesis: the Mass matched in form the historical events described by Scripture.

If theater and drama figured in Amalarius's allegorical thinking or sensibilities at all, they were tangential to the hermeneutics of the Mass itself as an agent in the salvation of Christian souls. While he covered the whole range of Christian history, Amalarius did not develop a linear narrative in the classical sense of story *(fabulae)* or history *(historia)*. The allegorical method presented the Mass as a series of moments, each with its own immediate significance in salvation history. The spiritual conflict between Christianity and its opposition, for example, was pervasive but was presented as ongoing, lived experience rather than as the inciting device in a narrative structure. Individual moments of the Mass thus described Christians fighting their common enemies (presumably heretics, pagans, and non-Christians as well as the devil), just as ancient theatrical spectacles served Rabanus Maurus as an analogy for the same struggle.

> But blessings are asked for us over the table like a prayer and an evangelical hymn, which Christ sang according to John, in commending his disciples to the Father before his Passion. In that last one, the people are blessed. What does this blessing mean? It means fight, at least against the devil and his treachery.[58]

Nevertheless—and this point has fascinated theater historians—Amalarius's descriptions also emphasized meanings derived from the performance of the Mass. Whereas Isidore had cataloged a straightforward description of the words of the sacrament and their meaning, Amalarius transferred the meaning of the scriptural accounts to the immediacy of its ritual representation—sights, sounds, gestures, and bodies in motion. Amalarius, starting with the ceremony rather than the theology, essentially focused on the representational capacity of the Eucharist within the Mass.[59] He proposed a mode of thinking in which the Mass reconfigured and reorganized the material, tangible, earthly world in the image of God's intervention at a moment in human history, not unlike Rabanus Maurus's reorganization and reinterpretation of Isidore's unembellished transcriptions of historical information in *De universo*.

Amalarius presumed the relationship between the Eucharistic elements and the historical blood and body of Christ—what Rainer Warning calls the tension between "the bloody sacrifice and the bloodless repetition"[60]—to be that described in the Scriptures. The correspondence was contingent on faith in the Word of God. In this sense, Amalarius's thinking was quite different from the theatrical performances described by Augustine and documented by Isidore, in which performers' actions and gestures by definition represented fictions and (in dance or mime) used narration to explain the story line.

The pretense, masking, and fictions associated with classical theater were as much anathema to Amalarius's idea of perceptual likeness between the celebrant and Christ as they were to Augustine's zealous proselytizing. Only the hierarchical relationship to Christ in the ecclesiastical chain of command, coupled with faith in the spiritual immediacy of the historical event, gave that likeness its authority as an aid to understanding the Eucharist as an act commemorating the past and confirming Christ's presence in the present. Amalarius's emphasis on the disciples' eating and drinking "in remembrance" of Christ reinforced the commemorative function of the Eucharist. Beyond visual "likeness," however, Amalarius's *Prooemium* expands the conditions of faith that must undergird the visual image if it is to make sense.

> Christ rose from death and he did not die. By the body of Christ that he eats, man is worthy, the soul lives—received in the resurrection, following baptism or penitence—completely and continuously until the resurrection is made full on the eighth day.[61]

In Amalarius's interpretation, the sacrifice at the altar drew participants together in the communal act of eating and drinking that historically had taken place before the Crucifixion. The celebrant led the meal, rather than demonstrating a full-scale reenactment of the Crucifixion or the Last Supper. The intended effect was transformative and sustaining not because of a mimetic replication of the event but because the original act of Christ's last meal with his disciples gave future Christians an act to repeat, secure in the promise of salvation if they do. Thus, the priest was "like Christ" to the extent that his visual image reinforced the idea that the congregants themselves were part of Christ's community, as Christ's disciples had been. Otherwise, the priest was another Christian soul who, like the other communicants, lived week to week filled with Christ's spirit. That mystical moment, in which the bread and wine were consecrated, was screened from congregants' eyes and was not visible or performative in any theatrical sense. Amalarius described in *De secreta* the imitation of a Hebrew sacrifice.

> . . . what relates to the priest alone—that is the offering of bread and wine—is done in secret. For as much as a victim was present at the Lord's sacrifice in the Old Testament, after he has led him to the door of the temple, just as much does the sacrament stand in the first place on the altar; now it cannot be changed either for better or for worse.[62]

The *Prooemium* moved from describing a "likeness" between the celebrant and Christ to describing the priest's function in the ceremony. "Likeness," in the sense of visual representation, gave way to a discussion of the reciprocity between the perception of worldly things (the physical components of the Mass) and communication with the divine. Amalarius's allegorical interpretations posited the materiality of the altar, Communion wafer, wine goblet, paten, and celebrant and allowed them to become a permeable membrane between the Christian past and the ninth-century present, between the ritual performance and its transcendent meaning.

This reciprocity was not characteristic of theater as it was understood through the texts transmitted to Amalarius. Medieval thought had placed ancient theater solidly in the realm of society, idolatry, and representational perfidy. If, for Amalarius, the priest's actions and words were done *in imitatio Christi* in the Mass, it was done with the already agreed on meanings produced from true Christian faith, not, as Augustine had observed in the theaters, as a combination of gesture and action with a narrated story. Christian knowledge was the a priori condition that gave allegorical referents their meaning. That meaning was specific to Christian believers.

> The present office brings back to memory for us that time, when Christ went up into the great covered dining room, for the meal and there spoke many things with the disciples, and repeated a hymn to God the Father, which John reports, until he went out to the Mount of Olives. There he thanked God; there he sang a hymn, in which he prayed to the Father that he keep his disciples from evil, saying, "I do not ask that you remove them from the world, but that you keep them

from evil"; and so that they might remain holy, he adds, "Sanctify them in truth," and again, "And for them I sanctify myself, that they also might be sanctified in truth"; and so that they might pass over into heaven, he says in what follows, "Father, those whom you have given me, I wish that where I am, they also mat be with me, that they might see my brightness, which you have given me." According to this sense, the altar is the table of God, on which he dined with his disciples; physically the linen cloth is that with which he girded himself; the handkerchief is the work of Judas the betrayer.[63]

Already by the ninth century, certain customs in the Roman and Gallican rites indicated an accepted practice of reenacting biblical events mimetically. Reenactments that involved the entire congregation were especially prominent during the observances of Easter week. Christ's entry into Jerusalem was celebrated with a procession (Palm Sunday); Christ's Passover meal with his disciples was observed with ritual foot washing (Maundy Thursday). Allen Cabaniss calls particular attention to the observance of Mary Salome, Mary Magdalene, and Mary the Virgin approaching the tomb on Easter morning. As described in the *Liber officialis,* priests and deacons walked down the aisle in an attitude of modesty as if walking to Christ's tomb. As much as this example reinforces the argument that early rituals were mimetic in the direction of realistic theater, Amalarius took the ritual from Scripture and transformed it into an example of proper Christian behavior.[64]

Amalarius focused first on the proper attitude that the celebrants and the congregation should bring to the celebration of the office, then on the actual meaning of the rubrics as they relate to the biblical account.

This office recalls those very devout souls who came to the burial-place of the Lord. When the holy women (*mulieribus*) arrived and found that the spirit had returned to the body and that a vision of angels was at the sepulchre, they told the Apostles what they had seen. . . . the subdeacon presents himself at the Lord's tomb [the altar] with his paten which he received from another subdeacon. The subdeacon reminds us of the zeal of the holy women concerning the Lord's burial. Nor is it to be marveled at if holy women are joined to deacons in their duty, since Paul joins the two together in ordination in his remarks to Timothy: in every admonition of the ordination, he wishes the women to be like the deacons. . . . After the priest says, *Pax vobis,* the oblations are placed on the paten. For after Christ by His own salutation made the hearts of His disciples joyful, the prayers of the women were fulfilled in the joy of the Resurrection.[65]

Cabaniss suggests that this allegory anticipated the tenth-century *Quem quaeritis* trope described with quasi-dramatic rubrics in the English *Regularis concordia,* which is generally considered the first example of liturgical drama in practice.[66]

Though Amalarius's description of the ceremony added an experiential dimension to biblical exegesis in the form of the ritual, he did not conflate such ritual mimesis with classical theater. Given the early medieval understanding of classical theater, Amalarius's description of deacons as holy women (cf. 1 Timothy 3.8–13) was quite distinct from medieval concepts of Greco-Roman theater, in that he emphasized Christian knowledge as conditions for perceiving the likenesses he suggested. Likeness in form was not merely a matter of visual similarity referenced to the material, social world; the visual likeness, as well as the meaning of the ritual, depended on the participants' belief in Christ as savior. Whereas Augustine had recoiled from the correlation of his own lust with stage action, Amalarius posited the memory of a historical event as written in Scripture, recalled in the Mass, and internalized in the participants.[67]

But for Amalarius's critics, the problem with constructing such imaginative visual likenesses as a mnemonic aid to the historical event and its salvific meaning was theological, rather than representational. The confusion of identity that the allegories suggested disrupted both the singularity of biblical figures in their historical moments and the distinction between the commemorative ritual and the sacred events themselves. Thus, Florus wrote sarcastically against Amalarius:

And so the aforementioned doctor asserts, among other things, that the Body of Christ is of three shapes and three parts, or rather that there are three bodies of Christ. He thinks that the body of Christ that is taken up by the faithful in the sacrament either is received invisibly into heaven; or remains, up to the day of burial, in the bodies of those who take it; or flows with blood from a cutting of the veins; or slips into a recess. He claims that the deacons, when they assist bowed at the altar, indicate the apostles, fearing and lurking at the Passion of the Lord. The subdeacons are the women standing by the cross without fear. The presbyter is Joseph of Arimathea. The archdeacon is Nicodemus. The cup is the tomb. He calls the offering of the body of the Lord a crucifixion. He says that the wood itself designates teachers; the wood from which he hangs is the cross; the rope by which it is dragged is faith; the tinkling by which it echoes is the tongue; the hand of the one who drags it is, when it is lifted up, the contemplative life and, when it is put down, the active life. He turns the exorcisms of catechumens simply offered for the spiritual affection of cleansing, into the five bodily senses, with far too much carnality.[68]

Set against prevailing ideas about ancient theatrical performance, Amalarius's aim was explanation, not rubrics for spectacle. Amalarius's descriptions of the Mass thus differed radically from the conventional image of ancient theater: the ritual required no critical distance from its subject matter (e.g., mockery of men), the history represented was already invested with Christian meaning (not fictions about pagan mythology), the connection between the rite and a spiritual world was a priori, and the congregation participated rather than observed. Even the aforementioned approach to the altar during the Easter service was imitative only insofar as the deacons evoked the historical event as already known from the Scriptures and demonstrated the reverential attitude proper to Christians. With a completely different understanding of embodied representation from that known of ancient theater, Amalarius had found correspondences between the material immediacy of the Mass and the abstractions of Christian salvation.

Amalarius's allegorical interpretations raised concern on three main issues: the theology of Christ's body, the representation of Christ's body in the Eucharist, and the meaning of the bread and wine consumed in the celebration of the Eucharist.[69] Partisan squabbling aside, the issue for the clerical establishment was how the Mass presented the physical and spiritual body of Christ as unified and the consistency of liturgical reform. The debate set Amalarius's quest for effective ways of presenting and interpreting the Mass opposite notions of theater as representational heresy.

As we have seen, the ninth-century image of ancient theater was of large-scale entertainments, purpose-built spaces, and professional performers; theater was by definition meretricious, in that theaters might be places for prostitution and in that the stories presented were fictions presented with false scenery. That theater was thought to represent only the actions of men or the pagan gods put further distance between the Mass and classical theater. While there might have been superficial overlaps between ninth-century rituals and images of ancient theatrical performance (in that both used gesture and narration), no positive value in such a comparison was possible within Christian thought at this time.

The terms in which Amalarius's critics accused him of theatricality and promoting pagan rites were rooted in a concept of theater, which, unlike rhetoric, logic, and poetry, could not be integrated into Christian thought as a form of reasoning or exegesis. "Theatricality" was a loaded critique, entirely fitting for an accusation of theological heresy because it covered a range of transgressions. Further, though the *Liber officialis* and the *Eclogae de ordine Romano* were widely known during Amalarius's lifetime,[70] their appeal was suspect. It is possible that Remigius of Auxerre himself contributed damning words against Amalarius, calling attention to the heretical effects of allowing congregants to understand the Mass as immediate and experiential.

> [Amalarius] has by his words, his lying books, his errors, and his fanciful and heretical discussion infected and corrupted almost all the churches in France and many in other regions. . . . All of his books should have been burned after his death so that the more simple folk *[simpliciores]*, who are reputed to love them and read them assiduously, might not be thus foolishly occupied and so dangerously deceived.[71]

But at the heart of the controversy over Amalarius's allegories was the representation of the body of Christ. Recent scholarship finds tight connections between changing theologies on the body of Christ and its presence in the Eucharist and medieval representational practices, particularly in light of current theoretical models.[72] This current emphasis on signification and the liminal spaces between representations and referents was not necessarily operative in the early allegorical method. But allegorical interpretation of the Eucharistic ceremony did shift emphasis from the substantial change of bread and wine into body and blood at the moment the elements are consecrated to the affective significance of individual moments in the Mass.[73]

The very idea that the objects and rubrics of the Mass might have the same transcendental properties as Christ's original body threatened the special status of that body. This conceptual shift decoupled the performance of the Mass, as Amalarius interpreted and described it, from the true meaning found in Scripture. For Amalarius's critics, Amalarius allowed the Mass to be perceived as theater rather than ritual and as dangerously pagan rather than wholly Christian. Amalarius's allegories proposed that the Eucharist made the workings of the Holy Spirit visible in material form, that the Mass was not representational in a mimetic sense but functioned as an extension of the invisible world of Christian salvation promised by Christ's sacrifice. As effective as allegory might be for illiterate congregants, from the point of view of his colleagues in theology, Amalarius had introduced a disturbing materiality to the otherwise spiritual effects of the bread and wine by implying that the material world itself (including human bodies), not just the Eucharistic wafer, was infused with the divine power of Christ's salvation.

Amalarius found this infusion of the material with the spiritual a useful and effective means of explaining salvation and privileged the materiality of the Mass. For others, it was profoundly disturbing. "Do we not see," wrote Florus

> to what animals, and what dirty animals, and in what places, human blood lies open when it has been poured out? May such stupid and dirty thoughts be absent from a faithful mind concerning the heavenly mystery of salvation. Surely that bread of the holy offering is the body of Christ, not with visible material or form, but in virtue and spiritual power. For the body of Christ is not born for us in a field, nor does his blood come into being in a vineyard or squeezed out by a wine-press. Simple bread is made from grains, simple wine is squeezed from grapes, and added to this is the faith of the Church, which offers it. Added is the consecration of the mystic prayer and the infusion of the divine virtue; and so, in a wonderful and unspeakable method, bread and wine, which is naturally of earthly origin, becomes spiritually the body of Christ—that is, the mystery of our life and salvation, in which we see one thing by the eyes of the body, another by the veil of faith; nor do we taste only that which we perceive by our mouth, but what we believe in our mind.[74]

Florus argues that the sacraments and their ritual presentation should be free of anything corporeal that would stain the uncorrupted body of Christ, which had escaped a human body's limitations. The argument uses the familiar Christian antipathy toward the body against Amalarius's allegories, which linked spiritual truths to physical objects and the human body in the Mass. The argument suspects what is the visible and demonstrable in favor of God's invisible authority and the unseen interior of the Christian heart.

> For Christ is the virtue of God, and the wisdom of God is taken up in him, which wisdom, as Scripture, bears witness to the brightness of

eternal light and is a kind of emanation of the clarity of the pure God, and therefore nothing stained runs into it, but it attains its purity everywhere. For the body of Christ, as was said before, is not in visible appearance but in spiritual virtue, nor can it be stained by the dregs of the body, because it is accustomed to clean the sins both of souls and of bodies.[75]

Certainly, Florus and Agobard opposed the performative excesses Amalarius suggested, with their emphasis on the bodies of the "performers" themselves (which modern scholarship values as evidence of an emerging dramatic or theatrical tradition). More important, however, the centrality of Christ's unified body to the effectiveness of Christian worship and the presentation of a single, unfractured symbol of belief in that body were paramount.

Amalarius's emphasis on the visual and experiential aspects of the Mass, which led to accusations of theatricality, were also bound to concern for indigenous pagan practices among the laity. Amalarius's use of pagan sources thus became an issue. Florus put Amalarius in the company of a list of early Christian thinkers whose experiments had led them to theological error: Sabellius and Arius, who misread the Trinity; Nestorius and Eutyche, who misunderstood the Incarnation; the Cataphrigians, Manichaeans, Adamites, Artonitae, and Aquarians, whose thought and practice betrayed the Fathers' zeal for truth and efforts to purify the Church of impiety, error, and superstition. "Therefore, these things," Florus asserted in the *Opuscula adversus Amalarium*, "rightly disapproved in the sacraments, seem to have been properly punished, inasmuch as by them, so great a mystery is impiously violated."[76]

Some of the criticism was not far removed from Augustine's observation that Roman theater was merely a man-made artifice that represented man-made things. Florus raised the concern that Amalarius presented his own interpretations as authoritative rather than deferring to the church or Scripture.

For in the church mentioned just above, through its prelate, Amalarius, there preceded an insane and vain error, hostile to faith and truth, contrary to religion and salvation, which actually at first he tried to sow by assembling a synod of presbyters: while the people sat in a circle and listened to him as their teacher, in his own voice—no, I should say, with all of his energy and zeal—for three whole days he proposed it, he set it forth, he laid it out in detail, he pressed it on them, he expounded it, like a minister of the New Testament wishing to engrave indelibly on the fleshly tablets of the heart everything he was claiming. Then he actually handed over to be read and transcribed a kind of great codex spread out over four volumes, written and arranged by himself, claiming that it should be called "official" as though it discussed sacred offices very wisely and very fully, but it is stuffed with such huge mistakes and madness as to appear to anyone, no matter how unskilled, plainly laughable and worthy of being spat upon.[77]

Contra libros quatuor Amalarii criticized the kaleidoscopic meanings Amalarius gave the Mass and found Amalarius's recommendations for performance heretical.[78] Because the rite itself was done differently in different churches, allegorical interpretation could not possibly account for all the variations in how the Mass was performed. The value of the ceremony, for Agobard, was in the spiritual reality that existed apart from any material representation. By proposing multiple meanings for the persons, gestures, and rubrics of the Mass, allegorical interpretation constructed false meanings around material artifice.[79] *De divina psalmodia*, for example, presented the Augustinian argument that humans could only praise God with Scripture and that Amalarius's antiphonary was the product of human inventiveness, not fidelity to the Bible.[80] But the *Liber de correctione antiphonarii* raises the issue of the kind of singing appropriate for representing Christian truths.[81] Contrary to the monophony Pope Gregory had authorized for standard liturgical practice, Agobard found theatricality that focused attention on the singers rather than God.

Saint Jerome, when he was expounding on the precept of the Apostle, where he says, "Be filled with the spirit, speaking with one another in psalms and hymns and spiritual songs, singing and playing the harp in your hearts to the Lord" [Colossians 3:16], he did not fail to mention that he found deserved reproof in the singers. "Therefore," he said, "we ought to sing and play the harp and praise the Lord more by the mind than by the voice. In fact, this is what is said: "Sing and play the harp in your hearts to the Lord." Let the young people listen to this, let those hear it whose duty is to play music in the sanctuary: they should sing to God not with the voice but with the heart; nor in the manner of tragic actors should the throat and jaws be smeared with sweet medicine, so that theatrical tunes and songs may be heard in church, but in fear, in work, in knowledge of Scripture. Although someone might be (as they are accustomed to call them) "tone-deaf" [*cacophonos*], yet, if he has good works, his song is sweet in the eyes of God. Let the servant of Christ sing in such a way that not the voice of the singer but the words that are read please, that the evil spirit which was in Saul be cast out by those who were possessed similarly by it; and let it not be introduced into those who, out of the house of God, have made a stage of the people." In these words, one must greatly consider that he confirms that those who sing in the manner of David playing the harp with fear and spiritual gravity can drive out a malignant spirit even from their listeners; as for those, however, who with theatrical noises and stage modulations, though their words may be divine, they take two intemperate delight in the sweetness of the voice, he bears witness that not only does he exclude them from others but—what is awful— he shows them to others.[82]

These critiques were thus not simply efforts to curtail liturgical excess and keep the church's appointed clerics in charge of disseminating truth; they were attempts to show that theatricality and Christian ritual were incompatible modes of representation. When Remigius of Auxerre (ca. 841–908) took up the topic of ancient theater less than half a century later, he did so with modes of representation in mind. Remigius added a layer of theological speculation that outlined precisely how theatrical representation was incompatible with Christian thought and practice. Though he found Christian symbolism in the ancient practice of theater, he stopped far short of recommending theater as a pedagogical tool or model for liturgy.

Remigius of Auxerre: Ancient Theater and Christian Perspective

Remigius's descriptions of the technical details of theatrical performance have provided theater historians with more detailed evidence for Greek and Roman theatrical practices than is available even in the *Etymologiae*.[83] Given the available descriptions of pagan theater and the categories of thought developed to this point, there was little reason for a commentator such as Remigius of Auxerre to link Christian ritual with classical theater. Whereas Amalarius's critics had seen liturgical allegory as theatrical and thus as the imposition of ancient pagan customs on the sacred rite, Remigius explored theatrical representation from a Christian perspective.

But more important, in his seemingly contradictory descriptions of masks and masked performance, Remigius refined the distinction between true and false representation and blurred the boundaries between Christian truth and pagan falsehood, by investigating the distinction between characters and the men who perform them. *Commentum in Boethii opuscula* describes ancient players imitating men by imitating their gestures (eventually with masks) and distinguishes between reasoning beings and nonsentient creatures.[84] Following Boethius's *Against Eutyches and Nestorius* in what would become a topos in discussions of the three aspects of the Trinity, Remigius holds that an audience could identify an individual both by substance of his character and by his appearance. A person, like a theatrical character, could be identified and known by his visible self-presentation. "Person" and "mask" are thus closely related, for a mask both conceals the actor's face and represents another man.

> For among the ancients it was the custom of actors to mock any people they wanted to with bare faces; but when this fell out of favor, masks were put on, in which a louder sound would be given forth because of the concave shape, and no one would be openly mocked. Therefore these masks were called "persons" because actors in them used to represent the essential natures [substances] of individual people. Whence they were called *"personae"* as though *"per se sonantes,"* making a sound by [or through] themselves. And you must know that those whose essential natures they represented also had their words and actions mocked by plots and physical gestures. And so from these *personae*—that is, masks—it so happened that the individual essential natures of all men were called *personae*.[85]

Augustine's concern with true and false representations of true and false things held firm in Remigius's conflation of masks (appearances) and the substance of a person. Remigius made a categorical distinction between *persona* meaning a person and *persona* meaning a theatrical mask. Masks could represent the contingent or transient qualities of a person, but not a person's substance or true nature.[86] *Persona* also took on a nonmaterial quality in Remigius's synonym for "mask," *id est larvis,* implying that a performer could represent only a skeleton, ghost, shadow, or shade of a human being.[87] Remigius, like Isidore, described theaters not only as places for playing games and singing songs but also as sites of false representation, if not outright harlotry, where deceptive and meretricious Muses intoxicated audiences *(scenicas meretriculas)*.[88]

Persona could thus refer both to characters in tragic or comic plays and to the substance of a person. While Augustine considered how theater's signs could not point to truth, Remigius continues with a speculation on the relationships between masks, *histriones,* and the characters they depicted. Remigius's presentation emphasized individual men as both subjects and stage performers, rather than focusing on the spectacles, portrayals of gods, or romantic fictions that had so disturbed Augustine or on the mockery of Christians described by Rabanus Maurus.

Remigius's commentary on Boethius, though invested in Christianizing pagan practices, still kept theater well outside Christian purview.[89] Remigius clearly construed theater as false, though its subjects (including Christians) might well have been living people. As H. A. Kelly observes, when Remigius commented on the meretricious scenes presented on the ancient stages, Remigius defined *scaenicae* as referring to the theater but identified the *scene* as the place where plays were performed and poems were recited.[90]

> Stage scenes. [Boethius] calls these meretricious scenes "Muses" because their poems were recited on the stages. But the stage is the place where plays/games were practiced and songs recited; or he calls the Muses themselves deceivers, because the stage, as they say, is the fragrant ointment with which prostitutes would anoint themselves so that they might present a pleasant smell to their lovers and so turn them to their own pleasure. So, therefore, they entice them to make love who themselves read the poems of poets.[91]

Not only did Remigius continue to link theater and sex (drawing from Tertullian, Boethius, and Augustine), but he also reinforced the idea that theater reproduced a material world that was anathema to Christianity's internal, spiritual reality. Remigius judged that scenic painting, for example, constructed a false visual image of the world. He thus used theater as a metaphor for the transience of the material world and the impermanence of humans' activities on earth. Remigius assumed that the shapes and forms created on the ancient stages were no less ephemeral and transient than earthly life. Petronius's lament that all the world is a stage was indeed a theological condition of the ninth century.

> The stage scene, in its variety, signifies the world. For it [a stage scene] could be turned around and drawn out [manipulated] in such a way that just as diverse tragedies were recited, thus different shapes could

be put before the eyes of those who sat idly, and they would be delighted by the variety of shapes just as by the diversity of tragedies. This was also done by double paintings. When [the scene] had been drawn in a circle, paintings [flats] were placed first so that those who sat there might be delighted also by the figures on the inside. Or it was being done for this reason, that the shapes themselves might coincide with the different persons there represented by comedians. He [who] proves by the greater that it is not surprising if there is no true firmness in human affairs, because not even man himself endures long but is quickly dissolved—he proves also that fortune changes, because, though it may not depart in the life of a man, yet it will depart when the man himself dies.[92]

Quite possibly Remigius conceived of recited tragedies as well as tragedies acted out with gestures. In the commentary on Martianus Capella, he placed poets in the theaters performing recitations. But he also connected the *scaena* with the Greek word for "shadow" and interpreted the *scene* as a shaded area or structure. The stage is metaphorically a shadow *(umbraculum)* of life, as well as a description of the arbor that covered the ancient Greek stage, which represented life itself.[93] In keeping with Rabanus Maurus's symbolic interpretations of the pagan past, Remigius made direct comparisons between the stories of Greek tragedies and the Christian narrative. Without faith, the entire significance of the Christian story would be merely a poetic fiction.[94]

Whereas it had been impossible for Augustine to speak of the Christian tradition in the same breath as pagan beliefs, Remigius, surrounded and supported by a Christian community in the ninth century, could treat the Incarnation as a narrative akin to Greek legends. If Greek and Roman tragedies lacked the true knowledge offered by the Christian Scriptures, Christ's birth could fill that lack. The comparison between fiction and faith served to prove the distinction between the Christian present and the pagan past, pointing to a vast chasm between the stories told in ancient cultures and the truth of Christianity's historical narrative. Christian history was not a tragedy and thus was not fit for the illusion of theatrical representation. By contrasting the visible contests of endurance performed in the ancient arenas, amphitheaters, and stages with the ongoing invisible struggle of Christians against pervasive evil and untruth, Remigius initiated an interplay between athletic contests, theater, dramatic narratives, and Christian eschatology.

The representational issue at this point, coming to the turn of the tenth century, focused less on signification than on visibility. If theater could show the earthly world, which was only a shadow of God's promised world, and if theater itself was of the earthly world, theater must still be false. For Remigius, however, the problem with theater was not only its immersion in and representation of pagan culture but its suggestion that Christian suffering—which should be kept silent, private, and invisible (or perhaps only shown in the Mass)—could be put on display. The spectacle of Christian suffering, in the artificial constructions of pagan theaters, was disturbing for Remigius because it gave Christian spiritual struggles visual and material form.

Remigius's descriptions of ancient theatrical practices were consistent with Isidore's categories insofar as Remigius construed theater as a form of entertainment that presented stories via some kind of human performance. Like Augustine and Isidore, Remigius saw no correspondence between Christian forms of representation (e.g., iconography, rituals, and liturgies) and pagan theater. But his interest in theater's representation of its subject matter further nuanced pagan theater's incompatibility with Christian representation. Remigius again asserted that theater, as a kind of representation, could not express the relationship between the material world and the ultimate Christian reality (God and salvation in Christ), because, ultimately, it was the work of humans, not God.

> The work of nature is double: when something either grows up from scattered seeds, like man from man and trees from trees, or grows up by itself, like certain trees rise by themselves without the scattering of seed. Or it is the work of a craftsman imitating nature, like the statue of someone. Therefore the sensible world is the work of God, made out of that material that was called *hyle*—that is, of a mixing of elements, which once was called chaos—and from the shape, "idea," or form that was in the divine mind, that is, from the figure coming forth from the image and concept of the divine mind. Behold, you have it—whose work is this world, whence it was made and how.[95]

While they continued Augustine's suspicion of theater (less virulently) and generally held to Isidore's categories, the writings of Rabanus Maurus and Remigius of Auxerre differed in their approach to theater and theatricality. Theater, like sports and games, remained bereft of any inherent potential for carrying information or advancing knowledge. Its value in the ancient world was construed as physical. The intellectual issue for theater, however, was not mimesis but the meaning of corporeal representation. Despite the obvious links with poetry, Christianity could not adapt theater or theatrical performance into Christian practice in the same way that poetry, rhetoric, grammar, dialectic, and allegory could be made to serve Christian thought. The very physical quality of ancient theatrical practice as it was understood through late classical sources—the requirements of buildings and perform-ers, spectators and prostitutes, scenery and costumes; its social function—set theater apart from the texts and language that constituted knowledge or the-ories of knowledge for Christian thinkers. Still, the idea of theater as a site of contest began to serve as a metaphor for the spiritual struggles of Christians against evil. Twelfth-century thought would adapt the idea of ancient theater to illustrate Christian behavior on earth.

CHAPTER THREE

Renaissance and Reorientation

Ancient Theater Revisited in the Twelfth Century

CAROLINGIAN WRITERS HAD carried the idea of ancient theater forward from the Fathers as a denigrated and false mode of representation (whatever Christian values might be imposed on the historical records). The revival of focus on classical texts in the eleventh century, as they both matched and challenged Christian beliefs, allowed for a more complex representation of ancient theater in Christian writings from the twelfth century. Terence's comedies continued to provide literature for study, as they had for Hrotswitha of Gandersheim (ca. 935–ca. 1002), who had reworked them as demonstrations of Christian morality and female virtue. School comedies based on Roman plays were composed in France; some of them commented on current events, such as the scandal of Peter Abelard, and may have received performances at court. These comedies include Vitalis of Blois's *Geta*, William of Blois's *Alda*, the anonymous *Pamphilus*, and *Babio*.[1] While they were treated and referred to as literature, that Terence's plays were mentioned in other kinds of writing suggests that the idea of a theatrical mise-en-scène was not entirely anathema to Christian thinking. The tradition of literary dialogue, allegorical and nonallegorical, also flourished in the twelfth century.[2] The Young Woman in the epistolary dialogues attributed to Heloise goes so far as to liken her own feelings to those of Antiphila in Terence's *Heautontimorumenos* (The self-torturer). [3]

By the early twelfth century, the expressive conventions of Christian worship had expanded to include what is now generally recognized as liturgical drama.[4] With liturgical drama and vernacular preaching bringing Christian learning more directly to laypeople and with new devotional forms prolifer-ating, the hermeneutics of embodiment discussed in chapter 2 entered dis-cussions of Christian spirituality. Far from registering an "antitheatrical" bias, however, critiques of liturgical developments spoke across different reg-isters. With the emergence of impersonated characters in ritual settings, the issues of persona and masking raised a practical concern for maintaining the integrity of a Christian body and its soul in the fictional portrayal of a less than Christian person.[5] Some criticisms focused on the dangers of role-play-ing. The polyphonic settings of traditional chants, which introduced combi-natory musical structures into the Mass and offices, earned criticism for heightening emotion through excessive gesturing that called attention to the performer instead of the worship.[6] In tandem with liturgical experimentation and its discontents, vitality in the liberal arts shifted the reception and use of classical learning. The educational reforms that blurred categorical distinc-tions between pagan, Christian, and vernacular literature generated new applications for the poetry, literature, and philosophy of the ancient world—and for its theater.[7]

The theaters and performances of the ancient world, however, remained a matter of conjecture. The theatrical conventions of the ancients were not directly imitated, nor were liturgical dramas discussed according to what was known of ancient theater. But Christian thought in the twelfth century began to adapt the idea of ancient theater without the stigma of Roman or barbar-ian paganism. Rather than being rejected, adapted, or explained in relation-ship to Christian thought, the idea of ancient theater was integrated into and, more important, as this chapter will show, compared favorably with Christ-ian thought and practices.

The twelfth-century move to extract from ancient texts the ethical princi-ples of Christianity differed, as Richard Southern famously argued, from the "literary humanism" of the Renaissance, which valued classical texts apart from their importance to Christian theology.[8] But the awareness of human dignity emerging in the twelfth century can quite properly be called a kind of humanism oriented toward restoring a closer likeness between God and man, whether the effort is to make God more human or humans more godlike.[9] Ancient theater, its aura of paganism growing dimmer and dimmer, offered twelfth-century thinkers a template for notions that spirituality might unfold from human beings.[10]

In this changing relationship to the pagan past and with embodiment of biblical events an increasing force in Christian worship, references to Greco-Roman theater (the performance practice attached to, but distinct from, literary drama) appear in distinct registers. In the twelfth century emerge thinkers who treat theater with more flexibility in relation to both the classical past and the Christian present. Honorius Augustodunensis of Regensburg used the image of a theatrical tragedian in his allegorical explanation of the Mass in the *Gemma animae* of 1100. In the *Didascalicon* of 1125, Hugh of St. Victor added theater to the catalog of mechanical arts, describing theater as a useful, productive, and physically cathartic (albeit ancient) activity. John of Salisbury's *Policraticus* (ca. 1156/59) invoked ancient plays and players in his social criticism of social and religious institutions. Each of these three texts assumes theater to be a performance practice and, as such, a product of human ingenuity with a part in man's progression toward a likeness to God. Ancient theater shifts in Christian theories of knowledge by the twelfth century. It is not a method or site of inquiry but becomes a positive example for Christian reorientations of self toward God.

Honorius Augustodunensis: Augustine's Theater Reimagined

Unlike Amalarius of Metz, whose life and writings were almost exclusively devoted to the inner workings and explanations of Catholic ceremonies, Honorius Augustodunensis (1075/1080–ca. 1156) wrote on a range of theological topics, drawing frequently from Augustine.[11] Among his writings is an allegorical treatment of the liturgies, the *Gemma animae*. Each of the 243 entries in book 1 of the *Gemma animae*, like the entries of Amalarius's *Liber officialis*, details how individual parts of the ceremony reinforce the eschatological meaning of the Mass. It is part of the broader project to systematize belief and practice in service of Benedictine reform, rather than introduce a creative or new interpretation of the liturgy. With the daily celebration of the liturgy a primary medium for scriptural exegesis, Honorius's allegories assume the importance of humans' active participation in understanding Scripture and the significance of the material world in God's redemptive plan. The interplay between the spiritual world of belief and the material world of human existence moves to the foreground. The simple dialogue *Elucidarium* and the *Eucharistion* focus on the Eucharist and its relationship to the body of Christ.[12] But as Caroline Walker Bynum has noted, while the *Elucidarium* "materializes the spiritual," Honorius's *Clavis physicae* "spiritualizes the material."[13] Thus, though Honorius took numerous allegories directly from Amalarius, the *Gemma animae* was part of the intellectual move toward medieval "humanism," part of which was motivated by debates over Christ's physical presence and human qualities.

For Amalarius's critics, attention to the physical performance of the ritual had confused the ceremony's spiritual significance; allegorical interpretations of the Mass stole authority from the Scriptures. Florus had concerns that Amalarius's allegories drew too much attention to the material components of the Mass, to the detriment of true faith, biblical history, and the mystery of salvation. Agobard's accusations that Amalarius encouraged "theatrical" and "tragic" singing, with implications of paganism inherent in the choice of adjectives, voiced the same fear. Amalarius had proposed embodying historical events as a way of giving them meaning in the present. For Amalarius's opponents, the emphasis on the physical components of the Mass (its objects, images, and rubrics) made the Eucharist an ongoing, repeatable activity rather than the commemoration of a single, monumental event in Christian history.[14] If Amalarius's allegories had described correspondences between the physical components of the Mass and their spiritual referents, as discussed in chapter 2, Honorius described the interplay between human culture and knowledge of God. Ancient theater could function in the *Gemma animae*—without stigma—as an example of how the human craft at work in the performance of the Mass might carry meaning and of how the Mass might effectively communicate God's ongoing renewal of the world.

Chapter 83 of the *Gemma animae, De tragoediis,* stands out as unusual in its approach to explaining how the entire Mass works effectively as a ritual.

It must be known that those who recited tragedies in theaters represented the actions of warriors by gestures to the people. In this same way, our tragic poet [tragedian] represents by his gestures the fight of Christ to the Christian people in the theatre of the church and teaches to them the victory of his redemption. Thus, when the elder [celebrant] says "Pray" [the *Orate*], he expresses for us Christ in the position of agony, as when he instructed his apostles to pray. By the silence of the *Secreta*, he signifies Christ as a lamb without voice, being led to the sacrifice. By the spreading out of his hands, he denotes the stretching out of Christ on the cross. By the chant of the preface, he expresses the cry of Christ hanging on the cross. For he sang the ten Psalms, that is, from *Deus meus respice* [My God, behold] to *In manus tuas commendo spiritum meum* [Into your hands I commend my spirit], and then he died. By the secret prayers of the canon, he suggests the silence of Holy Saturday. By sharing the *Pax* [the "kiss of peace"], he represents the peace given after Christ's resurrection and participation in its joy. At the completion of the sacrifice [sacrament], peace and Communion is given by the celebrant to the people, because after our accuser has been humbled in war by our hero [*agonotheta,* "president of contests," meaning Christ] peace is announced by the judge to the people, and they are invited to a banquet. Then, by the *Ite, missa est* [Go, the mass is ended], they are instructed to return to their own concerns with joy. They sing *Deo gratias* [Thanks be to God] and may go home rejoicing.[15]

Given the transmission of the idea of ancient theater as a contest and as a metaphor for Christian struggle, Honorius's construction of the allegory is consistent with the gradual transformation of theater from a practice to an idea. Rabanus Maurus, in *De universo,* for example, had made God the judge *(agonotheta)* of Christians' spiritual fitness.[16] Like Amalarius's *Liber officialis,* though with less claim to official interpretation, the *Gemma animae* also presented the Mass as a ceremonial reconstruction of Christ's sacrificial death, as told by the celebrating priest. Honorius expanded Amalarius's eschatological emphasis by making the daily Mass part of lay Christians' everyday lives. The "exodus" of laypeople from the sanctuary after Mass takes Christ's death and resurrection from symbolic representation to part of the continually unfolding narrative of human history.

Amalarius had treated the ritual of the Mass as a mode of scriptural exegesis, as does Honorius, and employed classical references. But *De tragoediis* introduces a distinctly Greco-Roman practice into the typology. The passage does not simply engage the conventional interpretive scheme (prefigurement, fulfillment, and ritual actualization) but explains the dynamics of the Mass and its overall effects on lay congregants—how the ceremony works as an experience of perception and sensation.[17] *De tragoediis* gives the Mass a dimension of conscious performativity, but that dimension is as distinct from the embodied hermeneutics of "liturgical dramas" as it is from scriptural exegesis.[18]

O. B. Hardison, Jr., in his 1965 interpretation of *De tragoediis* (discussed briefly in chapter 2), showed how Honorius's analogy revealed Aristotelian dramatic structure in the Mass. For Hardison, Honorius's phrase *tragoedias in theatris recitabant, actus pugnatium gestibus populo repraesentabant* implied a medieval understanding of the Mass as a crisis-resolution narrative, performed mimetically with the roles of protagonist and antagonist clearly identified and ending with a cathartic release (more similar in narrative structure to the *komos* of comedy than to traditional tragedy). Hardison maintained that Honorius construed the Christian story in a language of dramatic criticism:[19] *Christi resurrectionem et gaudii communicationem* implies a reversal of fortune, and *Qui gratias Deo jubilat et gaudens domum remeat* indicates the narrative catharsis.[20]

Honorius's analogy with ancient tragedy, as a literary genre, is not especially unusual. Classical sources, as noted at the start of this chapter, were regularly plundered for their pedagogical value, with the awareness that Christ's death and resurrection had redeemed the past. The preface to the *Gemma animae* is no exception, with its deployment of references ranging from Platonic disputations to the battles of Hector.[21] In this respect, ancient theatrical tragedy serves as one of many strategies for explaining how the Mass expresses the meaning of Christian salvation and history. The specificity of the analogy with ancient theater in *De tragoediis* suggests that it does more than reveal a conflict-structured hero narrative in the Mass, the potential of the Mass for dramatic spectacle, and a consciousness of theatrical mimesis in the history of Western theater.

In the *Gemma animae*, Christianity's conflict with evil and untruth are typological and related directly to Christian Scripture. Chapter 72, *De pugna Christianorum spirituli*, for example, emphasizes Christian triumph over evil, in language nearly identical to that of *De tragoediis*. But the references reinforce the prefiguration of Christ's battle against evil in the Old Testament (Genesis 36:12–16). In *De pugna Christianorum spirituli*, the New Testament demonstrates God's restoration of humankind. Christ is still the vanquishing warrior, and the Mass is still described as mimetic, yet here the Mass is not explained by classical tragedy but by reference to the Christian history.

> The Mass also imitates the conflict of the same fight, and the triumph of victory, by which our enemy Amalech is laid low, and a way is opened up for us to the Father through Jesus. Indeed, Jesus, our commander, fought with the devil and restored to man the heavenly republic, destroyed by the enemy . . . [22]

The analogy with ancient theater thus draws together already prevalent notions of conflict, the significance of matter, and human agency in a central narrator, while the comparison with tragedy supports the narrative structure already established by the annual cycle of liturgical readings in which the celebration of the Eucharist takes place. The use of *theatrum* in *De tragoediis* also

marks many of the intellectual changes in Christian thinking about the classical past that are associated with the twelfth century, by bringing the idea of
theater as a social, institutionalized practice (as opposed to drama as literature) into Christian knowledge.

The potential for spectacle in the Mass was, by the twelfth century, already
realized in episodic reenactments within the liturgy, which bore little resemblance to classical dramas. Nancy van Deusen's analysis of the epiphany
Officium stellae from Nevers Cathedral, for example, points directly to the
structural incongruity of classical and liturgical drama.[23] Van Deusen's analysis hints at distinctions in twelfth-century thinking between the embodied
reenactments sometimes referred to as *ludi* and concepts of ancient theater.
The combinatory structure of medieval liturgical dramas, in which individual
units are not bound by a causal plot, central theme, or genre, is distinctly different from the classical notion of a unified plot. As functions of the liturgy,
these short dramatizations were episodic. They worked dramatically as individual units, without making biblical history a coherent narrative of an ongoing history, but emphasized individual events as taking place again in the present moment. Through composition was not a priority in musical settings,
nor was logical progression of events necessary for either dramatic effect or
plot development. Liturgical plays required no dialectical center, presented
no new conclusions, and represented only parts of the whole of Christian
eschatology.[24]

If we follow van Deusen, the form of church reenactment thus did not
readily lend itself to thinking of the entire Mass as unified—whole and complete in itself. Classical tragedy, however, offered Honorius not only the intellectual cache of a classical reference but a metaphor for presenting the Mass
to the priests, who would perform it as a logical chain of events leading from
despair to celebration, from struggle to victory. The comparison suggests that
the practice of liturgical drama and ideas of ancient theater still functioned in
different registers, despite the emergence of what are today called "liturgical
dramas."

Hardison's fundamental question in *Christian Rite and Christian Drama* is
a concern of modern understandings of theatrical mimesis as realistic impersonation of character, which seems to be at work in liturgical drama. Hardison asked of *De tragoediis*, "How far did the celebrant [as a tragedian] carry
his role as *repraesentatione Christi*?"[25] This question has undergone revision as
postmodern dramatic theories have challenged notions of theatrical mimesis
in general. Michal Kobialka, for example, identifies the representational
strategies at work in *De tragoediis* rather than assuming that the passage sug-

gests anything about theater (ancient or twelfth-century).[26] In contrast to Hardison's emphasis on dramatic structure and the origins of theater in ritual, Kobialka deals with the discursive strategies that regulated the appearance (or disappearance) of the body of Christ, established monastic power relations, and negotiated between representation and the real, and he examines the processes by which representational practices produce and authorize meaning.

With reference to Honorius's *Eucharistion* and *Elucidarium,* rather than Amalarius's *Liber officialis,* Kobialka places *De tragoediis* in the context of eleventh-century debates over transubstantiation, which he suggests constituted a pervasive process "of clarifying the *logos,* which calls back the body that had disappeared, and of establishing the practices, which secured the presence of Christ."[27] Honorius's analogy with ancient theater structured the presence of Christ in the celebration of the Eucharist by uniting corporeal, spiritual, and theological discourses.

> The passage from *De trageodiis* is an example par excellence of the appearance of the real in the sacrament of the Eucharist, which structured the whole system of representations. It did so by describing the authority (the priest), the site of delimitation (the church), and the position of the faithful within it. More importantly, without the presence of the real in the sacrament of the Eucharist, the entire field of ecclesiastic practices could not function as it was envisioned by Honorius or other theologians. . . . the language used of *De trageodiis* gave *Hoc est corpus meum* a narrative structure that, in the universe of material codification, becomes both the intelligible sign of a Paschasian understanding of the Eucharist and a proof of both reality and the real.[28]

But in the tradition of Amalarius, objects as loaded with meaning as the sacramental Host could be given purely practical explanations that do not lend themselves to the complexity of theological controversies for pedagogical effect. Chapter 66 of the *Gemma animae,* for example, describes the shape of the wafer as an expression of Christians' everyday concerns for charity and the necessity of donations to the Church.

> It is reported that once priests received wheat from individual homes or families. The Greeks still preserve this [custom] and hence they made the "Lord's Bread" which they offered the people and distrib-

uted consecrated to them. . . . But after the Church increased in number, but lessened in sanctity because of the carnal, it was determined
that those who could [on certain days] should communicate, so that
they would not take on themselves judgment for any crime before confession and penitence. And because, with the people not communing,
it was not necessary that such a large bread be made, it was decreed
that it be shaped or made in the manner of a *denarius,* and that the
people should offer *denarii* for the offering of wheat, for which they
would understand that the Lord was handed over, and that these
denarii be given for the use of the poor, who are the members of
Christ, or for something which relates to this sacrifice.[29]

With a similar emphasis on the materiality of the Eucharistic elements and
their relation to everyday things, chapter 33 describes the sacramental wine
with a biblical reference to Christ as the vine of life (John 15:1–5). The "vine of
life" combines with the practical image of a winepress to explain Christian
suffering and the triumph of Christianity over its adversaries.

Therefore, moreover, this sacrament is made of wine, because Christ
said he was the vine, and Scripture has confirmed him as the wine of
pleasure. But the grape, pressed out on a stake, by two planks, is
liquified into wine, and Christ pressed on two planks of the cross, his
blood poured out as a drink for the faithful. . . . The Church of Christ
is restored, which is assembled out of many righteous people. This is
trampled underfoot by those who press down the world as though in a
winepress, and [it is] incorporated into Christ by passions.[30]

The interplay between the unusual analogy in *De tragoediis* and more conventional allegories is a reminder of the *Gemma animae*'s explanatory purpose and the fluidity of meanings that liturgical objects, even those as loaded
as the communion bread and wine, could have without losing their spiritual
value. But whereas chapters 66 and 33, just cited, are fairly clear in their analogies between liturgical objects and Christian life, *De tragoediis,* because it
invokes a non-Christian practice and mode of representation, is somewhat
more challenging.

Honorius (in the tradition of Lanfranc and Anselm) worked well within
the parameters of Christian logic, and Anselm's Platonism assured that, in
John Marenbon's words, "the most real things are those which are contem-
plated by the mind, rather than by the senses."[31] But while eleventh- and

twelfth-century arguments over the presence of Christ in the Eucharist, the incarnation of Christ in human form, and the Trinity of God-spirit-flesh took place in the arena of grammar and dialectic, the *Gemma animae* turned to the effects of ritual worship for congregants and celebrants. By the twelfth century, in the wake of *Cur Deus homo,* the corporeality of Christ's body had been given positive value, which was not the case in the ninth century.[32] In the *Gemma animae,* the relationships between spirit and matter in the understanding of Christ's presence were grounded less in logical arguments or the problem of grammar and God than in experience and perception.

The two prominent twentieth-century readings of *De tragoediis* summarized here focus on how *De tragoediis* articulated or structured Christian history in the present moment.[33] Hardison concludes that the Mass was thought of and presented as a dramatic narrative of Christ's suffering, death, and resurrection; Kobialka considers *De tragoediis* itself to be a representational practice that, in its description of the Eucharist, made the absent body of Christ "speak."[34] Even two such divergent interpretations of *De tragoediis* evince a modern interest in representation—in how far the priest took his role as Christ in the cosmic drama of the Mass and in how the theater foregrounds the absent body of Christ.

But what gave this analogy a particular resonance for a twelfth-century audience of practicing Benedictine priests? I suggest two possibilities. First, the twelfth-century interpretation of human craft as inherently meaningful in the expression of God's creation opens the possibility that the Mass (here likened to ancient theater) might be considered a kind of cathartic physical labor on the order of ancient games, as described by Isidore, Rabanus Maurus, and Remigius. Second, is the emphasis in Honorius's commitment to Benedictine (possibly connected to Hirsau) reform on priests' ability to communicate with laypeople. Practicing priests and their congregants were to think of the Mass as Honorius described it in his title, as a handcrafted jewel, a material manifestation of the ideal Christian world.[35] The analogy with theater might well construe the twelfth-century Mass as a work of humans—a kind of artifice akin to painting, music, and liturgical objects—and thus as a method for making God real and immediate.

For Honorius, human invention could indeed represent, with no theological dissonance, the intersection of the natural world, the spiritual world, and the material world of human experience. In contrast to Augustine's suspicion of man-made signs, Honorius valued humans' capacity to give meaning to the material world. Though Honorius himself did not include theater in his classification of the *artes mechanicae,* as would Hugh of St. Victor's in the

Didascalicon (slightly more than two decades later), the *Gemma animae* comfortably posited the performance of the Mass as artifice.[36]

Given the breadth of Honorius's classical references and the specificity of the analogy in *De tragoediis*, it is highly unlikely that he was unaware of theater's pagan origins or of the suspicion in which Christian theology held false representation. The idea of representing Christ with the gestures of an actor would have sent Augustine to the edge of reason and Amalarius over the brink of liturgical propriety. Yet *De tragoediis* presumed ancient theater to be a viable mode for signification and a perfectly suitable model for Christian representation. Elsewhere, the idea of classical theater sat less comfortably with Christian worship.

From Isidore, Rabanus Maurus, and Remigius, the image of masked actors in an amphitheater putting gestures to a speaker's recitation had become common knowledge.[37] Like his contemporary Gilbert de la Poirée, Honorius imagined ancient theatrical tragedy as a kind of formal recitation, a combination of mimed gesture, accompanying narrative, and music. Honorius's analogy relied on theater's well-established association with the everyday entertainments of the ancient world—public games, athletic events, and forensic contests—as well as with tragic poetry. For Honorius's purposes, the tragedies performed in the ancient world had represented these war games and warriors and (like the games) were presided over by a judge (Christ in the analogy).

Honorius layered over Rabanus Maurus's interpretations of spectacles in *De universo* a reinterpretation of these ancient practices as fully redeemed by Christian ritual, just as Christ redeemed the pagan world. Mediated by a well-transmitted knowledge of ancient spectacles and their reinterpretation in Christian terms, theatrical tragedy could now provide a legitimate analogy for Christians' ongoing struggle against evil. Three centuries after the Council of Kierzy, Honorius could assume that comparing Christian ritual with pagan entertainments would not incite accusations of heresy. While his other treatises were criticized by his contemporaries, the *Gemma animae,* with its overt claim that the Christian Mass could be explained with reference to a pagan practice, seems to have been received with benign acceptance.

Honorius did not likely intend to suggest that the Mass displayed what should be kept secret, set Christians up for mockery, told lies, constructed false worlds, or supported prostitution—all associations with ancient theater. By the twelfth century, the analogy with theater serves to demonstrate the importance of the Mass as a human construct, as well as a representational practice. Ancient theater—which categories of medieval thought had already construed as a physical, rather than intellectual, practice—thus functioned as an appropriate metaphor both for the Mass as a demonstration of God's history playing out and for the importance of human craft in representing that history. According to Honorius, the activities of everyday life, such as leaving the sanctuary after Mass, and the effective presentation of sermons and ceremony, were ways Christians might participate in God's plan.

This theme runs through numerous passages in the *Gemma animae*. Some allegories seem to imply Platonic doubling, with the Mass reconstructing the prophetic Old Testament past or the imagined future after the return of Christ. In other passages, especially in allegories dealing with artifice, the Mass seems to replicate existing (rather than ideal) forms, in the manner of manuscript copying. Thus, as much as Honorius's allegorical method was intended to explain the Mass to people who might be confused by theological abstractions, it also reinforced the idea that the entire material world, including human artifice, was infused with Christian divinity.

Honorius had justified visual artifice as the literature of the laity, suitable for beautifying people's homes and useful as a mnemonic aid to recalling the lives of patriarchs.[38] Painting and sculpture (and even classical theater) could be as potentially meaningful as the banners and candles of the entry procession. The positive value of artifice in the twelfth-century and throughout the *Gemma animae* was likely part of what allowed the tragedy analogy to work successfully. But human artifice, such as iconography, did require more complicated exegesis.[39] In chapter 133, *De corono in ecclesia* (On the crown in church), for example, painted light is just as powerful a symbol as the light generated by candles, even though the painting is only a representation. Halos painted around the heads of the saints show how saints enjoy the light of eternal splendor; halos are painted in circles to resemble shields in form and so show that the saints are fortified with divine protection. The imitation of light painted in halos demonstrates the eternal light of Christian faith and ensures divine protection for people who see it.[40]

Honorius's phrase *tragicus noster* was thus not a definitive description but one of many descriptions of how liturgical participants stood for eschatological realities or historical persons. Chapter 16 of the *Gemma animae* presents readers and singers as God's workers *(negotiatores)* on earth, as well as symbols for the apostles who had first taught God's praises to the Church, and their singing demonstrates their commitment to serving Christ. Similarly, the organization of choral voices symbolizes categories of Christians, grouped together by how they worship. Honorius posits the choir as an earthly double for the hierarchical organization of angels in heaven and the order of things at the end of Christian time. Performers of the Gradual (literally, a "stepped hymn") signify people who serve Christ with an active life; singers of the Alleluia signify people who praised Christ in private contemplation. Their higher voices, ascending in the alleluia, symbolize people who in their worship ascend to heavenly heights through contemplation and are thus higher in their virtues. Sequences are done antiphonally because angels and humans will eventually sing in alternation in the house of God.[41] Choristers thus had a quadruple function: they served the ritual (by singing), illustrated biblical history (apostolic proselytizing), reinforced spiritual practices in monastic life, and, finally, provided a visual and aural symbol for the end of days.

In chapter 20, *De diacano,* another example of an allegorical interpretation of liturgical participants, the bishop and deacons symbolize biblical figures. The presiding bishop, as head of the church, is Christ's earthly double. Deacons represent the apostolic order, with the reader taking the position of the apostle Peter. The bishop blesses the deacon's reading in the Mass because, says Honorius, Christ filled the apostles with his blessing and gave them power over all demons. Deacons' gestures were likewise symbolic: the deacon carried the book on his left arm because the left side indicates the present life of Christians.[42] Allegories such as this suggest imitation not in the Aristotelian sense of role-playing or impersonation but, rather, as a doubling of heavenly forms.

The complication in *De tragoediis,* of course, is the introduction of a kind of artifice not usually associated with Christian worship and the association of celebrants with referents from pagan, rather than Christian and Jewish, history. The direct analogy between the celebrant and a tragic poet or actor in the narrative structure of classical drama illustrates the Mass as a particular form of expressive artifice.[43] Given the appearance of Hugh of St. Victor's classification of theater with the mechanical arts twenty-five years later, Honorius may have used the analogy to suggest that the Mass could have the cathartic effect of physical labor. Work and human artifice figure prominently in several allegories, including a fascinating interpretation of singing as equivalent to agricultural labor, based on the parable of the plowing servants returning from the fields (Luke 17:7–10). The Word of God was eaten and expelled in song so that the work of the Mass could continue joyfully.

> They plow who, by the plowing of repentance, split their hearts; in the reading, the listener is fed like a kind of ox. An ox is fed for this purpose, that in him the work of agriculture may be performed. An ox is

for the speaker, the cantor, a kind of plowman, who shouts to the oxen with joy so that they may draw the plow more cheerfully; that is, he drives on the singers to sing more cheerfully.[44]

It is quite possible that Honorius, like Hugh, who wrote in the first half of the twelfth century, incorporated theater into the category of craft, or labor of the soul, in service of God's kingdom on earth.

Hugh of St. Victor and the Social Value of Ancient Theater

Hugh of St. Victor's *Didascalicon* (ca. 1125) cataloged how skill in the arts, broadly construed, could lead to knowledge of the divine, very much in the way that Honorius described the Mass as uniting the physical and the spiritual.[45] As C. Stephen Jaeger notes, Hugh "thought of spiritual formation in terms of the model of human handcraft"; a finished, reformed human is an artwork.[46] As the third division of philosophy, accompanying theoretical and practical modes of knowing, the *artes mechanicae* offered ways of dealing with physical existence, a process through which mankind could restore its collective soul to a pure state of divine likeness.[47] If *ars* required manipulating matter, as opposed to the abstractions of reason, the mechanical arts testified to man's ingenuity, just as reason testified to man's ability to acquire knowledge. Though somewhat less sophisticated, the mechanical arts were no less valuable than logic in restoring man to his original likeness to God.[48]

The *artes mechanicae* belonged to "that science to which [the ancients] declare the manufacture of all articles to belong;" the ancients' products were "adulterate" copies.[49] Honorius's analogy proposed a circle of imitation: in the performance of the Mass, a priest imitates an actor who imitates Christ, whom all Christians imitate directly in the course of their daily lives. But Hugh's conception of ancient theater is rooted in pedagogy: discipline of the body and mind through the disciplines of the liberal arts ends with inner order, synchronicity between body and mind, the correct ethical orientation, and similitude to God (leaving aside the issue of Christ's body).[50]

In its categorization as a mechanical art, however, ancient theater bore neither the stigma attached to twelfth-century entertainers nor the well-rehearsed associations with prostitution, perfidy, and mockery. The *Didascalicon* maintains ancient theater's association with games, contests, and forensic oratory but recasts theater's value as physical labor.

The science of entertainments is called "theatrics" from the theatre, to which the people once used to gather for the performance: not that a theatre was the only place in which entertainment took place, but it was a more popular place for entertainment than any other. Some entertainment took place in theatres, some in the entrance porches of buildings, some in gymnasia, some in amphitheatres, some in arenas, some at feasts, some at shrines. In the theatre, epics were presented either by recitals or by acting out dramatic roles or using masks or puppets; they held choral processions and dances in the porches. In the gymnasia they wrestled; in the amphitheatres they raced on foot or on horses or in chariots; in the arenas boxers performed; at banquets they made music with songs and instruments and chants, and they played at dice; in the temples at solemn seasons they sang the praises of the gods. Moreover, they numbered these entertainments among legitimate activities because by temperate motion natural heat is stimulated in the body and by enjoyment the mind is refreshed; or, as is more likely, seeing that people necessarily gathered together for occasional amusement, they desired that places for such amusement might be established to forestall the people's coming together at public houses, where they might commit lewd or criminal acts.[51]

Both the *Didascalicon* and *De tragoediis* place theater and drama in the distant past. Of Hugh's seven categories of mechanical arts, only theater appears in the past tense, and Honorius also describes tragic acting as an ancient practice. When Honorius defines the liberal arts, he includes (beyond the usual quadrivium and trivium) *physica, economia,* and *mechanica,* as ongoing practices. The mechanical arts, those done with the hands, included painting *(insuper picturas)* and sculpture *(sculpturas)* as vehicles for translating and teaching Christian history.[52] (It would certainly be convenient for my argument if he had included theater.) Still, if doing the liturgy could be analogous to the kind of work that produced craft or artifice and if work was attributed the power to right the soul, then Honorius's use of theater as a metaphor for the Mass implies that performing the ritual was a kind of legitimate physical labor. Ancient theater, according to Hugh of St. Victor and Honorius, was clearly distinct from liturgical reenactments or the secular performances of jongleurs, mimes, dancers, gymnasts, mummers, bards, poets, and players. The "catharsis" implied in *Ita missa est* likely evoked not the intellectual catharsis of an Aristotelian tragic narrative but the release after the physical exertion and spiritual concentration of the ceremonial commemoration of Christian history, including Christ's death and resurrection.

Honorius's commitment to the pastoral role of monks and to appropriate payment for their services also gave the *Gemma animae* a decidedly practical purpose.[53] As a supplement to his sermon anthology, the *Speculum ecclesiae,* the *Gemma animae* served the priests who conducted masses for laypeople, by explaining the ritual settings in which the sermons would be preached according to the standard liturgical calendar.[54] Once committed to memory, the allegories would be used pedagogically. The image of an ancient tragedian whose gestures and voice carried tremendous signifying power (issues of false representation aside) thus could have provided a useful model for priests to follow in service of communicating more effectively with lay congregants. Unlike Gerhoh of Reichersberg, who shared Augustine's concerns in his criticism of liturgical reenactments, Honorius did not pass judgment on the immorality of ancient stages, plays, actors, and mimes; rather, he pressed the idea of theater into Christian service, with an emphasis on the value of human invention and the craft of conducting the Mass rather than on elaborate embellishments of the ceremony itself.[55] The concern for theater's inability to represent truth is notably absent in the works of both Honorius and Hugh, as is any connection between ancient theater and contemporary performance practices. Honorius emphasizes theater's effectiveness as communicative performance, with the assumption that the Christian truth represented by the Mass will override or counter any residual paganism in the form itself. Similarly, Hugh set aside issues of representation to focus on theater as a physically demanding social event that contributed to health of the community.

John of Salisbury, the Ancients' Theater, and the Performance of Everyday Life

John of Salisbury (d. 1180), writing a critique of courtly life in the *Policraticus,* was, like Gerhoh of Reichersberg, acutely aware of theater as a mode of representation and imitation. Like Honorius and Hugh, John relies on the accumulated information about the ancient past but brings it to bear in yet another discursive arena. John's employ in the Canterbury court of Archbishop Theobald gave John access to an intimate circle of similarly educated clerics (including Thomas Becket) in prominent political positions.[56] Begun in 1156, after a falling out with Henry II left John with plenty of time for reflection and correspondence with Peter of Celle, the *Policraticus* is a prose work of self-reflexive consolation aiming to "demonstrate the foundations of

the good human life and to demystify the false images of happiness pro-
pounded by" John's colleagues in bureaucracy.[57] In this particular treatise,
the impetus for which remains ambiguous, John's commitment to reasoned
ethics overrides his duties to partisan politics. He approaches his topics—the
vicissitudes of fortune, flattery, tyranny, the duties of a prince, the exercise of
princely power, Epicureanism—with the nondogmatic moderation of the
Ciceronian New Academy and in the conservative spirit of preserving ethics
the school disciplines espoused.[58] John, always working across the gap
between the realities of the Christian commonwealth and its ideal, invokes
classical theatrical performances and contemporary court entertainments in
the context of political dissent.

The authoritative pagan and Christian texts provide John with a foundation for his arguments and offer guidance to clerical servants who, like himself, must attempt to preserve some degree of spiritual integrity and moral
decorum while working in institutional bureaucracies—and who all too often
lose their better judgment in unwitting Epicureanism.[59] Like Augustine, John
is aware of the difference between proper Christian self-love that leads to
charitable acts and solipsism. With concern for moderation in behavior, dignity in self-presentation, and uncorrupted ethics (concerns shared in Hugh of
St. Victor's *De institutione*), John treats the problem of vain flattery as a widespread social mechanism by which men are seduced into abandoning their
true and better selves.[60]

John's knowledge of pagan and patristic texts apparently gave him a fairly
clear image of tragic and comic plays as having been performed with gesture
and vocal inflection, as well as giving him an understanding of drama as a
form of poetic literature.[61] Augustine, one of John's privileged sources, had
found theatrical representation inadequate for Christian learning. John's
twelfth-century mind finds in that inadequacy an illustration of the effects of
compromised ethics on Christians serving political institutions. The illusion,
feigning, deception, and distraction Augustine found in theatricality are, for
John, the very qualities of a life informed by human institutions rather than
by Christian knowledge. John deals with theater in books 1 and 3 of the *Policraticus*. In book 1, theater is one of several interweaving metaphors for man's
passage through earthly life. In book 3, John takes the debauchery of contemporary entertainments as an indication of how far twelfth-century society has
fallen from the accomplishments of the ancients.

In chapter 7 of book 1, a famous passage from Petronius's *Satyricon* provides John with an often cited exemplum that compares friendship to stage
acting, which leaves truth in its wake when the performance is over.[62] In

chapter 8, John extends the simile of the performers' illusion to Christians' earthly life, spinning an elaborate comparison between the material world of the courts and the frivolous illusions of ancient theater. He finds the thronging of profane multitudes to be more like a stage comedy than real life (*quia fere quicquid in turba prophanae multitudinis agitur, comediae quam rei gestae similius est*), and he judges a life lived in service of earthly things no more real than a performed comedy—a person forgets his own role and acts out another's (*diceretur egregie quia comedia est vita hominis super terram, ubi quisque sui oblitus personam exprimit alienam*).[63]

Drawing on Petronius's lament, John observes that all the world's people live as if merely playing the parts of actors (*mimum*) on a stage. People become so engrossed in watching themselves play out their comedies that they cannot free themselves from the stage illusion and return to the lived reality of their daily lives.[64] John's application of classical theater stands in precise opposition to that of Honorius. For Honorius, a classical tragedian provided an effective image for conveying Christianity's truth in the Mass; for John, theatrical acting is like the material world constructed by men—inherently false. The image of ancient comic actors drives John's critique of men who live out lives as if existence itself was merely a matter of performing social roles. If Honorius began *De tragoediis* by comparing the Mass to classical tragedy, the description ends with comedy: the Mass concludes with a banquet, a blessing, a *Komos*—the congregation's joyful release from the danger of Christianity's enemies. John reverses the analogy. Comedy has captured the thoughts and lives of otherwise great men. Those same men experience changes of fortune as if the events were merely plot points in a comic play acted out on a stage for spectators' amusement.[65] Life, John asserts, is not a comedy but a tragedy. The end of life will be, as the long-suffering Job predicted, inevitably and invariably disastrous, regardless of whatever good fortunes have marked a person's earthly existence.[66]

Honorius had capitalized on theater's presentational and communicative qualities as a way of describing the communicative power of the Christian ritual. John goes more subtly to theatrical mimesis and its potential dangers for the Christian soul when men choose to imitate the acts of lesser men rather than to live in imitation of Christ. For John, life becomes a kind of false performance all too easily. Performing instead of living one's life is not, for John, acceptable Christian conduct. But John does not here follow Horace and discuss plays as didactic narratives designed to set out plots and characters for the scrutiny of a discerning audience. John complains that people live their lives as actors play roles. Men play out the conventions of the institutions they serve without awareness that they are only playing parts. The problem for John is that whatever actions people imitate in their own behavior, however artificial or imposed, will begin to seem so natural as to be indistinguishable from their true Christian selves. Awareness of one's role in life is crucial—the masks one wears—will come to define one's self.[67] John returns again and again to Petronius's lamentation that almost all the world is playing out as staged comedies or tragedies. A person must choose carefully, for the character he acts out in life is what he will eventually become. For John, as for Augustine, this false, theatrical world is the world of unbelievers.

> It is surprising how nearly coextensive with the world is the stage on which this tragedy, so immense, marvelous and indescribable a tragedy, or comedy, can be done; its domain is in reality the entire world.[68]

John is not thinking here of didactic performances designed to instruct. He uses theater as a metaphor for human behavior, with Augustinian distinctions between truth and falsehood and between the self as represented in the conventions of society and the true Christian self. Theater is defined as a practice of the past and so works as a metaphor, but it is not thought of as a Christian activity.

Chapter 8 of book 1 of the *Policraticus,* however, deals with theater as a past and present practice. The pagan past compares favorably to the declining present. John idealizes the more respectable performers of ancient theater in comparison with what he considers to be the debauched state of contemporary twelfth-century performance. Following Horace on theater's moral utility, John lauds the ancient actors who performed plays by Menander, Plautus, and Terence and who reproduced fact and fiction by the magic of gesture, of language, and of voice.[69] Slaves though these ancient actors might have been, their craft enhanced the art of poetry and brought it to life. Far from Augustine's condemnation of Roman theater, John puts the responsibility for choosing appropriate entertainment solidly in the individual mind or soul. A wise person will be able to choose stories or spectacles that are instructive and that meet Christian requirements for virtue.[70]

But while John holds up the ideals of ancient comedians, he complains about the temptations of performances that offer excessive "delights" of eye, ear, and heart and about the "romances and similar folly" that "inflame wantonness" and give "incentive to vice." Music, storytelling, and singing are the diversions of shiftless people; as much as they are diversions from virtue, they encourage idleness. Contemporary theatrical performances are fit only for occasional indulgence in "reasonable mirth." John's particular target is not pagan theater but the indecent and rude spectacles (performed by mimics, jumping or leaping priests, buffoons, Aemilian gladiators, wrestlers, sorcerers, jugglers, musicians, and jesters) that otherwise dignified men invite into their homes.[71] John finds the debauched state of twelfth-century performance an indication of moral decline parallel to the decline of legitimate Roman drama at the end of the empire.

The underlying assumption of verisimilitude in John's approach to theater is not evident in the approaches of Honorius or Hugh of St. Victor. John presumes that stage acting in the ancient world was a dignified craft, so much so that he prefers poetic stage performances to the lewd tumult of contemporary mimes and musicians.[72] The problem as he sees it is not theater as a mode of representation but the subject matter of performers' representations (bawdy acts, low comedy), which in turn makes actors and mimics participants in an "evil career" and rightly bars them from Christian sacraments. A wise man might better turn his eyes elsewhere, but the illusion of frivolous stage tricks is only a temporary blindness. Who would not be glad to find his true sight restored when a juggler's tricks are revealed?[73]

The problem with contemporary performance, then, is social rather than representational. The baseness of common popular performance—urine-drenched jugglers and indecently exposed jesters—puts unguarded minds in danger. The performers themselves, whose energy is spent (or misspent) in creating frivolities for the idle courtiers of John's critique, are too easily invited to intimacy with those in power. The effects of their performances can only compromise the judgments and souls of those to whom power has been entrusted.

Here, imitation is at the center of John's suspicion of theater. If repeated behavior alters a Christian's internal moral compass and if theatrical entertainments encourage men to squander learning and civility, then John's issue is less the value of theatrical representation itself than the decline of dignified performances and performers. Like Hugh of St. Victor, John opposes what Richard Southern sees as the "disorganized and disorientated" condition of human beings when reason and instinct clash.[74] In the foundation of John's critique is the idea that the representation of human foibles is unworthy entertainment; seeing oneself so represented is a form of vanity.[75]

In John's criticism of courtiers' frivolousness, the *Policraticus* delivers an inherent critique of theatrical representation. Theater presents illusions that are powerful enough to sway reason, coerce judgment, and manipulate human tendencies toward lasciviousness (as Augustine had observed) and, more important for John of Salisbury, idleness. John remains suspicious of the common theatrical practice of imitating undesirable human traits, though he readily admits that performances of the ancients were indeed of a higher order. Theatrical likeness conceals, rather than reveals, truth (seeing is not believing); thus, there is no pedagogical value in theater as there is in reading the comedies of Menander, Plautus, and Terence. The responsibility for seeing through theatrical illusion rests with the courtier who judges it folly.

Twelfth-Century Transformations

Though the stigma of excessive spectacle was never far away, twelfth-century uses of ancient theater drew more freely on a tradition of incorporating the ancient world into the redeemed world of the Christian present. Horace and Terence remained useful and viable referents for twelfth-century concepts of literary genre and dramatic poetry, especially for John of Salisbury. Theater itself—as a social practice—also begins to figure positively in the twelfth century.

But twelfth-century thought operated without the Aristotelian model of mimetic drama that later provided a foundation for modern dramatic criticism. While an Aristotelian model can be mapped onto *De tragoediis*, Honorius's description of a celebratory *gaudium* emphasizes the expression of Christ's victory over evil and false belief, including the pagan past. In the context of Benedictine reform, pagan theater offered a useful, practical image for priests trying to communicate to lay congregations. That Honorius's use of theater was not pejorative suggests that the idea of ancient theater had been absorbed into other kinds of artifice—painting, iconography, and architecture—which functioned as expressions of the Scriptures' true meaning.[76] With regard to mimesis, *De tragoediis* suggests that the true imitation is life lived *imitatio Christi* outside the ritual. For Amalarius, the final benediction commemorates Christ's prayer with his disciples, which the disciples were to pray after his Passion. The "new benediction" of Roman rite commemorates Christ's fight with and triumph over the devil and his insidious works.[77] In the context of twelfth-century thought, the final hymn and exit from the church marks Christians' reentry into a world infused with anti-Christian forces. Amalarius's response to *Quid est namque "Ite missa est?"* assured that the Mass offered participants spiritual peace; for Honorius, *Ite missa est* is the punctuation that ends the formal gathering of Christians and gives them permission to leave the meeting.[78] Having watched the priest commemorate Christ's historical triumph by performing the ritual, congregants are released from the sanctuary to again participate actively in that world, secure in their own salvation and closer in spirit to God. This is less a literary catharsis than a sensual experience. Congregants, like the Host, have been transformed and then liberated to reengage the ongoing Christian battle against the devil. That fight takes place not in the literary structure of the Christian narrative but in daily life outside the ritual.

For Hugh of St. Victor, the ancient theater was also a communal experience. The *Didascalicon* considered the practical value of collective physical labor in releasing the Christian mind for contemplation and in achieving a likeness to God. The traditional classification of theater with Roman games and sports allowed Hugh to suggest that attending the theaters (as opposed to bars and brothels) had had potential physical benefits for the ancients. While Christian knowledge would not be found in a play or performance, exercise of the body such as men engaged in when they attended the ancient theaters and amphitheaters would produce, for Christians, a state of receptivity to God's word. Hugh of St. Victor, like Honorius, associated theater with a collective, physical experience. Both men interpreted that experience as useful to man's effort to know God by becoming like God or Christ.

John of Salisbury was consistent with Hugh in the assumption that ancient theater was legitimate entertainment. But he found the theatrics and false representations of the contemporary papal and royal courts neither cathartic nor edifying. In practice, he judged the in-house entertainments popular with the courts to be both a waste of time and a waste of Christian virtue. Not only did such contemporary performances lack moral utility, but they offered spectators dangerous invitations to compromise the human dignity necessary for ethical administration of church and civil affairs. John, more in sympathy with Plato than with Aristotle, found that contemporary entertainments failed to meet the literary and performative standards of their pagan predecessors. Though a critic of performative excess in Christian worship, John of Salisbury championed ancient practices against the less erudite secular entertainments popular with the well-positioned aristocrats with whom he circulated.

In the works of Honorius, Hugh of St. Victor, and John of Salisbury, ancient theater appears as a function of—even incidental to—larger concerns (ritual and scriptural exegesis, pedagogy, and social critique). As classical knowledge was pulled into the broader project of connecting human and divine (less an issue of interpreting texts than of demonstrating man's capacity for perfection), even the theater of the ancients could, by the twelfth century, be made to serve Christian programs for human reform. Theater was not set out as an object of inquiry in itself but, rather, served intellectual projects aimed at understanding the relationship of the material world and human behavior to the ultimate (though sometimes veiled) truths offered by the Scriptures. For John and Hugh, that relationship was expressed in the acts of daily life and in their connection to the knowledge that reveals truth and that could bring a person to more accurately resemble God. For Honorius, the Mass was an expression of God's truth as revealed in the Scriptures and a direct experience of a Christian's ongoing struggle in the material world. Though distinct from each other in their treatment and use of classical theater, these three texts allowed that theater (conceived as a pagan practice) belongs in the domain of the material world of human practice. As part of that world, artifice can function in Christ's service as a critique of worldly attachments (John). Further, collective human activity can yield the proper conditions for knowing God through *imitatio Christi* (Honorius) or by clearing away worldly distractions to achieve a more precise likeness to God (Hugh). By the twelfth century, pagan theater had begun to function positively in Christian thought. Theater expanded to include praxis, but the true source of knowledge remained the Scriptures, and its proof was the internal, invisible rightness of the Christian soul's relationship to God.

Though twelfth-century writings on theater acknowledged human participation in theater as a potential vehicle for Christian knowledge—a departure from an Augustinian world in which theater and its gods were banned—the practice of theater did not enter Christian theories of knowledge as a site of inquiry. Classical poetry remained a division of the trivium, and its connection to physical realization in theatrical performance went unnoticed. Ancient theater, with the display of counterfeit emotions and contrived actions that characterized its mode of representation, did not find intellectual ground in which to take root. Nor would the idea of a connection between ancient theater, classical poetry, and performative mimesis take root in the fertile inquiries of the thirteenth-century Scholastics.

CHAPTER FOUR

From Poetics to Performance

The Reception and Interpretation of Aristotle's
Poetics to the Early Fourteenth Century

———— ❧ ————

THROUGHOUT THE TWELFTH CENTURY, vernacular and sacred *ludi*
had emerged in tandem with new religious orders, preaching styles, and liturgical practices. By the beginning of the fourteenth century, elaborate, scripted
Passion plays; secular *ludi*, such as Adam de la Halle's *Le jeu de Robin et Mar-
ion;* and prototypes of guild-sponsored cycle plays were performed out of
doors with temporary scenery and platform stages. Modern theater criticism
has moved steadily away from privileging texts and toward greater attention
to the semiotics and dynamics of live performances in their cultural contexts.
It would seem that thirteenth-century Christian thinking already considered
live performance as a practice. As such, however, dramatizations, reenactments, and spectacles were occasional and situational rather than products of
an ongoing cultural institution. Perhaps going back to the old classification of
theatrum with athletics or to the Augustinian antipathy to Roman theater as a
Christian activity, what is today recognized and discussed as theatrical performance was of no evident value in the intellectual pursuits of the twelfth
and thirteenth centuries. There was criticism of theatrics, but there was no
method for theater or drama criticism.

Despite the influence of newly translated Aristotelian treatises on thirteenth-century learning,[1] Aristotle's *Poetics* (the likely source for an inquiry
into the purpose, structure, and effects of theatrical performance) found little
sympathy with the topics or methods of Scholastic inquiries. Unlike the con-

tested interplay between allegory, scriptural exegesis, and liturgy, Aristotle's method for analyzing Attic drama seems not to have resonated with medieval entertainments or liturgical dramas.[2] By the early fourteenth century, however, Aristotle's *Poetics* was available in three Latin versions. The most recent hints at a shift in Scholastic thought. Of the three—the translation of Averroës's *Middle Commentary on the Poetics* from Arabic by Herman the German (1256), the translation of Aristotle from the Greek by William of Moerbeke (1278), and the *Brevis expositio supra poetriam Aristotelis* (based on a recension of Herman the German) by Bartholomew of Bruges (1307)—Bartholomew's *Brevis expositio* shows a distinct movement toward the Renaissance interest in dramatic imitation as an inquiry into human nature and behavior.

Early Modern and Modern Poetics

An Aristotelian model of written and performed drama based on Renaissance reinterpretations of the *Poetics* remains a foundation for modern Western concepts of narrative drama. In H. A. Kelly's words, the *Poetics* has been, since the Renaissance, "an indispensable element in discussions of tragedy."[3] John Wesley Harris's recent introduction to medieval theater draws implicitly on Aristotle's criteria (a consciously constructed plot that imitates an action; produces an emotional response; and adheres to the unities of time, place, and action) when he suggests that medieval Passion images satisfied a "theatrical need for display in their sheer physicality, dramatic tension in their emotional content, and thematic unity through their allusive reference to the author's larger vision."[4]

In modern scholarship, these qualities—display, dramatic tension, emotional content, and thematic unity—have been applied to liturgical texts, such as the *Quem quaeritis* dialogues and *Visitatio sepulchri* ceremonies, when the aim is to identify them as drama or theater. The characteristics of drama as Aristotle defined it have also been mapped onto Honorius Augustodunensis's description of the Mass in *De tragoediis:* tragedy has a history *(Propter quod et magis philosophicum et studiosius poesis quam hystoria est);*[5] Christ becomes a tragic hero *(corporibus et in animalibus habere quidem magnitudinem);*[6] the Mass imitates the action of Christ's life *(quoniam autem actio est imitatio),*[7] with a single plotline centered on a crisis (the Crucifixion and entombment), a reversal of fortune in the Resurrection *(Dico autem simplicem quidem actionem qua existente, ut determinatum continua et una sine peripetia et anagnorismo transitio fit)*,[8] and "something like a dramatic cathar-sis" in the final *gaudium*.[9] The expectation for increasingly realistic represen-tation—the close relationship between a representation and its real-world referent—has long been regarded as a mark of sophistication in Western drama and performances.[10]

Early modern readings of the *Poetics*, as Brian Vickers points out, studied poetics as didactic rhetoric aimed at moral improvement. Though such read-ings did not catch the Aristotelian concept of an autonomous artwork, six-teenth-century commentaries did question the extent to which truth could be verified by the senses and emotions.[11] Thus, the stage tradition developing in the sixteenth century, aiming at an aesthetic of "true-to-life" representation and the stimulation of emotions, began to define mimesis not in Plato's pejo-rative terms, with human imitation falling short of ideal forms, but in terms of likeness to what is already known, that which exists in the phenomenal world.

Early in the sixteenth century, theatrical versions of Roman comedies had replaced the "ancient" style recitation-and-mime performances previously popular among Italy's educated classes.[12] Neoclassical plays from the late fifteenth century—for example, Ludovico Ariosto's comedy *La Cassaria* (1508) and Angelo Poliziano's *Orfeo* (1480)—mark this transition from rhetorical performance to mimetic dialogue. With Giorgio Valla's 1498 trans-lation of the *Poetics* from Greek to Latin and with the availability of the Greek text published in Venice a decade later, the intellectual project shifted from reconciling Aristotle's *Poetics* with rhetoric or logic to applying the idea of pleasurable instruction from Horace's *Ars poetica* to descriptions of ancient theatrical practice. Such principles as a twelve- or twenty-four-hour time frame, a single location for a play's action, the construction of a simple or complex central action, depiction of a noble protagonist, the central charac-ter's recognition and the plot's reversal, and a chorus—gleaned in part from Aristotle's *Poetics*—became topics for argument and debate.[13]

With an increasing value on the ability of staged performance to produce the appearance of truth—on images that were at once real, morally instruc-tive, and universal in their themes—dramatic presentations began to set human behavior (quite literally) in perspective. The rediscovery of Roman theater architecture through Vitruvius's first-century B.C.E. treatise *De archi-tectura* also made possible a range of techniques for the accurate depiction of human life in stage performance. The second book of Sebastiano Serlio's 1545 *Architettura* laid out designs for generic settings against which comedies, tragedies, and satires should be set, as well as stock visual scenes for plays with rural and urban settings. Neo-Roman proscenium theaters, such as the Teatro Olympico in Vincenza, originally designed by Serlio, gave the stage new visual depth by adding painted perspective scenery and raked floors to the three openings in the facade, the raised stage, the semicircular *cavea*, and columns described by Vitruvius as characteristic of Roman theater buildings. Imitation became a source of pleasure and an end in itself: theater could give human experience the appeal of artifice and the appearance of reality.

By the end of the sixteenth century, interpretations of Herman the German's translation of Averroës, as well as translations of the full *Poetics* from the Greek, had also prompted theories of drama. Efforts to recoup the pagan past meant reconstructing Greco-Roman theater with an emphasis on verisimilitude and human behavior in a rational world. This approach to theater and drama proved to be a foundation for the development of a new theatrical tradition. For theater historians, the revival of Greco-Roman theater, newly authored plays, and verisimilitude as an aesthetic value have marked a break with medieval drama.[14] Marvin Carlson's foundational survey of theater criticism, as one example, holds that Renaissance dramatic criticism is "essentially the story of the rediscovery of Aristotle, of the establishment of his *Poetics* as a central reference point in dramatic theory, and of attempts to relate this work to the already established critical tradition."[15]

A treatise on a par with the early modern treatment of Aristotle's *Poetics* has yet to be found in the records of the Latin Middle Ages. Other cultures flourishing at the same time produced elaborate analyses of their theatrical practices and aesthetics. The Indian *Natyasastra*, attributed to the Hindu sage Bharata and composed sometime between 200 B.C.E. and 200 C.E., analyzed the conventions of Sanskrit drama, including its history, music, dance, gestures, training of performers, playwriting, symbolism, and theater architecture. The *Natyasastra* also detailed a complex aesthetics of sensual perception involving eight *bhavas* (or emotions) and *rasas* (or moods) that performers expressed in performance to elicit specific feelings in audience members. By the early fifteenth century in Japan, the treatises of the highly skilled court performer Zeami Motokiyo had described, again in elaborate detail, the history and aesthetics of the Buddhist Noh theater. Writing at the court of the shogun Yoshimitsu Ashikaga, Zeami set down the history of the emergence of single-plot Noh drama from popular *sarugaku* and *kuse-mai* performances, describing character types and five categories of plays based on the content of their stories. Zeami explained Noh's expressive aesthetics, including the concept of *yugen*, the suggestive beauty and subtle grace of an actor's masked performance. Here, too, aesthetic responses and the symbolism of the theater architecture, performance practices, music, dance, and masks appear in sophisticated detail.

Certainly some examples of medieval drama had roots in Greco-Roman traditions: Hrotswitha's literary adaptations of Terence and Hildegard of Bingen's use of Prudentius in her quasi-liturgical *Ordo virtutum* stand as witnesses to the adaptation of pagan plays for Christian purposes. In a more general sense of theatrical mimesis, Amalarius of Metz veered into the hermeneutics of embodied imitation in his typological approach to Christian worship. The tendency toward this particular kind of ritual mimesis gained credibility in the late tenth century in rubrics for the performance of the *Quem quaeritis* trope and *Visitatio sepulchri* ceremonies, though not without criticism. That Honorius Augustodunensis made an unusual link between pagan theater and Christian ritual when he described the Mass as a kind of performed spectacle without reference to liturgical drama is also undeniable.

Nevertheless, the absence in medieval Europe of a treatise like the *Natyasastra* or the writings of Zeami offers negative proof for what Nils Holger Petersen identifies as the lack of a "consciousness of a concept of drama" in the Latin Middle Ages.[16] Thus, the attention to mimetic drama and theatricality in Europe in the late sixteenth century often distinguishes "medieval" from "early modern" intellectual sensibilities.[17] How and why, then, was the *Poetics* so benign in the Scholastic period?

Mimesis and Dramatic Poetry to the Fourteenth Century

The status of dramatic poetry in the medieval trivium had never been precise or stable. No specific place had been created for the "science of [human] creation."[18] When it was mentioned at all in intellectual discourse, theater continued to be classified with the mechanical arts as a physical, rather than representational, activity.[19] Poetics, however, took a variety of places in the context of logic, as in the thought of the Spanish translator Dominicus Gundisalvi (Gundissalinus) and Ralph of Longchamps (Radulphus de Longo Campo).

For Gundisalvi, rhetoric and poetics fell into pedagogy, wrapped in the Greek-Arabic *Organon* on the authority of al-Farabi.[20] Gundisalvi's divisions made dialectic a category midway between language *(scientiae eloquentiae)* and theoretical philosophy *(scientiae sapientiae)*. As one species of logic, poetry could verify truth through the imagination at the same time it operated as a kind of syllogistic logic, because it was a science of how words con-structed images from and for the imagination *(Proprium est poetice ser-monibus suis facere ymaginari).*[21]

> The making of syllogisms is a species of elocution by which men can verify all things, and this species can be given five names: decision making, thought or consideration, discerning mistakes, making sub-stitutions, constructing imaginative likenesses.[22]

In the mid–twelfth century, language could function as an instrument for sci-entific inquiry (or theoretical philosophy, including science, mathematics, and divinity). Language could be part of logic and also its method; because logic could neither be taught nor learned without language, logical thinking happened at the juncture of knowledge *(scienciis)* and its instrument, words *(sermonicales).*[23] But if logic was a method for discerning universals in truth and goodness from the particulars of a situation, it was the business of rhetoric to persuade and that of poetry to delight the mind.[24]

In the natural order of language inquiries, grammar taught direction of speech, poetry taught delight, rhetoric taught persuasion, argumentation cre-ated beliefs (propositions), and demonstrative reasoning proved certainties.[25] Poetry also functioned (again, as a kind of logic) in the realm of practical knowledge *(pratice philosophie)* of everyday social life *(civilis ratio),* where it was part of social communication.[26] Though it is not clear whether or not Gundisalvi had access to Avicenna's commentary or to any other version of the Aristotelian *Poetics,* he apparently devised a complex classification for poetry as a form of demonstrative reasoning whose process was indeed the creation of forms from the imagination and the use of those (albeit linguistic, not theatrical) forms to verify truth and goodness.[27]

Another classification of poetics with logic that accommodates human creation and imagination appears in Ralph of Longchamp's early-thirteenth-century *Commentary on the Anticlaudianus of Alan of Lille* (1216). Radulphus organizes knowledge into four principal parts: language (grammar, logic, and rhetoric), philosophy (theoretical and practical), and the mechanical arts (agriculture, navigation, theater, armaments, clothing, etc.).[28] Here, poetics becomes an independent branch of knowledge composed of four species—history, stories, disputation, and comedy—all of which assume that language represents something other than itself. Poetry functioned to represent virtue and expel sin from the reader, speaker, or listener, "now by history, now by story, now by disputation."[29] In this schema, theater and poetics not only are different representational practices but also produce different kinds of knowledge. For Thomas Aquinas, however, whose reliance on Aristotle is well known, poetics became a science of invention, that is, a process that "invites judgment based on the 'estimation' of something as represented through similitude."[30] In Aquinas's commentary on Aristotle's *Posterior Analytics*, poetry earned a place as an act of reasoning involving construction of probabilities and possibilities. As an "inventive" mode of reasoning in the *Topics*, *Rhetoric*, and *Poetics*, poetic invention could be distinguished from sophistic arguments—which were based on false premises (the *Sophistical Refutations*)—because poetics relied on existing things as the basis for linguistic images.[31]

Presence and Absence of Theater: Herman the German (fl. 1240–56) and William of Moerbeke (1215–86)

The two earliest versions of the *Poetics* did not easily find a niche in Christian thought, but for somewhat different reasons. Latin translations of the Aristotelian treatises from Arabic kept the Arabic classification; the *Poetics* and the *Rhetoric* belonged in the *Organon*. This classification implied that the science of words *(scientia sermonicales)*—a lesser form of reasoning than logical propositions, hypothetical propositions, or syllogisms—was understood to be a method for discerning truth from falsehood by means of logic.[32] Herman the German had accepted this arrangement uncritically in his translation of Averroës's *Middle Commentary on the Poetics*.[33] The 1256 translation was received into the fourteenth century as a treatise on logic.[34] In contrast, William of Moerbeke's 1278 translation of Aristotle's *Poetics* from the Greek is marked by an absence of copies, commentaries, *expositio*, or florilegia. Aristotle's analysis of tragic poetry as mimetic theater apparently generated no scholarly interest.[35] The lack of interest in William of Moerbeke's translation, coupled with the fact that it made no apparent contribution to medieval philosophy, has long been acknowledged in modern scholarship.[36] But why the *Poetics* was dismissed as a treatise on performance remains an open question.

Modern scholarship generally maintains that the problem of the medieval treatment of poetics as a logical method was solved when poetics was joined to rhetoric in the early modern period and finally liberated from logic into the domain of art.[37] Against this convention, however, Deborah Black argues that the value of the *Poetics* as a treatise on logic has been unfairly neglected precisely because of its annexation to literature and theater in the sixteenth century.[38] But keeping the Aristotelian *Poetics* in its medieval classification as a treatise on logic reveals exactly how, in this case, Greco-Roman theater was left out of the medieval consideration of dramatic poetry. The differences between Herman the German's translation of the *Middle Commentary* and William of Moerbeke's translation of the *Poetics* point to the precise aspects of theatrical tragedy that could not be adapted into Scholastic inquiries.

Herman the German, a monk in Toledo, considered poetics to be a method of nondemonstrative logic, a counterpart to rhetoric.[39] He understood that the universal rules of poetry could be applied in service of discerning truth from falsehood—even when language was acknowledged to represent things existing only in the imagination.[40] The introduction to the translation of the *Middle Commentary* is unambiguous in its placement of poetics with logic.

> Serious men may undertake this translation of the *Poetics* if it seems good, and they may be glad to gain that which completes Aristotle's thought on logic.[41]

The "poetry" discussed in the *Poetics* could not be confused with the theaters in Carthage that Augustine had first enjoyed and then rejected.

According to principles of syllogistic logic, Herman the German assumed poetics to be the science of discerning truth through the imitations of poetry. He presents poetry as a kind of linguistic artifice that makes effective likenesses *(modi ymaginationis et assimilationis)*[42] in two ways: either by replacing one thing for another *(assimilatio rei ad rem et exemplio)* or by establishing comparisons by tropes *(concambium)*. Substitution *(transumptio)* and figuration *(translatio)* are subspecies of poetic tropes. The performed poems to which Aristotle referred were song lyrics of praise *(laudatio)* or blame *(vituperatio)*. Poetry thus assumed both ethical and rhetorical components, following Horace and Cicero *(intellectus Poetrie Oratii, sicut intelectus Rethoricarum Tullii Ciceronis adiuvans est ad intelligendum negotium aristotelicale Rethorice)*.[43]

But Herman the German's translation of the *Middle Commentary* incorporated Aristotle's three components of poetry—melody, meter, and the composition of representative statements—into a medieval hierarchy that privileged rational speech *(ars consonandi, et ars metrificandi, et arts componendi semones representativos)*. Poetry became the art of making statements in imitation of ideas, images, and aspects of human conduct *(erunt artes imagi-*

native vel que faciunt effectum imaginandi tres). As such, poetry was the study of the composition of imitative statements and how they presented truth: "That last [imitative statements] is the art of logic, which is considered in this book."[44]

The Latin *Middle Commentary* describes poetry, unlike demonstrative statements (which could themselves be judged as true or false), as imitating men's actions in color, figure, sounds, and statements. But the construction of poetic statements—the direct link between poetics and logic—stays in the foreground in both the Arabic and Latin texts.[45] Poetics, as a linguistic art, becomes a rational process by which the actions of men are made known and, through comparison with their likenesses in poetic imitation, judged. Further, the propensity for creating likenesses of other men is an innate human impulse.

> And some men some naturally make images of men and so represent other men in action [the actions of men] in color, figured images, and voice either through artistry or convention or long practicing; some men also naturally make linguistic representations.[46]

After describing the impulse to imitate as an innate human capacity, Herman the German incorporated the Aristotelian modes of poetic representation into the three species of medieval terms: mental concepts (natural), spoken concepts (derivative), and written concepts (also derivative). Thus, he foregrounds the logical ends of poetic imitation, rather than how dramatic tragedy imitates action and character through plot.

The overlap between rhetoric and poetics carried over from Cicero, Horace, and other late classical authors distinguished poetry as a more oblique or circumstantial form of linguistic representation, or *res ficta*.[47] These authors were clear in their methods: rhetoric was a tool for argumentation and persuasion based on existing matter and conditions; poetic statements required comparison between an imitation and its referent. As defined in the Latin *Middle Commentary,* then, poetic imitation could easily be fitted with rhetoric in the Scholastic organization of knowledge. Therefore, given the categories of knowledge established by the mid-thirteenth century, connecting poetry to theatrical performance or the physicality of the Roman theaters was not an obvious or necessary intellectual leap.

How Aristotle's *Poetics* found a place in European logic is clearest in Herman the German's discussion of Aristotle's third part of tragedy: thought that is articulated through characters' language. The Latin translation of the *Middle Commentary* construed thought as a person's belief in the object of representation.

> The third part of tragedy is belief; this is the ability to represent a thing that is or a thing that is not. This is similar to the undertaking in rhetoric that makes clear what thing exists and what thing does not exist, except that rhetoric undertakes it by words that persuade, poetry by words that represent.[48]

Poetry was not pure artifice, nor was it entirely the product of an individual poet's flights of imagination: *Ideo poete non pertinet loqui nisi in rebus que sunt aut quas possibile est esse.*[49] With this understanding of poetry as representing things that are conceptually possible but not always verifiable by the senses, the Latin *Middle Commentary* posited poetics as a kind of argumentation organized by comparison of a linguistic image with its referent.[50]

The Latin *Middle Commentary* further enumerated how poetic imitations could be juxtaposed with observation to result in proper judgments of good or bad actions and human character.

> And because those who represent and make comparisons intend to incite taking a voluntary position in some actions and pulling back from other kinds of actions, they necessarily intend by their representations to represent virtues or vices.[51]

This process of representing and comparing constituted a method of reasoning precisely because poetry's medium is language, not music or rhythm. Language is the carrier of meaning.

> Therefore, finally, in all likenesses two differences are discovered: approval of comely figures and a detesting of ugliness; indeed, these two differences are only discovered in likenesses and representations that are made in words, not in representations that are made in meter and not in representations made in harmonious sounds.[52]

Language, a manifestation of reason, was distinct from performance, either as oratory or recitation. Thus, Aristotle's sixth part of tragedy becomes contemplation of or argument for correct beliefs through linguistic representation, not performance.

And the sixth part is contemplation, that is to say, argument for proof of right belief or work not by persuasive words (for that does not pertain to this art and is not in agreement with it) but by representative words; the art of poetry as is characteristic of tragedy truly does not consist of arguing or in observation of contemplation. That is why the art of praise songs also does not use the art of gesture or facial expression acceptable for use in rhetoric.[53]

The aims of poetry were also distinguished from those of rhetoric by poetry's capacity to move the soul, or will, to produce correct judgment. A soul can be moved by two kinds of representation: direct representation (praising the thing itself) or circular representation (representing the opposite of what is to be praised so that the object of praise is known by its antithesis).[54] Thus, when writing on Aristotle's two parts of mythic statements, Herman the German translated poetry as a method of reasoning.

Every representation is caused from the same place as a representation of its opposite; later it changes into its own direction (this was called, according to them, "indirect representation") or the thing is represented without making mention of the contrary (and this is what they called a "direct sign").[55]

The truth of an argument, according to Herman the German's translation, resided in how a poem represented a thought progression that led to a conclusion.

Man uses direct and indirect reasoning only in inquiry and refutation; this species of direct reasoning is what moves the soul to feel pity at times and fear at times.[56]

The Latin *Middle Commentary* constructed a poem's visual presentation as a metaphor for the internal images a poem might create in a person's imagination. A poem's action must be convincing to an individual's mind, not in the collective view of an audience, to move a reader or listener to pity or fear; the action will not be effective if not believed.[57] This internal movement of the soul to pity and fear in response to linguistic representation happens as a result of the kind of argument the poem presents, not as a response to the sad or pitiable actions represented. Men will be naturally moved, Herman the German translates, by two kinds of language: demonstrative and nondemonstrative.[58]

Herman the German's *Middle Commentary,* following the Arabic tradition, thus presents poetry as the composition of imitative statements, rather than the delivery of persuasive statements as in rhetoric. Poetics, then, was the science of analyzing a particular practice of linguistic imitation within the discipline of logic.

> And knowledge that shows or teaches what poems are made of and how they are made is more completely authoritative than making poems. Indeed, any knowledge that is aware of the way other kinds of knowledge are subordinate to its function is more authoritative than those that are subordinate.[59]

Given the well-established Arabic tradition and existing categories of Scholastic knowledge, Herman the German's description of poetics as a species of nondemonstrative logic was rendered recognizable, if not especially useful, in the tradition of Aristotelian exegesis and logic in Paris.[60]

In contrast, William of Moerbeke's translation did not position the *Poetics* as a treatise on logic at all. Unlike the translation of Averroës's *Middle Commentary* and its recensions, William of Moerbeke's translation from the Greek presented poetry specifically as theatrical.[61] William of Moerbeke made no attempt to reconcile Aristotle's analysis of theatrical tragedy with the logical methods of Scholasticism. His translation presented the *Poetics* as an inquiry into the form, nature, and performance of tragic poetry, with the idea that a poetic drama stood on its own as an autonomous work of craft (if not art) whose components could be identified and analyzed.

Both translators located the two natural causes of poetic representation in the human capacity for imitation and ability to enjoy and learn from imitation. Both described the knowledge derived from representation as pleasurable to all observers, not just philosophers.[62] Both texts acknowledge that poetic representation makes objects that would be repugnant in the natural world tolerable in representation (an issue Augustine had not been able to reconcile).[63] But the subject of the *Middle Commentary* would have appeared to its Scholastic readers as the exposition of a method for discerning truth from representations of human nature in lyric poetry by the poem's effect on a listener. William of Moerbeke's *Poetics,* in contrast, deals with poetics as a scientific inquiry into poetry as an autonomous, material object in and of itself.

In William of Moerbeke's translation, Aristotle's treatise offered neither ethical nor intellectual rewards for the labor of analysis. Poetics could yield only a more refined knowledge of Attic drama (not productive knowledge), the ability to distinguish good from bad poetry (not useful without a moral dimension leading to improvement of the soul), and a set of categories on which to base an analysis of dramatic tragedy (for Christian thinkers, a method with no object). Whereas the *Middle Commentary* at least made poetic statements a cognitive process leading to the soul's perfection, William of Moerbeke's translation placed the source of poetic imitation directly in a human proclivity for "formless" activity *(a principio apti nati et ipsa maxime paulative adducentes produxerunt poesim ex informibus).*[64]

William's *Poetics* does not allude to familiar medieval topics—the perfection of the soul, Horatian and Ciceronian poetic traditions, or how a comparison between imitations and objects of imitation might improve human knowledge. In sharp contrast to the opening of Herman the German's *Middle Commentary*, William of Moerbeke's *Poetics* introduces Aristotle's description of poetic species—tragedy, comedy, and dithyrambs—and the method by which they could be parsed.

On poetry in general and of the kinds of poetry, its virtues, and the kinds of stories proper to good poetry, thus far, the number and nature of its parts, and similar questions of its methods, we say at the beginning following naturally with first principles. Epic and also tragic poetry, and also comedy and dithyrambic poetry . . . [65]

For a Scholastic reading audience, William's *Poetics* made action the object of imitation, represented by narration and impersonation, narration only, or dramatic imitation. That Greco-Roman theater represented human actions was certainly not new information for medieval thinkers. But that poetry would do so was a less accessible concept. The philosophical problem presented in the *Poetics*—the criteria on which poetry (rather than people) might be judged as good or bad—was incongruous with Christian thought on the methods for distinguishing truth from falsehood. William of Moerbeke's literal translation further allowed that all forms of imitation—including dance and music *(omnes existunt entes imitationes secundum totum)*—could be distinguished and analyzed by their media, their objects of imitation, and their specific mode of imitation *(aut enim per genere alteris imitari, aut per altera, aut per aliter et non eodem modo).* Each form could function as a discrete human craft.[66]

William of Moerbeke's *Poetics* thus broadened the category of imitative representations in (for Scholastic thought) unexpected ways. Aristotle, for example, observed that Greek had no common name to describe the mime performances of Sofronis and Xenarchi (at one extreme) and Socratic discourse (at the other) under the general category of verbal arts *(Nichil enim habemus nominare commune Sofronis et Xenarchi mymos et Socraticos sermones)*. The point is illustrated in the contrast between Homeric poetry (imitative) and the scientific writing of Empedocles (natural philosophy).[67] With Aristotle's Greek references covering the full spectrum of Attic poetry—written, spoken, and performed—William of Moerbeke presented the *Poetics* as an analytical guide to Attic poetry, significantly limiting its relevance for medieval thinkers whose references were largely from Roman culture and literature.

Herman the German's *Middle Commentary* presented meter as characteristic of imitative statements and as a component of written poetry: many statements otherwise called poems are not poetic except for their meter, as in the metered statements of Socrates and the statements of Empedocles on natural things, both of which are unlike Homeric poetry.[68] But the *ars metrica* was a subordinate, though unavoidable, issue. William of Moerbeke's *Poetics* referred repeatedly to species of poetic writing that were neither clearly defined nor performed in Christian Europe.[69]

The *Middle Commentary* proposes two kinds of oral poetry, accessible in two forms (*laudatio* for tragedy and *vituperatio* for comedy). These represented either honorable things or despicable things *(rebus voluntariis, scilicet honestis et turpibus)* and constituted a kind of inductive reasoning *(Et hoc patet per inductionem poematum)*.[70] In contrast, William of Moerbeke's translation analyzes four species of poetry that together constitute an entire genre of imitation *(omnes existunt entes imitationes secundum totum)* in which the medium, objects, and modes of imitation were not the same *(aut enim per genere alteris imitari, aut per altera, aut per aliter et non eodem modo)*.[71] Based on this initial presentation of tragic and comic poetry and the science of its composition in metrical language, rhythm, and melody, Aristotle's *Poetics* as rendered by William of Moerbeke would have required extensive commentary to fit into the *Organon* as a treatise on logic.

In William of Moerbeke's *Poetics*, there was a potential for linking Attic poetry with Roman theater, especially given the translation's composition and limited circulation in Italy, in proximity to Roman theater ruins. But the border between the science of language and the sport of theatrics was perhaps, in the Christian intellectual tradition, drawn so firmly that it could not be crossed. Though Aristotle places the internal logic of a dramatic plot in its language, the performative aspect of Attic tragedy is unmistakable throughout the *Poetics*. Tragedy is grounded solidly in the physical practice of poetry, and its roots are deep in improvisational performances.[72] Aristotle presents the disputed history of the origins of tragedy and comedy, including the word for "tragedy," with active verbs: the Dorian *dran* and the Athenian *prattin*. William of Moerbeke's Latin equivalents also present tragic poetry as an activity. Dramatic poetry goes beyond spoken and written texts but is not precisely rhetorical: *et poein ipsi quidem 'dran' (idest actitare), Athenienses autem 'prattin' (idest agere) appellant.*[73] While tragedy's pagan history would not necessarily present a conceptual obstacle for Scholastic thinkers, the concept of tragedy as dramatized action would have been incongruous with the concept of lyric poetry as linguistic.

The *Middle Commentary* adapts the structural elements of tragedy into oratory. The "first part" functions as an introduction in a rhetorical speech *(Prima est que se habet apud ipsos in poemate ad modum exordii in rethorica)*, the "second part" is a song *(Et pars secunda est ipsa laus)*, and the "third part" functions as the conclusion to a speech *(Et tertia pars est que habet se ad modum conclusionis in rethorica)*.[74] William of Moerbeke translates without explanation the original terms in Aristotle's list of the quantitative parts of tragic performances *(prologus, episodion, exitus, khoricon, parodus, stasimon)*, the function of the tragic chorus *(khori)*, and the choral meters appropriate to tragedy *(anapesto et trocheo)*, allowing the terms to stand for structural parts of Greek tragedies, which readers were unlikely to have at hand.[75] The translation of the *Middle Commentary* gave poetics some relevance to medieval representational practices, by linking it with rhetorical delivery. But without a tradition of dramatizing classical poetry in theaters, without the Athenian plays (e.g., *Oedipus Rex, Medea, Thyestes,* and *The Chorephorai*) at hand, and without a reason to analyze them as performance, Aristotle's presentation of poetry as theater translated by William of Moerbeke had, again, little application in the effort to reconcile classical knowledge with Christian belief through rational inquiry.

Recognitions and Reversals: The Logic of Poetry and Theatrical Performance

The difference in how the versions presented poetics with respect to logic and performance is nowhere clearer than in the treatments of anagnorisis (recognition) and peripeteia (reversal). Herman, as I have already discussed, presented anagnorisis and peripeteia as functions of poetic logic (indirect and direct reasoning). Having acknowledged that when the art of praise refers to things that already exist (as opposed to naming things already represented in poems), poems had greater power to provoke voluntary action, the *Middle Commentary* follows Aristotle's analysis of simple and complex plots: "[S]imple imitation is that in which two kinds of thinking are used, either the kind called indirect or the kind called direct."[76] Throughout the *Middle Commentary*, poetics is assumed to be a method for deducing how poetic statements represented truths and/or falsehoods in the world of human behavior, as well as for identifying subjects appropriate to a poetic genre.[77]

William of Moerbeke's *Poetics* offers a radically different presentation of the analysis of dramatic tragedy: the analytical goal of poetics is the ability to mask aesthetic judgments. Plot *(fabula)*, in William of Moerbeke's translation, represents an action that could be identified as either simple or complex *(Sunt autem fabularum hee quidem simplices, hee autem complexe; et enim actiones, quarum imitationes sunt fabule, existunt mox entes tales)* according to the placement of the recognition (anagnorisis) and reversal (peripeteia) in the story.[78]

> I say also that a simple action exists and determine that it continues without *peripeteia* or *anagnorisis* to make a transition; and also complex expressions transition with *anagnorisis* or *peripeteia* or both. These must also be done from a unified story, [showing] how preceding events follow from necessity or probability; it is different whether these many things are done before or after [reversal or recognition]. Also, a reversal is a contrary transition, which, as we say, must also follow probability or necessity.[79]

In William of Moerbeke's translation of Aristotle's simple and complex plots, anagnorisis and peripeteia appear as what would now be called "plot points" in a script. A poet's skill in depicting a character's change in fortune and self-recognition indicates that the action of the story is well structured and effective. In the discussion of anagnorisis and peripeteia, William of Moerbeke's *Poetics* preserves Aristotle's references to Sophocles's *Oedipus Rex* as an illustration of how a dramatic character's self-recognition occurs simultaneously with the turning point of the action (specifically from good fortune to bad) in the narrative and in the acted performance. The use of *Oedipus Rex* and other Attic dramas as reference points for structural principles took Aristotle's analysis well out of the realm of ethics, grammar, rhetoric and logic, and biblical referents.

The Latin translations of the *Middle Commentary* and the *Poetics* thus differed markedly in their presentations of poetics as a scientific inquiry for Scholastic readers. For Herman, poetics was the analysis of the logic of imitative statements and their ability to represent truths and/or falsehoods. But William of Moerbeke presented poetics as a method for analyzing the qualitative and quantitative components of dramatized poetry, which might include characters' good or bad reasoning. The *Middle Commentary* gave the science of poetics at least some resonance in Scholastic logic, while the *Poetics* itself, as a method for analyzing Attic theatrical poetry, had no such resonance. The Aristotelian *Poetics* thus fell outside existing intellectual traditions in which poetics and rhetoric were classified with nondemonstrative logic in the tradition of dialectic and rhetoric taught in the trivium. Linking the *Poetics* with existing knowledge of ancient theatrical performance would indeed have created a fascinating tension between language as method for discerning truth and language as ancillary to mimetic representation of human behavior.[80]

In a departure from the Arabic source, for example, Herman the German's *Middle Commentary* suggests that Aristotle's breakdown of the six parts of dramatic tragedy refers to its literary form:

And it is proper that tragedy, the same as the art of praise, has six parts: language representing myths, the customs of men, weighted rhythm, belief, speculation, and sound.[81]

In his comment on chapter 4 of the *Poetics,* tragedy is equated with praise poetry and the representation of virtuous things. Here, tragedy is a genre based on the content of the story, not a method.

It is proper, therefore that the appearance of reciting and representing words in tragedy should take the form of certain and not doubtful things, in serious and not jocular speaking, such that they are the words of men who are honorable in morals and opinions and actions . . .[82]

But Herman's translation does not always distinguish tragedy from praise poetry. He reverts to terms meaning "poetry," "arts of praise," and "poetic words" when following Averroës's examples of Homeric poetry, the Old Testament story of Abraham (an example of epic poetry), and Arabic songs. Following Herman's interpretation of Averroës, "tragedy" refers to the words that tell the story of a myth and the narration of men's behavior that represents correct belief through rhythmic tones. There is no evidence (of which I am aware) that the rules for poetry discussed in *Middle Commentary* were ever directly applied to Latin poems or, for that matter, to liturgical dramas. However, the concept of performed poetry in the *Middle Commentary* was certainly not incompatible with the *ars poetica* tradition.

William of Moerbeke's translation of the *Poetics* suggests no such possible parallel to poetic or dramatic forms current in thirteenth-century Europe. William presents tragedy as an exclusively Greek practice, somewhat incongruous with the more familiar medieval grounding in Roman poetry. It is clear from William's translation that Aristotle assumed that tragic poetry was acted mimetically, rather than recited or read silently. Poetry's value was in the demonstration of human behavior as action represented in a visual and aural medium.

> Tragedy, therefore, is the imitation of an action that is serious and complete and has magnitude, in delightful words, its form separated into parts, acted out and not spoken, which concludes with the purgation of pity and fear. . . . Since agents make imitations, it is first necessary to consider the visual ornamentation of tragedy.[83]

Whereas the *Middle Commentary* presents poetry as written *(poema)* or spoken *(oratio poetica),* with genre defined by content (poems of blame or poems of praise)[84] and by rhythm, meter, and tonality as properties of language, the *Poetics* makes mimetic action the central component of performed tragic poetry. Poetry does not require the facial expressions and gestures required for rhetorical persuasion,[85] but a narrator's conviction in the presentation of a poem affected the believability of poetic statements, as in rhetoric, and hence affected the validity of the argument presented by a poem's representation of real or possible things.

> One [element of representation] is the form indicating character and customs, as one who speaks in words of insight/understanding or in words of anger, and the other is the appearance of signifying a person's belief or his opinion; the appearance of one who speaks with certainty of the existence of things is not the same as one who speaks doubtfully of the existence of things.[86]

By contrast, in the *Middle Commentary,* inflections used in rhetorical argumentation (e.g., elongating vowels or accelerating and slowing speech) do not originate in poetic meter but are properties of a narrator's delivery.[87]

The idea of tragedy as one of three genres of narrative performance (with epic and comedy) is well established in the first section of William of Moerbeke's translation. But tragic and comic poetry are intended for mimetic performance, as imitations of human behavior.

> In this way Sophocles is an imitator like Homer, both imitating zealous men and also both like Aristophanes, who imitates acts being done. Wherefore it is called *drama* (it is active), that is, imitation of action.[88]

The idea of tragedy as action in William of Moerbeke's translation contradicts the familiar concept of poetry as linguistic. This concept of tragedy would have required expanding medieval notions of tragedy beyond the boundaries of logic, rhetoric and grammar, the *artes poeticae,* and theater as a mechanical art. Had there been a place for such an inquiry in the classifications of knowledge in the thirteenth century, the difference between the two presentations of tragedy was sharp enough to have provoked a reassessment of the traditions of classical tragedy.

The Latin *Poetics* located knowledge not in human perception but in tragic poetry itself, irrespective of previously held beliefs, a priori truths, or the state of a Christian soul. Tragedy has a soul *(anima),* which is its carefully arranged plot (not its narrative content or representation of virtue and vice). Plot—the schematic arrangement of events of a story *(fabula)*—leads Aristotle's list of tragedy's six elements and is followed by character and thought. Thought and action reveal the moral qualities of the fictional people represented by performers in the tragedy. Plot was not described in relation to the (Christian) person's reading or hearing, then interpreting, the poem.

> The first principle is therefore the plot and is the soul of tragedy, followed by character. . . . [T]ragedy is the imitation of action and therefore imitates the agents of action. Third is thought, which can speak relevant and congruous speeches, as is needed in the language of politics and rhetoric.[89]

If a presentation of poetics that emphasized the artifice of plot construction as action was incompatible with late thirteenth-century discussions of poetics, the use of "theater" as a performative venue for tragedy was even more difficult to reconcile with Scholastic categories. Where Herman the German uses the word for "theater," he follows the suggestion of the Arabic commentary that poems should be presented without the external artifice of "dissimulation and delivery."[90] H. A. Kelly suggests that Herman most likely used *theatralis* as a generic term to refer loosely to any number of kinds of public performances (minstrels, mimes and recitations, etc.) rather than, as in the *Didascalicon*, to refer to a formal theatrical performance in the classical sense.[91] *Theatralis* functions as a descriptive term, not a reference to Greek social or civic performance practice.[92] A poet's theatrical gestures could be appropriate or inappropriate depending on the content and goal of a poem.

> Nor is it necessary for an experienced poet to complete his imitation with external devices, theatrical gesture, or arrangement of facial expressions. . . . External devices aid their imitation when the aim is imitation of belief.[93]

The specificity of William of Moerbeke's use of the term for "theater" throughout his translation, however, established a categorical divide between the general and generic *theatricalibus* of the *Middle Commentary* and the performative *theatrum* of the *Poetics*. In William of Moerbeke's Latin, theatrical tragedy is by definition mimetic *(imitationes actitivas fecit)*, and its development as a theatrical tradition is specific: the number of actors was increased to three, they performed with added scenery *(ypocritarum multitudinem ex uno in duo primus Eschylus produxit; . . . tres autem et skenografiam Sophocles)*, the chorus was reduced *(et que chori minoravit)*, and the spoken word increased in importance *(et sermonem protagonistam disposuit)*.[94] Tragedy's origins and modes of imitation came not from texts but from dance and satire *(primo quidem enim tetrametro utebantur propter satyricam et magis saltativam esse poesim)*.[95] Theatrical performance was an unequivocal (if undeveloped) component in the evolution of tragedy.[96]

The *Poetics* thus veered sharply from a logocentric approach to poetry. Against the presentation of poetry as the conscious formation of poetic statements without rhetorical gesture or facial expression in Herman the German, William of Moerbeke presented poetry as a visual art and presented a poet's skill as the ability to visualize the poem as a three-dimensional performance as he composes it.

> A poet must compose a story by putting it in front of his eyes (for by putting the story before his eyes as if it were taking place, the poet can best discover what is incongruous and obscured; a sign of this is the critique of Carcinus as Amphlarus came in from the temple; the poet

did not visualize it, and on stage the audience was annoyed and the play failed); as far as possible a poet should include gesture in composing.[97]

The two thirteenth-century versions of Aristotle's *Poetics* offered radically different approaches to poetics and poetry. Herman the German's *Middle Commentary* made poetics a mode of thought leading to the discernment of truth and applicable in current practice as a method for discerning truth. The responsibility for discerning truth rested with the reader's or hearer's ability to reckon the relationship between a probable event and its representation and to judge not the quality of the presentation but the value of what a poem represents. Poetry constituted a form of nondemonstrative logic. In contrast, William of Moerbeke's *Poetics* presented a method for analyzing tragedy as a species of theatrical performance, specific to Attic drama. Translation from the Greek emphasized modes of imitation and foregrounded a concept of dramatic tragedy far beyond the models of ancient tragedy available to Scholastic thinkers. Any interest in the *Poetics* as a treatise on the art of performed poetry would have been dependent on an intimate knowledge of Greek plays and the conventions of their performance.

By presenting tragedy as inseparable from its theatrical performance, William of Moerbeke's *Poetics* allowed little maneuverability for a Scholastic trying to fit poetics and poetry into the parameters of grammar and rhetoric or the study of the Roman *artes poeticae*. The Aristotelian emphasis on visual spectacle, mimesis, human invention, tragedy's origins in unscripted improvisations, and Greek plays and conventions was (at best) incongruous with the aims of dialectic. The differences in the conception of poetry and poetics placed Moerbeke's *Poetics* outside the purview of Scholastic philosophy. The analysis presented in the *Poetics* alienated poetry from rhetoric, dialectic, and grammar, thus giving it no place in the liberal arts curriculum. Because classical theatrical performance had not warranted serious consideration in Christian thinking, its treatment as an object of analysis as explicitly detailed in the *Poetics* had no particular relevance either for knowledge of ancient theater or, for the Scholastics, to liturgy or liturgical drama. While the treatise did not fit existing concepts of tragedy, poetry, or performance, there is no indication that William of Moerbeke's translation of the *Poetics* presented a significant challenge either to prevailing methods of logical inquiry or as impetus to inquiry into Greco-Roman theater.

Greco-Roman Theater as a Method of Inquiry: The Early Modern Poetics

The intellectual move toward dramatic poetry as an autonomous theatrical form with the particular aesthetic values deduced in the late fifteenth and sixteenth centuries was perhaps not as revolutionary a change of position as Marvin Carlson's statement on the "rediscovery" of Aristotle would suggest. The conceptual roots of theatrical verisimilitude and "humanist" theater lie deep in the post-Aristotelian logic of fourteenth-century Scholasticism.[98] Bartholomew of Bruges, in his short commentary on Aristotle's headings in the *Middle Commentary,* hints at an interest in the *Poetics* as a method for analyzing the poetic representation of human behavior as mimetic performance. While Bartholomew is far from advocating or even recognizing the *Poetics* as a treatise on drama and theatrical spectacle, aspects of the text point in the conceptual directions from which the theatrical sensibilities of the early modern period would emerge.

By the time Bartholomew of Bruges wrote his *Brevis expositio supra poetriam Aristotelis* in the "post-Aristotelianism" brewing at the University of Paris in 1307, the placement of poetics in pedagogy could prompt a range of ideas about poetry. None of those ideas, however, connected poetry to any kind of staged drama, classical or medieval. Poetry could be an object of knowledge, a method of knowing (distinct from syllogistic logic), an act producing knowledge, a form of demonstrative or nondemonstrative reasoning, a means of communicating reasoned propositions, an end in itself, or an exposition on how language interacts with the reality it represents. But until Bartholomew's hints at a reevaluation of Herman's translation of "imitation" as "imagination," the science of poetics remained a science of imitative words.[99] Bartholomew, the *Brevis expositio* suggests, began to explore the logic of imitation by introducing the concept of mental mimesis, the imaginary imitation of forms as well as words and emotional responses to poetry, as crucial to how poetry functions.[100]

The radical aspect in early modern readings of the Aristotelian *Poetics* was in large part a matter of applying dramatic poetry to stage performance, with scenery and dialogue, rather than recitation. But if Aristotle's *Poetics* had warranted no such practical application in thirteenth-century Scholastic thought, the shift in the status of the *Poetics* was less a matter of reinterpreting Aristotle than a function of how the Aristotelian principles of poetic form were understood and applied.

One sign of a more gradual transition between the interpretation of the

Poetics as a pedagogical treatise on dialectics and its treatment as a blueprint for the aesthetics of dramatic poetry comes from Bartholomew's little-studied commentary on a recension of Herman the German's translation of Averroës.[101] Bartholomew's lecture notes suggest a late Scholastic interest in the Aristotelian text itself, coupled with a willingness to explore poetics beyond its classification with dialectic.

The Arabic commentary had provided a framework for interpreting the *Poetics* as a philosophical method, though not grounds for analyzing dramatic genres or performance practices. Placed with logic, poetry allowed for distinctions between truth and falsehood, as well as virtue and vice—distinctions thought to lighten burdens and expel sin from a Christian soul. Poetry produced knowledge by allowing the mind to juxtapose observations (in a process similar to that of demonstrative reasoning) between realities and hypotheticals and to draw universal principles from particular examples. The end product was, of course, rational Christian judgment.

Bartholomew's *Brevis expositio*, however, indicates an intellectual move toward and greater emphasis on human creativity and a glimmer of appreciation for Aristotelian theatrical mimesis. The manuscript of Bartholomew's notes and commentary is grouped with a series of lectures. It is unusual in two respects. First, the *Brevis expositio* seems to be the only extant example of a Latin commentary on the recension of Averroës's Latin translation of the Arabic *Middle Commentary*.[102] Second, Bartholomew's comments deal not with Averroës's observations but with the fragments of Aristotle's text preserved in the *Middle Commentary*. Bartholomew's interest in Aristotle rather than Averroës suggests that he might have preferred working with William of Moerbeke's 1278 translation of the *Poetics* rather than the Arabic commentary, had a copy been available in Paris at the time. Bartholomew does not link Aristotle's analysis of tragedy with the theatrical performances of the Greco-Roman past, but his notes indicate a subtle shift in the medieval interpretation of the *Poetics*.

The *Brevis expositio* is sketchy at best, and some of the manuscript is virtually unreadable. It suggests, however, that within half a century of Herman the German's translation of the *Middle Commentary*, Aristotle's major points on mimesis, the role of human invention in poetic writing, and poetry as an object (as well as a method) were being taught at Paris. Bartholomew's focus on the Aristotelian passages puts more weight on poetry itself than on poetry as a function of dialectic. Bartholomew also informs his reading of the *Poetics* with his knowledge of other Aristotelian texts, thereby bringing the issues of the *Poetics* into the context of the entire Aristotelian corpus.[103] The importance given to human imagination as a component of knowledge in the *Brevis expositio* begins to accommodate the idea that imaginary forms such as poetry constitute a kind of knowledge. Further, the knowledge imaginary forms produce is grounded in contingent experience.[104] Thus, human will becomes a factor in the production of knowledge.

Bartholomew's purpose in writing the *Brevis expositio* was to provide a detailed *divisio textus* of Aristotle's *Poetics,* based on the divisions of the Paris recension, to which his own prologue was attached. Unlike the recension he followed, however, Bartholomew's commentary both draws on and refers to the *Nicomachean Ethics, Politics, Rhetoric, Metaphysics,* and *De anima,* as well as Porphyri's *Isagoge,* in an effort to correlate the ideas in the *Poetics* to more familiar Aristotelian concepts. The prologue, for example, begins with a reference to *De anima* that asserts that the human soul is prima facie rational. As if a blank page on which nothing has been written, the soul contains all potential written figures *in potentia* and embodies all complete knowledge.[105]

Bartholomew's pedagogical purpose in lecturing on the *Poetics,* however, was clearly to teach the methods of logic—specifically the discernment of truth and falsehood, virtue and vice. With the *Metaphysics, Topics,* and *Posterior Analytics* as authorities, poetry could stand as an instrument of knowledge. But Bartholomew points out the need to fully understand how that instrument works, that is, how poetry teaches men to distinguish truth from falsehood through contemplation, good and evil in practice.[106] Similarly, Bartholomew interprets Aristotle's intent in the *Poetics* as instruction in the workings of poems as instruments of knowledge. Poetics stands as a method of inquiry into poetry as a product of human imagination that could not exist prior to its being imagined *(quo devenitur in existimationem seu imaginationem, prius non existematio neque ymaginatio).*[107] The *Brevis expositio* thus reinforces the basic presentation of poetic imitation outlined in Herman the German's translation, but it further develops the workings of poetic writing to assert that by representing likenesses of men, poetry gives goodness material form and shows that goodness proceeds not from natural virtue but from knowledge and human will.

While Bartholomew clearly inherited and accepted the Arabic tradition of placing the *Poetics* with logic, his commentary suggests that the methods of logic might expand to include poetry as a specific kind of imitation designed to prove universal principles by presenting imitations of men doing particular actions. Observation of represented actions can yield moral judgments, which can then be applied to lived situations. He is equally interested in the practical, moral uses of poetry and the imagined characters, scenarios, and ideas to which poetry gives form. He is also attentive to the ability of poetry to produce emotional responses that in themselves might factor into the process of making intellectual judgments.

By the early fourteenth century, the *Poetics* was read not only as a strategy of nondemonstrative argumentation but as the representation of hypothetical examples from which general principles of morality could be derived.[108] Following Bartholomew's commentary, poetry allows for judgment of human actions precisely because it produces directly, as if without mediation, images that represent goodness and evil, honesty and dishonesty, truth and falsehood. Poetry thus becomes a species of logical argumentation when it constructs an imagined image of a person who is good and honest or bad and dishonest, rather than representations of the qualities themselves in poetic descriptions of people's behavior. This is the mode by which poetry, still set within the frame of logic, is productive rather than persuasive. Poetry's method for dispelling ignorance is grounded in its ability to give material form to moral qualities—to set them out for observation—and to invite critique by presenting persons who embody them *(et est ad removendam ignorantiam dispositionis, que est quando aliquis distincte et determinate nescit rem).*[109]

Bartholomew continues to define poetic imitation within the discipline of logic, but he also begins to develop a way of thinking that distinguishes poetry from logic: they are interdependent but distinct modes of reasoning.[110] With the advantage of more of the Aristotelian corpus than was available to Herman the German or William of Moerbeke, Bartholomew could compare the *Poetics* directly with the *Rhetoric.* The *Rhetoric,* Bartholomew says, reports that the art of persuasion is good and honorable. Though poetics is a viable method for distinguishing truth from falsehood, poetic method (which Bartholomew takes the *Poetics* to be) is itself a necessary discipline.

> Likewise, however, because in all [logical] processes of this kind it happens that there is diversion from the process of reason, therefore there was need of a kind of knowledge to teach avoidance of diversions and removal of the reasons that have been made up by the quibbler. And thus is complete the knowledge about the method of knowing or about the instrument of knowing, which is the same thing as was evident elsewhere.[111]

One of the conceptual shifts in the *Brevis expositio,* then, is Bartholomew's distinction between the knowledge that poetry produces—the moral judgment of what is good, bad, true, or false in the realm of human behavior—and poetry as an instrument of that knowledge, which must itself be understood. If Aristotle's intention in the *Poetics* was to define the causes behind ideas and images, the immediate goal of the treatise was the understanding of spoken poetry as one instrument of knowing. Understanding the causes would lead to the perfect understanding of performed poetry as an instrument of knowing.

> . . . the immediate and intrinsic cause is the perfect understanding of the spoken instrument or of the spoken composition. The final remote cause is the perfect understanding of the instruments of knowing and the completion of philosophy universally.[112]

Bartholomew interprets Aristotle to say that the purpose of poetry is to provide an instrument of knowledge whose formal properties readers can analyze. More important, however, poetry produces the material characteristics of an argument *(tam materialia quam efficientia, quam formalia, quam finalia, et de eius proprietatibus determinare)*, from which a spectator can derive philosophical principles.[113]

A second shift in the *Brevis expositio* is in Bartholomew's presentation of mimesis. The *Brevis expositio* presents poetry as a representational practice, with attention to the gap between a poetic representation and its referent. Poetry's particular species of logic, as presented in the *Brevis expositio*, works by approximation and likeness. Poetry constructs a specific kind of similitudinous relationship between spoken words and what they represent. Whereas Herman the German was bound to a discussion of indirect reasoning, Bartholomew introduces human imagination as the variable. In Bartholomew's comments, Aristotle distinguishes poetry from other imaginative arts *(vel possit dici quod hic distinguit artem poeticam ab aliis artibus imaginativis, et patebit ibi diviso)*.[114] For Bartholomew, Aristotle's criteria for plot structure are a matter not of inferred logic but of how poetic speech proceeds from the abstractions of human imagination to material form.

> Likewise [Aristotle's] notes say that poetic speeches are assimilative, in that they express a thing not directly but in their own likeness or proportion, or because they use similes and proportions—the opposite of demonstrative speeches, which directly express a thing. Or [Aristotle] says this because they proceed from assimilations, as is clear in a letter. Likewise he calls them imaginative, either because they express a thing

in their image—that is, likeness—or because they proceed not always from things which are but also from things that are possible to imagine . . . [115]

Bartholomew's lecture thus suggests that while the structure of poetry is rational and can be analyzed, the imagery poetry produces proceeds not from things that already exist but from things that are possible, *in potentia,* in the soul.

The *Brevis expositio* still presents poetics as a form of reasoning, but it takes its process to be distinct from demonstrative statements, experimentation, and even, to an extent, rhetorical persuasion. Here, the referents for poetic representation are not necessarily objects perceived by the senses; they may be products of human imagination. The images produced by poetry must be referred back to the sensual world: its method is representation rather than demonstration, and it presents universals by imitating particulars. Poetry can also be separated from unexamined, habitual expression by virtue of its particular mode of representation. At the same time, poetry itself is the object of analysis.

> It seems to me that the habit of custom seems the same as experiment and is the same in thought as in subject; and this habit differs from art because art is of universals and this is not but, rather, is of single things. Even art recognizes a working thing from its own beginnings, and habit does not, because through such beginnings, it seems to discover everything, working by recognition; for otherwise it could not work.[116]

In Bartholomew's interpretation of Aristotle, then, poetry operates by representing actions imagined by the poet, which yield information by which moral judgments can be made. Poetry presents the imagined action directly, in its own image *(vel quia exprimunt rem in sua imagine).*[117] Bartholomew's acknowledgment that poetry represents the world of the senses in material form is perhaps the most significant intellectual move in the *Brevis expositio* with regard to an emerging consciousness of the theatrical presentation of dramatic poetry. While far from the Renaissance concept of verisimilitude as a classical ideal, here is a perception of poetry as direct representation of material realities and human will, a core concept for realistic representation.

The *Brevis expositio* does not take poetic mimesis as theatrical; there is no reason to do so given Averroës's commentary, Herman's translation, and the fragments of Aristotle that Bartholomew had to work with. But Bartholomew did begin to develop the criteria by which poetic imitations are rendered, with the idea that the ability to imagine likenesses and draw from them moral principles is the primary operation of—and the beginning of reason in—all animals *(id est similiter imaginatntur; si enim similes operationes per imagina-tionem debent producere, necesse est eos similiter imaginari; est enim imaginatio principium operationis in animalibus).*[118] Human artifice, that which is not a natural or perfect beginning, is the basis for poetic representation.

The intense interest in an emotional catharsis in response to the depiction of human crises is, as William F. Boggess pointed out in 1969, largely a twen-tieth-century innovation.[119] Nevertheless, a large part of a poem's believabil-ity as discussed in the *Brevis expositio* rests in a poem's ability to incite emo-tions, specifically pity and fear. With assimilative knowledge as the major component of the poetic art, Bartholomew takes the affective aspect of Aris-totelian poetics further toward the importance of human response than in previous presentations in the *Middle Commentary.* Herman had translated from Averroës that the effectiveness of a poem depended on the clarity of its narrative and its presentation. A poem would not be credible, nor would it move an audience either to pity or to fear, if the invented story it presented before the eyes of an audience did not match what those eyes would see in the natural world. The Latin *Middle Commentary* hinted at truthful representa-tion in the spoken recitation of poetry.

> And it is right that the composition of stories be an invention full of fear and grief, as though set up before the eyes, which gets its credibil-ity as though from sight. For when the telling of stories has been doubtful and with doubtful composition, it will not set its intended action in motion. For what someone has not believed, it will not move him, neither to fear or to pity.[120]

For Herman the German, in contrast, it was demonstrative or nondemon-strative speech that had the power to move emotions. When Bartholomew comes to Aristotle's six parts of tragedy, however, he, like William of Moer-beke, uses Aristotle's term *tragedie.* Tragic catharsis, the capacity of poetry to generate a response, is not presented in the *Brevis expositio* as a function of a poem's credibility as a story. Rather, through Aristotle, Bartholomew con-ceives of a direct relationship between the emotion produced in an audience member when he perceives poetic depictions of virtuous or evil men and the poetic representation of the fictional character. The evidence presented by the poem itself (rather than the mode of reasoning) and the order of the story (the structure of the plot), together with the depiction of character, provoke an emotional response.

> And it is right that poetry be of stories and, on account of those stories, should stimulate fear and sadness in men. . . . The representation of fear incites the feeling of fear. That which is a true likeness to what is seen [incites feeling]; that stories move people has motivations: presenting evidence and bringing together order.[121]

Drawing on the *Ethics*, Bartholomew thus expands imitation of emotions and fidelity to visual images to include both knowledge and human will. From the *Ethics*, he acknowledges that the virtues represented in poems are not natural phenomena. Rather, an individual consciously constructs will and knowledge just as a poet consciously makes a poem.

> And it is fitting that [poetry] be of stories, which must be arranged from men's passions; here in the third [part] he shows which and what sort of virtues, because from virtues are shaped knowledge and will and not from natural virtues, which can be outside of knowledge and will, as is evident in books 3 and 4 of the *Ethics*, about justice . . .[122]

Bartholomew also acknowledges that tragedy is based directly on men's emotions. Men's emotions are its subject matter, as well as its product. Men's actions are still subject to right judgment, but the subject matter of poetry is the human subject.

> And it is right that it be of stories, because there he shows of what sort of passions tragedy is made. Or it could be said that since the actions of men are various, he shows here from which actions is his praise, because it is from voluntary and conscious actions that are good.[123]

Bartholomew links the emotions represented in characters in poems with human responses to fiction and allows that those responses factor into the production of knowledge. Bartholomew's version of catharsis binds the representation of fear directly with the experience of fear.

The *Brevis expositio* posits the Aristotelian *Poetics* both as an analysis of ancient performed poetry and as a guide to how poetry is a method for representing human actions. It would seem that Bartholomew is neither entirely within the interpretive tradition of the Arabic commentators and Herman the German nor directly applying the principles of the *Poetics* to existing poetry or *ludi*. The *Brevis expositio* does suggest that by the beginning of the fourteenth century the classification of poetic writing as a form of disputation was being transformed into a recognition of poetry as a mode of human invention enmeshed in logic but singular in its reliance on the resources of the imagination.

Perhaps the most important distinction—one that has been overlooked in discussion of performance history in the medieval and early modern period—is the Scholastic effort to reconcile pagan learning with Christian faith and reason. While the classification of the *Poetics* with logic could not yield any kind of aesthetic theory in medieval times, as it would two centuries later, Bartholomew's 1307 commentary suggests quite clearly an expansion of the category of logic to include a concept (however undefined) of performed poetry that is rooted in the exegetical project of Herman the German and that foreshadows the conscious development of a new poetic drama.

Within two decades of the *Brevis expositio*, Matthias of Linkoping, also writing in Paris, would distinguish poetry from logic in his *Poetria*. Mathias's interest in poetry as an autonomous, human creation divorced the science of poetics from its traditional categorization with logic. The *Poetria* also distinguished between poetry and rhetoric, allowing poetry to present a thing as it exists in nature—or contrasting things—and to excite emotions.[124] Bartholomew's *divisio textus* appears as part of a gradual reorientation of thinking about classical poetry. The conception of poetry, though not tied to Greek or Roman theatrics, moves gently toward a concept of poetry as dramatic, a human doing *(dram)*, the purpose of which is to move the soul. This foundation, beginning as early as the first decade of the fourteenth century, suggests a much more gradual shift from "medieval" to "early modern" thought about classical dramatic poetry as a practice.

The neo-Roman Renaissance theater drew some of its performance practices from the cathedral spectacles, civic cycle plays, curtained booth stages of the chambers of rhetoric, and *mansions* (platforms) of the Passion plays. But the integration of theatrical practice with a kind of rational inquiry apart from overtly religious quests has been attributed to the "rediscovery" of Aristotle and the emergence of European dramaturgy based on Greco-Roman architecture and playwriting. The evidence presented here, working backward from the late fifteenth century, suggests a much earlier reorientation of Christian thought around the *Poetics*.

CHAPTER FIVE

Afterword

From Idea to Practice

ONE OF THE FRUSTRATIONS—or perhaps one of the joys—for historians who study medieval performance practices has been the lack of a critical tradition to explain how medieval minds perceived and understood activities now easily folded into modern, Western notions of theatrical drama. Since the early twentieth century, modern expectations for drama have presumed drama's presentation as theater: dramas are acted out in designated performance spaces; actors play characters and speak scripted dialogue in narratives of conflict and resolution with recognizable reference to the "real" world of daily activities and human emotions. But the idea of theater itself has now expanded to the extent that the discipline of performance studies recognizes an increasingly wide range of human behaviors as overtly performative. As I noted in my introduction, this expansion has had a tremendous, often liberating effect on studies of such medieval activities as festivals, rituals, processions, and executions, as well as on studies of activities more easily labeled "theatrical," such as cycle plays and liturgical reenactments.

Modern historiography has, in its many phases, romanticized, dismissed, criticized, or championed the roles that Christian beliefs and institutional structures played in the development of Western theatrical traditions. Intellectual inquiries independent of Christian belief were clearly not solely responsible for the secularization of the European liturgical *ludi,* cycle plays, and morality plays. But within the restructuring of knowledge beginning in the late fifteenth century, the *scholas,* academies, and schools did reconstitute classical drama and theater as valuable artifacts of the ancient world in a way medieval universities and monasteries had not. Classical drama and theater took on the status of an intellectual discipline, neither dependent on Christian narratives and rituals nor emerging directly from the less structured mummings, disguisings, folk performances, and festivals of everyday practice. Drama and theater were set apart, defined, made independent objects of study rather than by-products of other activities, such as worship.

What survives to constitute a kind of medieval dramatic criticism (itself a post-Renaissance idea) is thus ambiguous at best. At one extreme, Augustine's diatribes against Roman theater seem to have provided a foundation for ecclesiastical resistance to excessive spectacle. Augustine's concerns that theatrical representation proferred and encouraged false emotions, as well as theater's inextricability from pagan culture, kept theater well out of Christianity's purview. At the other extreme, Honorius Augustodunensis freely reincorporated the image of a classical actor to explain the positive value of human artifice in the performance of the Mass, and John of Salisbury championed the acting on the ancient stages against the debauched spectacles popular in the twelfth-century courts.

This study has attempted to break apart two conventions in medieval theater historiography by casting writings about classical theater in the medieval intellectual tradition rather than in the history of a developing theatrical tradition. The first convention is the tendency to anthologize these writings as dramatic criticism or evidence of theatrical practice without attention to their internal arguments, textual context, or purpose. Thus, we find in Augustine a sophisticated analysis of theatrical signification running through his severe critique of theater as a Roman institution, and we find in Amalarius of Metz indications of mimesis in Christian ritual that is not intended as theater *(theatrum)*, though some liturgical practices at the time clearly evoked concern that worship might come to resemble ancient theatrical shows and so set back Christianity's progress over pagan religions.

The second convention challenged herein is the question of continuity or discontinuity between the Middle Ages and the Renaissance along the axis of an artistic tradition. As a relic of the past, accessible through such texts as Isidore's *Etymologiae*, the theaters of the ancient world generally remained in a separate category from the rituals and *ludi* performed on temporary booth stages or pageant wagons and from the Roman plays read as literature and rhetoric (the ancient techniques of which were absorbed into medieval oratory, later evident in the so-called Terence stages and chambers of rhetoric). The effects of medieval categories of thought on the potential for recouping classical theater for Christian purposes is especially evident in the treatment of Aristotle's *Poetics* in the thirteenth century. Early fourteenth-century thought suggests some of the sensitivities to theatrical mimesis that opened Aristotle's *Poetics* to reinterpretation as a document of literary and theatrical practice in the sixteenth century. As Bartholomew's brief treatment of the *Poetics* indicates, the categories of thought that separated theater (as a practice) and drama (as literature) may have started shifting as early as the beginning of the fourteenth century. With regard to the intellectual fortunes of ancient theater, the question of transition between historical periods is a matter less of continuity or discontinuity than of the rate of change in intellectual categories, methods of inquiry, and sites of analysis.

Ancient theater was an idea in medieval intellectual culture. The content of the idea depended more on the intellectual context in which it was placed and the purposes for which it was invoked than on its relationship to actual performance practices of the Middle Ages. When ancient theater was included in medieval discourses, it could be shaped to fit into existing discursive formations (as in the case of the thirteenth-century *Poetics*) or filled with whatever images served the writer's purpose (as with Agobard and Florus, who took pagan theatricality as anathema to Christianity, or, three centuries later, John of Salisbury, who, reversing Augustine, condemned the *ludi* of his own day only to extol the theater of the ancients).

If medieval minds were keenly aware of theater as an ancient and pagan practice, they also incorporated—however fleetingly—ancient theater into larger intellectual projects. As this study indicates, there is a gradual integration of theater into Christian discourse (without Augustine's residual animosity). There is also a wide variance in approach to, interpretation of, and judgment passed on the idea of the ancients' theatrical performances. If a concept of theatrical drama and a critical tradition, as defined since the Renaissance, cannot be found in medieval texts, the mistake has been to consider this a lack or failure. As this study has shown, until classical theater was stabilized as an edifying practice in the sixteenth century, its place in Western thought was remarkably fluid, and its value was open to lively variation.

Notes

∞∞∞

INTRODUCTION

1. See Stephen G. Nichols, "The New Medievalism: Tradition and Discontinuity in Medieval Culture," in *The New Medievalism*, ed. Marina S. Brownlee, Kevin Brownlee, and Stephen G. Nichols (Baltimore: Johns Hopkins University Press, 1991), 1–26. Nichols examines a developing disciplinary interest in investigating medieval representation in its endless variety, free from privileging literature as the highest form of cultural expression and with equal attention to the differences and continuities between medieval, classical, and Renaissance mimesis (1–2).

2. This study focuses on the idea of theater as constructed in medieval texts and tracks changes in that idea. Closely related to this project are studies that follow changes in ways texts are written and read, as well as the relationships between writing and orality. See, for example, Patrick J. Geary, "Oblivion Between Orality and Textuality in the Tenth Century," in *Medieval Concepts of the Past: Ritual, Memory, Historiography*, ed. Gerd Althoff, Johannes Fried, and Patrick J. Geary (Cambridge: Cambridge University Press, 2002), 111–22.

3. Jody Enders, *The Medieval Theater of Cruelty: Rhetoric, Memory, Violence* (Ithaca: Cornell University Press, 1999); Claire Sponsler, *Drama and Resistance: Bodies, Goods, and Theatricality in Late Medieval England* (Minneapolis: University of Minnesota Press, 1997); Caroline Walker Bynum, *The Resurrection of the Body in Western Christianity, 200–1336* (New York: Columbia University Press, 1995); Bruce W. Holsinger, *Music, Body, and Desire in Medieval Culture: Hildegard of Bingen to Chaucer* (Stanford: Stanford University Press, 2001); Michal Kobialka, *This Is My Body: Representational Practices in the Early Middle Ages* (Ann Arbor: University of Michigan Press, 1999); Sarah Beckwith, *Signifying God: Social Relation and Symbolic Act in the York Corpus Christi Plays* (Chicago: University of Chicago Press, 2001); Gail McMurray Gibson, *The Theater of Devotion: East Anglian Drama and Society in the Late Middle Ages* (Chicago: University of Chicago Press, 1989); Clifford Davidson, ed., *Gesture in Medieval Drama and Art* (Kalamazoo: Medieval Institute Publications, Western Michi-

129

gan University, 2001); Victor I. Scherb, *Staging Faith: East Anglian Drama in the Later Middle Ages* (Madison: Fairleigh Dickinson University Press, 2001); Dunbar H. Ogden, *The Staging of Drama in the Medieval Church* (Newark: University of Delaware Press, 2002).

4. For this point with regard to the Carolingian period, see Giles Brown, "Introduction: The Carolingian Renaissance," in *Carolingian Culture: Emulation and Innovation,* ed. Rosamond McKitterick (Cambridge: Cambridge University Press, 1994), 1. For the twelfth century, see Bernard McGinn, "The Religious World of the Twelfth Century: Introduction," in *Christian Spirituality: Origins to the Twelfth Century,* ed. Bernard McGinn and John Meyendorff with Jean Leclercq (New York: Crossroad, 1985), 195.

5. Rodney Thomson, "John of Salisbury and William of Malmesbury: Currents in Twelfth-Century Humanism," in *The World of John of Salisbury,* ed. Michael Wilks (Oxford: Basil Blackwell, 1984), 117.

6. See Karl Young, *The Drama of the Medieval Church,* 2 vols. (Oxford: Clarendon Press, 1933). The historiography of medieval theater and drama to 1984 is well documented in Ronald W. Vince, *Ancient and Medieval Theatre: A Historiographical Handbook* (Westport, Conn.: Greenwood Press, 1984), 89–129. Vince surveys major trends in scholarship, noting especially the shift away from an evolutionary model in the 1960s, differing orientations toward literature (drama) and performance (theater), and changing perceptions of relationships between medieval theater or drama and folk traditions, art and iconography, vernacular expressions of culture, pagan and Christian rituals, rhetoric and oratory, music, historical records, and literary forms. Michal Kobialka gives a thorough assessment and sharp critique of the discipline's recent historiography, *This Is My Body,* 1–33.

7. Nils Hoger Petersen, "Music, Dramatic Extroversion, and Contemplative Introspection: Hildegard of Bingen's *Ordo virtutum,*" in *Ritual, Performance, Culture: Papers by C. Clifford Flanigan, His Students, and Colleagues,* ed. Robert Clark (Auckland: Wim Husken, forthcoming).

8. Nichols, "New Medievalism," 23 n. 3.

9. John Wesley Harris simply and eloquently summarizes medieval dramatic representation as part of a sensibility in which "the whole of creation was a book provided for man, in which he could read the wonderful works of God" (*Medieval Theatre in Context: An Introduction* [London: Routledge, 1992], 8).

10. Harold C. Gardiner's historical narrative of Protestant suppression of the Catholic religious drama in England, a revision of early twentieth-century evolutionary theory of the development of dramatic form (*Mysteries' End: An Investigation of the Last Days of the Medieval Religious Stage* [New Haven: Yale University Press, 1946; reprinted 1967]) has been revised in Beckwith, *Signifying God.*

11. Vince, *Ancient and Medieval Theatre,* ix.

12. The plays of Hrotswitha of Gandersheim, written in the tenth century, and the twelfth-century Latin *commedia* from France, Italy, and England are generally considered literary products based on Roman models. If they were read out loud at all, their purpose was educational. Hrotswitha's plays served as narratives demonstrating female virtue and as pedagogical exercises in Latin in the schools. See Vince, *Ancient and Medieval Theatre,* 132.

13. Marcia L. Colish, *Medieval Foundations of the Western Intellectual Tradition, 400–1400* (New Haven: Yale University Press, 1997), 206.

14. Vince, *Ancient and Medieval Theatre*, 111. Jonas Barish gives an overview of early Christian polemics against theater in *The Antitheatrical Prejudice* (Berkeley: University of California Press, 1981), 38–65. The idea that the Christian church consistently opposed theater is still pervasive, though as Ronald Vince pointed out three years after the publication of Barish's book, the perception is erroneous.

15. Jody Enders, *Rhetoric and the Origins of Medieval Drama* (Ithaca: Cornell University Press, 1992); Kobialka, *This Is My Body*.

16. David Bevington, *Medieval Drama* (Boston: Houghton Mifflin, 1975), 7. Rainer Warning points to the traditional distinction between drama as literature and theater as institution, and redirects the inquiry into religious drama to "the institutional setting to which it stood witness," in which the performance and its reception are inseparable and the presentation of fiction impossible. See Rainer Warning, "On the Alterity of Medieval Religious Drama," *New Literary History* 10 (1979): 265–92; here 266–67.

17. These characteristics have guided numerous discussions of medieval performance. See, for example, Harris, *Medieval Theatre in Context*, 8. Kobialka observes that the modern lexicon for tenth-century *Quem quaeritis* and *Visitatio sepulchri* ceremonies automatically applies these characteristics in medieval contexts; terms include "biblical drama," "liturgical drama," "play," "play of a ritual drama," "dramatic office," "liturgical music drama," "dramatic resurrection ceremony," and "performance ceremony." The lexicon itself, he argues, imposes a post-Renaissance concept of representation as an imitation of nature (Aristotle) or a doubling of ideal forms (Plato), made visible and ordered by the rules of linear perspective (*This Is My Body*, vii, 24).

18. The term *classical theater* when it is used today (and in the present study) generally refers to the Attic theater of the fifth century B.C.E. and to an extent the comedies of Plautus and Terence, Senecan drama, and other Roman adaptations of Greek plays. For a historiographical summary of source material that traces the influence of scholarly trends in classical studies (such as the Cambridge School of Anthropology) on studies of theater in Attic Greece, the Roman Republic and Empire, and Christian Europe, see Vince, *Ancient and Medieval Theatre*, 3–28. The number of extant scripts and evidence of performance has, since the mid–nineteenth century, suggested Attic theater as the root of modern Western theatrical practice. The Attic theater's ritual context (civic and religious) generated a theory of theater's origins in ritual in the 1960s that is still influential. Foundational sources for modern understandings of Greek theater and its Roman adaptations include Margarete Bieber, *The History of Greek and Roman Theatre*, 2d ed. (Princeton: Princeton University Press, 1961); H. D. F. Kitto, *Greek Tragedy*, 2d ed. (London: Methuen, 1950); William Beare, *The Roman Stage: A Short History of Latin Drama in the Time of the Republic*, 3d ed. (London: Methuen, 1964); and A. W. Pickard-Cambridge, *Dithyramb, Tragedy, and Comedy*, 2d ed., revised by T. B. L. Webster (Oxford: Clarendon Press, 1962), and *The Dramatic Festivals of Athens*, 2d ed., revised by John Gould and D. M. Lewis (London: Oxford University Press, 1968). Much work has since been done on unscripted, popular entertainments in Greece and Rome. The standard investigation of continuities between traditions of unscripted, improvisational performance from Roman to Western Christian culture is Allardyce Nicoll, *Masks,*

Mimes, and Miracles (London: G. C. Harrap, 1931). More recent studies have extended knowledge about the theaters and plays into the social world. See, for example, Ruth Scodel, *Theater and Society in the Classical World* (Ann Arbor: University of Michigan Press, 1993); the collection of essays edited by John J. Winkler and Froma I. Zietlin, *Nothing to Do with Dionysus? Athenian Drama in Its Social Context* (Princeton: Princeton University Press, 1990); and William J. Slater, ed., *Roman Theater and Society* (Ann Arbor: University of Michigan Press, 1995). For purposes of this study, I will use the term *Greco-Roman theater* or *ancient theater* to refer to medieval concepts of theater in Christianity's formative era. Use of the term *classical theater* in this study will indicate a modern or early modern concept of ancient theaters, plays, and theatrical practice.

CHAPTER 1

1. Jonas Barish opens his study of Western culture's antipathy toward theater with the observation that "a prejudice against the theater that goes back as far in European history as the theater itself can be traced" (*The Antitheatrical Prejudice* [Berkeley and Los Angeles: University of California Press, 1981], 1). For concerns about classical theater in Judaism and the Eastern church, see Shmuel Moreh, *Live Theatre and Dramatic Literature in the Medieval Arab World* (New York: New York University Press, 1992), 3–11. For the awareness of Greek and Roman theater in the Arab world, see ibid., 11–15; on the absence of institutionalized theater in the Near Eastern territories in the sixth century, see ibid., 21–25.

2. For a contrasting use of theater as a metaphor in Eastern Christianity, see Blake Leyerle, *Theatrical Shows and Ascetic Lives: John Chrysostom's Attack on Spiritual Marriage* (Berkeley and Los Angeles: University of California Press, 2001).

3. The issue of the relationship between dramatization (embodied representation of biblical events) or theatricality (spectacle) and the celebration of the liturgy will be taken up in chapters 2 and 3. For the development of the Roman rite and the varieties of liturgical expression into the eighth century as a liturgical context for this chapter, see James McKinnon, *The Advent Project: The Later-Seventh-Century Creation of the Roman Mass Proper* (Berkeley and Los Angeles: University of California Press, 2000).

4. See Richard C. Beacham, *The Roman Theatre and Its Audience* (Cambridge: Harvard University Press, 1992).

5. Michal Kobialka summarizes the Trinitarian distinctions between *signa propria* and *res* and among *allegoria theologica, allegoria historiae,* and *allegoria in factis* (*This Is My Body: Representational Practices in the Early Middle Ages* [Ann Arbor, MI: University of Michigan Press, 1999], 108–9).

6. Tertullian and St. John Chrysostom also emphasized the dangers of pleasure, specifically that of the theater. See Barish, *Antitheatrical Prejudice,* 50–51. In *Soliloquies,* in particular, Augustine submits his physical desires to Reason, ending with the importance of seeing the difference between knowledge contained in the intellect and that which is created by the mind (fantasy), or truth and falsehood. See *Soliloquies* (trans. Thomas F. Gilligan) 2:17–20; hereafter, *Soliloquies* (Gilligan).

7. Ramsay MacMullen points to the polarization of Christians in pagan society

and to Christianity's ongoing struggle against erroneous understanding of God and God's divine plan (*Christianity and Paganism in the Fourth to Eighth Centuries* [New Haven: Yale University Press, 1997], 5–6, 30–31).

8. For the denigrated position of actors in Roman society, the erosion of theater's link to pagan ritual, and prohibitions on actors becoming Christians in the fourth and fifth centuries, see Barish, *Antitheatrical Prejudice*, 41–43. For a fairly recent examination of the secularization of pagan performances, with a focus on the eastern empire, see Dorothea French, "Christian Emperors and Pagan Spectacles: The Secularization of the *Ludi*, A.D. 382–525" (Ph.D. diss., University of California, Berkeley, 1985).

9. See MacMullen, *Christianity and Paganism*, 32–33.

10. Augustine *City of God* (ed. and trans. R. W. Dyson) 6.7; hereafter, *City of God* (Dyson).

11. MacMullen, *Christianity and Paganism*, 34, 49–50.

12. Marcia L. Colish, *Medieval Foundations of the Western Intellectual Tradition, 400–1400* (New Haven: Yale University Press, 1997), 25–27.

13. On the Manichaean and Neoplatonic audience of the *Confessions* and on themes in earlier Augustinian writings, see Robert J. O'Connell, *St. Augustine's "Confessions": The Odyssey of the Soul*, 2d ed. (New York: Fordham University Press, 1989), 13–19, esp. 15–16, 18.

14. For the lineage of views on the infallible authority of the Christian Scriptures, from Tertullian through Philastrius of Brescia, see MacMullen, *Christianity and Paganism*, 87–88.

15. Augustine *Confessions* (trans. Vernon J. Bourke) 3.7; hereafter, *Confessions* (Bourke).

16. See ibid., 3.2. Robert J. O'Connell (*St. Augustine's "Confessions,"* 46–47, 51) traces Augustine's adaptation of the triplex concupiscentia (1 John 2:16).

17. *Confessions* (Bourke) 3.2.

18. Ibid., 3.2.

19. It can be argued that Augustine's Christian Platonism keeps him from an entirely negative view of the material world and the body and that his antipathy toward theater is not simply a rejection on ascetic grounds. See A. Hilary Armstrong's seminal essay, "St. Augustine and Christian Platonism," in *Augustine: A Collection of Critical Essays*, ed. Robert A. Markus (Garden City: Anchor Books, 1972), 9–11.

20. See Aristotle *Poetics* 14.1453b1 on the experience of pity and fear in response to a properly constructed tragic plot.

21. *Confessions* (Bourke) 3.2.

22. See Augustine's comparison of civil and mythic theologies through Varro and Seneca in *City of God* (Dyson) 6.10.

23. See Rita Copeland, *Rhetoric, Hermeneutics, and Translation in the Middle Ages: Academic Traditions and Vernacular Texts* (Cambridge: Cambridge University Press, 1991), 161.

24. See Marcia Colish, *The Mirror of Language: A Study in the Medieval Theory of Knowledge* (New Haven: Yale University Press, 1968), 16; Colish, *Medieval Foundations*, 29.

25. See Barish, *Antitheatrical Prejudice*, 60.

26. See *Confessions* (Bourke) 3.2.

27. Cf. Aristotle *Poetics* 1448b5 on the pleasure of observing in reproduction what would be horrific if experienced without mediation.

28. Cf. Barish, *Antitheatrical Prejudice*, 53; Aristotle *Poetics* 1448b5–1448b11 chap. 4.

29. *Confessions* (Bourke) 3.2.

30. See Colish, *Mirror*, 23.

31. *Confessions* (Bourke) 3.1. The issue of human perception in recognizing true objects from the similitudes produced by sensory and mental phenomena such as optical illusions, dreams, seeing reflected images, reproduction, and imitations of sounds is given extensive treatment in the *Soliloquies*. Barish (*Antitheatrical Prejudice*, 55) analyzes Augustine's Platonic argument against imitation and the intent of the theater to deceive by creating false images.

32. *Confessions* (Bourke) 3.6. On Augustine and the "food of Truth," cf. O'Connell, *St. Augustine's "Confessions,"* 29–30.

33. Barish suggests that Augustine also compares theater unfavorably to Christian ritual in *On Christian Doctrine* (1.29) and that similar comparisons in some sermons demonstrate his "antitheatrical" attitude. Though Barish sees in these comparisons Augustine's application of general characteristics of theater, such as crowd psychology and spectacle, to Christian ritual, I argue that the comparisons serve to keep theater distinct from Christian worship rather than indicating true similarities in their mode of representation. See Barish, *Antitheatrical Prejudice*, 57–59.

34. Though not a focus of this study's concern for the written transmission of ideas, the role of memory cannot be underestimated. See, in particular, Mary J. Carruthers, *The Book of Memory: A Study of Memory in Medieval Culture* (Cambridge: Cambridge University Press, 1990).

35. *City of God* (Dyson) 4.26.

36. See F. Edward Cranz, "*De Civitate Dei*, XV, 2, and Augustine's Idea of the Christian Society," in *Augustine: A Collection of Critical Essays*, ed. Robert A. Markus (Garden City: Anchor Books, 1972), 404–21.

37. See Frederick Van Fleteren, "*De Civitate Dei*: Miscellaneous Observations," in *The City of God: A Collection of Critical Essays*, ed. Dorothy F. Donnelly (New York: Peter Lang, 1995), 418; *City of God* (Dyson) 4.28.

38. *City of God* (Dyson) 2.25.

39. Ibid., 1.7, 1.3.

40. Ibid., 2.25.

41. MacMullen, *Christianity and Paganism*, 90–91.

42. *City of God* (Dyson) 2.4, 2.16.

43. Ibid., 6.6.

44. Ibid., 4.8–11, 4.14–24. In relation to theater, see esp. ibid., 4.26.

45. Ibid., 2.19, 2.14.

46. Ibid., 6.7.

47. Ibid., 4.26.

48. Ibid., 6.7.

49. Ibid., 2.9, 2.21.

50. Ibid., 2.14.

51. Ibid., 4.26.

52. Ibid., 4.1.

53. Ibid., 6.6.

54. Ibid., 2.26.

55. Ibid., 4.5.

56. Ibid., 2.25.

57. Ibid.

58. Ibid., 2.18.

59. Ibid., 2.11.

60. Ibid., 2.14.

61. Ibid., 2.12.

62. Ibid., 2.10.

63. Augustine also takes aim at a fourth-century "fan culture." He construes idolization of performers, despite their marginalization in Roman society, as a destructive social force. See *City of God* (Dyson) 2.32 and *De doctrina Christiana* (ed. and trans. R. P. H. Green) 9.24–25; hereafter, *De doctrina Christiana* (Green).

64. For the relationship between the thing of the sign, the perceiver or user of the sign (signifier), and the thing brought by reference or impression to the mind, see Robert A. Markus, "Signs, Communication, and Communities in Augustine's *De doctrina Christiana*," in *"De doctrina Christiana": A Classic of Western Culture*, ed. Duane W. H. Arnold and Pamela Bright (Notre Dame: University of Notre Dame Press, 1995), 98–99.

65. MacMullen, *Christianity and Paganism*, 150.

66. See Christoph Schäublin, *"De doctrina Christiana:* A Classic of Western Culture?" in *"De doctrina Christiana": A Classic of Western Culture*, ed. Duane W. H. Arnold and Pamela Bright (Notre Dame: University of Notre Dame Press, 1995), 47–67, esp. 48.

67. *De doctrina Christiana* (Green) 1.4–5.

68. Schäublin, *"De doctrina Christiana*," 49.

69. *De doctrina Christiana* (Green) 2.97.

70. Markus, "Signs," 98.

71. *De doctrina Christiana* (Green) 2.99.

72. Ibid., 2.130.

73. Edmund Hill, introduction and notes to *Teaching Christianity: "De Doctrina Christiana,"* vol. 11, The Works of St. Augustine: A Translation for the 21st Century, ed. John E. Rotelle, (Hyde Park, N.Y.: New City Press, 1990), 87.

74. *De doctrina Christiana* (Green) 2.71.

75. Augustine *Concerning the Teacher* (trans. George C. Leckie) 1.2.

76. Ibid., 3.6.

77. For the context in which theater slips into Augustine's language theory and for the relationship of *signa* to *res*, see Christopher Kirwan, "Augustine's Philosophy of Language," in *The Cambridge Companion to Augustine*, ed. Eleonore Stump and Norman Kretzmann (Cambridge: Cambridge University Press, 2001), 186–204, esp. 191–94.

78. Barish, *Antitheatrical Prejudice*, 57.

79. *Soliloquies* (Gilligan) 2.7.

80. Ibid., 2.9.

81. Ibid., 2.16.

82. Ibid., 2.18.

83. Ibid.

84. Representations of nonexistent things, such as Medea's chariot, cannot by definition be false, because these things do not exist in reality: "a thing which is absolutely non-existent cannot imitate anything" (*Soliloquies* [Gilligan] 2.15).

85. Barish, *Antitheatrical Prejudice*, 57.

86. The conclusion that Augustine's antipathy toward theater is a function of a prudish attitude toward sexuality and a myopic view of Christian ethics is generally accepted. Barish concludes his comparison of Augustine and Tertullian with the observation that Augustine does not have an ontological problem with theater as a "falling away from being" (dramatic impersonation as a betrayal of self) or that spectacle itself is a "calculated affront to the truth of creation." For Augustine, theater is an "aggravating agent" in Rome's ongoing degeneration. Barish sees Augustine's critique as grounded primarily in Christian morality: theater encourages imitation of indecency, general immorality, fan frenzy, and bad social behavior. See Barish, *Antitheatrical Prejudice*, 64–65.

87. Stephen G. Nichols, "The New Medievalism: Tradition and Discontinuity in Medieval Culture," in *The New Medievalism*, ed. Marina Scordilis Brownlee, Kevin Brownlee, and Stephen G. Nichols (Baltimore: John Hopkins University Press, 1991), 1.

88. See Colish, *Medieval Foundations*, 23.

89. The *Etymologiae* was written at the request of Bishop Baulio of Saragossa, who organized it into twenty books after Isidore's death. Sections of the *Etymologiae* circulated during Isidore's lifetime, though most of it was copied posthumously. See Ernest Brehaut, *An Encyclopedist of the Dark Ages: Isidore of Seville*, (New York: Columbia University; Longman, Green, and Company, 1912), 34.

90. For an overview of the schematic organization of the *Etymologiae*, especially with regard to poetics, see Ernst Robert Curtius, *European Literature and the Latin Middle Ages*, trans. Willard R. Trask (New York: Pantheon Books, 1953), 450–57.

91. See Mary Hatch Marshall, "Theatre in the Middle Ages: Evidence from Dictionaries and Glosses," *Symposium: A Journal Devoted to Modern Foreign Languages and Literatures* 4 (1950): 1–39, esp. 8. See also Brehaut, *Encyclopedist*, 16–17.

92. For Isidore's investment in preserving and illustrating Greco-Roman cultural identity and for his reliance on Varro for the connection between theater and pagan religion, see Jacques Fontaine, *Isidore de Séville: Genèse et originalité de la culture hispanique au temps de Wisigoths* (Turnhout: Brepols, 2000), 288–90.

93. For Isidore's Roman sources, see Brehaut, *Encyclopedist*, 37–38, 47–48. Brehaut attributes the inconsistencies in the *Etymologiae* to Isidore's eclectic use of sources, the attempt at a comprehensive compilation of existing knowledge, and a lack of deep consideration of the material (see also *Encyclopedist*, 32–33, 44; on Isidore's use of Varro, cf. Fontaine, *Isidore de Séville*, 291–92). See Joseph R. Jones, "Isidore and the Theatre," in *Drama in the Middle Ages: Comparative and Critical Essays*, ed. Clifford Davidson and John H. Stroupe, AMS Studies in the Middle Ages, no. 18 (New York: AMS Press, 1991), 1–23, for a survey of Isidore's data on drama and theater; his sources (especially Diomedes); his descriptions of theatrical practice; his use of such terms as *histrio, saltator, comici,* and *tragici;* and the authority of the *Etymologiae* into the fifteenth and sixteenth centuries. Jones sifts through Isidore's entries in search of accurate information

about, primarily, the performance of classical drama. For Isidore's sources on tragic and comic performance, including *De doctrina Christiana*, see Henry Ansgar Kelly, *Ideas and Forms of Tragedy from Aristotle to the Middle Ages* (Cambridge: Cambridge University Press, 1993), 43–48.

94. The definitions of *theatrum* and *scena* in the *Etymologiae* are an example of the kind of confusion Isidore's descriptions pose for modern scholars attempting to draw a picture of ancient theater from the terms Isidore uses in his descriptions. Marshall ("Theatre," 7–8) lays out uses of these terms (and the various associations of *scena* with shade, covering, small house, facade, or platform and of *theatrum* with "seeing place") in Cassiodorus, Boethius, Virgil, Placidus and pseudo-Placidus, and Tertullian. Marshall ("Theatre," 10) observes that in *Etymologiae* 18.42, Isidore assumes that the *scena* is part of the *theatrum*, whereas he uses the terms synonymously elsewhere (e.g., 10.253). Jones ("Isidore," 9) interprets *scena* as "stage-building" and *pulpitus* as "platform." Kelly (*Ideas and Forms*, 41–42) interprets *scena* to mean "the large roofed building at the rear of the open-air Roman theatre," including the stage, with the stage itself designated with the masculine form *pulpitus* and also identified as the *orchestra*. Modern discussions of numerous terms (most prominently *histriones, auctores, tragoedi, comoedi, ludi,* and *thymele,* as well as *fabulae* as performative or written) in service of reconstructing ancient theater reveal the ambiguity of Isidore's intended meaning and his diverse interpretation of his sources. See also William Tydeman, *The Theatre in the Middle Ages: Western European Stage Conditions, c. 800–1576* (Cambridge: Cambridge University Press, 1978), 184–85; Kelly, *Ideas and Forms,* 40, 43, 45–46. The ambiguity in terminology is part of the reason for my focus on the categories into which Isidore puts ideas, rather than on derivations or meanings of the words as they apply to theatrical practice.

95. See Brehaut, *Encyclopedist,* 34. Brehaut and, more recently, Jody Enders, for example, identify hierarchical patterns in Isidore's organization of dictionary-style entries. For Brehaut (196 n. 1), books 7 and 8 of the *Etymologiae* catalog divine, human, and demonic entities in a progression from highest value to lowest. Jody Enders, tracing the importance of forensic oratory to dramatic representation, identifies a degeneration in the structure of book 18. Enders notes "a progression from serious physical battle to bloodless verbal disputation to . . . silly dice games" (*Rhetoric and the Origins of Medieval Drama* [Ithaca: Cornell University Press, 1992], 81). Enders interprets Isidore's categories as a historical and etymological conflation of warfare, law, judgment, drama, sport, and spectacle, "rendered coherent by a focus on the *theatrical* space in which each combat ritual is played out" (78; italics added). The structure of the *Etymologiae* also separates ancient activities by category. Isidore distinguishes theatrical space as a particular kind of entertainment within the broad categories he sets up. The criteria he uses to do this, I argue, establish a concept of theater that makes it distinct from other forms of medieval entertainment.

96. On the emergence of categories in localized environments and out of embodied experience, as well as the flexibility of categories outside those parameters, see, George Lakoff, *Women, Fire, and Dangerous Things: What Categories Reveal about the Mind* (Chicago: University of Chicago Press, 1987), xiv.

97. Lakoff, *Women, Fire, and Dangerous Things,* 2.

98. See Brehaut, *Encyclopedist,* 33–34.

99. For the question of whether Isidore intended to chart the origins of words or the things designated by words, see Fontaine, *Isidore de Séville,* 285.

100. Brehaut (*Encyclopedist,* 33), emphasizing contradictions and inconsistencies throughout the *Etymologiae,* suggests that the binding thread of the *Etymologiae's* categories was Isidore's belief that knowledge lies in the origins of words and their transcendental meanings. Curtius (*European Literature,* 456) points out the origin of all knowledge in Hebraic sources, which Isidore harmonized with pagan learning in service of Christian learning.

101. See Katherine Nell MacFarlane, *Isidore of Seville on the Pagan Gods ("Origines" VIII.11),* Transactions of the American Philosophical Society, vol. 70, no. 3 (Philadelphia: American Philosophical Society, 1980), 11.

102. Kelly (*Ideas and Forms,* 37–38, 41) argues that Isidore might well have taken his evidence from architectural ruins as well as texts.

103. Isidore *Etymologiarum sive originum* (ed. W. M. Lindsay) 15.2; hereafter, *Etymologiae.*

104. *Etymologiae* 15.2.30. 15–20.

105. Ibid., 15.2.33.27.

106. Ibid., 15.2.35.4–7.

107. Ibid., 15.2.36.7–10.

108. Ibid., 15.4.2.15–24.

109. Ibid., 15.2.34.2–3: *Theatrum autem ab spectaculo nominatum ἀπὸ τῆς θεωρίας quod in eo populus stans desuper atque spectans ludos scenicos contemplaretur.*

110. The distinction between ritual and theater is also evident in Isidore's discussion of the *thymele,* now understood as a central altar in pre-Hellenic theaters. Isidore considered the *thymele* to be a place for musicians. See Kelly, *Ideas and Forms,* 46.

111. For a more detailed description of Isidore's composite picture of theater, see Jones, "Isidore," 16.

112. See Enders, *Rhetoric,* 74–89, esp. 87–89. Enders sifts from Isidore's entries criteria that have guided modern analyses of how theater evolved in the Middle Ages from religious ritual, ritual combat, agon, games, spectacle, performance space, oratory and debate, contests, and impersonation. Enders suggests that book 18 of the *Etymologiae* weaves together (rather than separates out) numerous qualities that today characterize theater and theatricality. Enders concludes that Isidore's "etymological justification of the interplay of legal oratory, drama, battle, circus, and spectacle attests to an intellectual climate in which the drama inherent in rhetorical conflict might readily have developed into conflictual drama as such" (87–89).

113. *Satanas in Latino sonat adversarius, sive transgressor. Ipse est enim adversarius, qui est veritatis inimicus, et semper sanctorum virtutibus contraire nititur. Ipse et transgressor, quia praevaricator effectus in veritate, qua conditus est, non stetit. Idem et temptator, quia temptandam iustorum innocentiam postulat, sicut in Job scribitur* (*Etymologiae* 8.11). For the sources see MacFarlane, *Isidore,* 15.19.

114. The entry *De spectaculis* concludes with a list of spectacles: *Ludus autem aut gymnicus est, aut circensis, aut gladiatorius, aut scenicus* (*Etymologiae* 18.16). Following Isidore, the origins of plays *(ludi)* would be in Etrurian rites imported by the Romans when professional performers were brought in to provide entertainments. Jody Enders

analyzes Isidore's use of *ludi, lusi,* and *luctae* as polysemous terms that function equally well in describing combat, debate, spectacle, and theater. These terms and their permutations continue to describe secular and sacred dramatic events through the sixteenth century. See Enders, *Rhetoric,* 80–81.

115. *Etymologiae,* 8.7 *De poetis.* The structure of the *Etymologiae* makes a categorical distinction between writing (book 1, *De Grammatica et partibus eius;* book 2, *De rhetorica et dialectica*) and spectacle performances (book 18, *De bello et ludi*).

116. *Etymologiae* 18.51, *Quid quo patrono agatur;* 18.59, *De horum exercitatione ludorum.* See Jones, "Isidore," 13–14.

117. *Etymologiae* 18.42, *De theatro.*

118. Ibid., 18.45, *De tragoediis;* 18.46, *De comoedis;* 18.48, *De histrionibus;* 18.49, *De mimis.* Tragedians sang in poetry of the deeds and sad crimes of evil kings, and comedians sang of mens' private affairs, the defilement of virgins, and sex lives of whores. Actors impersonated women and danced; mimes imitated human actions with their bodies to accompany poetry as the poets recited. For the patristic sources of Isidore's definition of sung poetry and for full translations of these passages, see Kelly, *Ideas and Forms,* 44, 46.

119. *Agonum genera fuisse: inmensitas virium, cursui celeritas, sagittandi peritia, standi patientia, ad citharam quoque vel tibias incedendi gestus, de moribus quoque, de forma, de cantandi modulatione, terrestris quoque belli et navalis proelii, perpetiendorumque suppliciorum certamina* (*Etymologiae* 18.26, *De generibus agonum*).

120. *Orchestra autem pulpitus erat scenae, ubi saltator agere posset, aut duo inter se disputare. Ibi enim poetae comoedi et tragoedi ad certamen conscendebant, hisque canentibus alii gestus edebant* (ibid., 18.44, *De orchestra*). Enders (*Rhetoric,* 86) notes, "The orchestra is the platform of the stage, where one dancer could perform or two could compete with each other." *Etymologiae* 18.43 describes *scena* as a backdrop.

121. *Etymologiae, De poetis,* 8.7.

122. *Apud poetas autem tres characteres esse dicendi: unum, in quo tantum poeta loquitur, ut est in libris Vergilii Georgicorum: alium dramaticum, in quo nusquam poeta loquitur, ut est in comoediis et tragoediis: tertium mixtum, ut est in Aeneide. Nam poeta illic et introductae personae loquuntur* (ibid., 8.7.11). Tragedy and comedy are prominent in Isidore's discussion of the church and his discussion of them follows. Kelly *(Ideas and Forms)* asserts that Isidore was here thinking not of theater but of literary dialogue (40) and that he did not conceive of two poets competing on stage (43). On the same passage, Jones ("Isidore," 8) concludes that Isidore viewed satire as a form of drama and that this borrowing from Diomedes would indeed have been understood as dramatic (i.e., theatrical).

123. *Tragoedi sunt qui antiqua gesta atque facinora sceleratorum regum luctuosa carmine spectante populo concinebant* and *Comoedi sunt qui privatorum hominum acta dictis aut gestu cantabant, atque stupra virginum et amores meretricum in suis fabulis exprimebant* (*Etymologiae* 18.45–46). For the grounding in Diomedes, see Jones, "Isidore," 8. For Isidore's use of Lactantius for these definitions, see Kelly, *Ideas and Forms,* 47. For Isidore's understanding of theater and tragedy as pantomime, see ibid., 36–50, esp. 49 (for a summary of Isidore's "unfavorable attitude toward tragedy") and 43 (for tragedy as narration accompanied by mimed gestures).

124. *[H]istriones sunt qui muliebri indumento gestus inpudicarum feminarum*

exprimebant; hi autem saltando etiam historias et res gestas demonstrabant. Dicti autem histriones sive quod ab Histria id genus sit adductum, sive quod perplexas historiis fabulas exprimerent, quasi historiones (*Etymologiae* 18.48). *De histrionibus.*

125. *Mimi sunt dicti Graeca appellatione quod rerum humanarum sint imitatores; nam habebant suum auctorem, qui antequam mimum agerent, fabulam pronuntiare[n]t. Nam fabulae ita conponebantur a poetis ut aptissimae essent motui corporis* (ibid., 18.49). *De mimis.*

126. *De scenae* defines the visual aspects of theatrical representation, emphasizing the likeness between theatrical backdrops and common homes as a site for performances of song, dance, and gesture: "The scene, however, was the place in the theater that was arranged in the manner of a house with a raised platform, which was called the orchestra, where comedians and tragedians sang and where actors and mimes danced" [*Scena autem erat locus infra theatrum in modum domus instructa cum pulpito, qui pulpitus orchestra vocabatur; ubi cantabant comici, tragici, atque saltabant histriones et mimi*] (ibid., 18.43).

127. Ibid., 10.119–20, 19.34. For a summary of Isidore's description of these technical details of the performances, see Kelly, *Ideas and Forms,* 48.

128. Brehaut (*Encyclopedist,* 75) observes (and the idea is not contested): "[T]oward pagan philosophy and poetry, then, Isidore's attitude is hostile, and it is very probable that he never wasted any time on them. But in the field of secular knowledge apart from these subjects, he has, within limits, a use for the inheritance left by pagan Rome."

129. *Etymologiae, De equitibus,* 18.38.

130. Ibid., *De desultoribus,* 18.39.

131. Ibid., *De peditibus,* 18.40.

132. Ibid., *De coloribus equorum,* 18.41.

133. *Unde animadvertere debes, Christiane, quod Circum numina inmunda possideant. Quapropter alienus erit tibi locus quem plurimi Satanae spiritus occupaverunt: totum enim illum diabolus et angeli eius repleverunt* (ibid., 18.41). Like Augustine, Isidore conceived of a natural world populated by demons, angels, and humans.

134. *Ludi Circenses sacrorum causa ac deorum gentilium celebrationibus instituti sunt: unde et qui eos spectant daemonum cultibus inservire videntur. Nam res equestris antea simplex agebatur, et utique communis usus reatus non erat; sed quum ad ludos coactus est naturalis usus, ad daemoniorum cultum translatus est* (ibid., 18.27). *De ludis circensibus.*

135. *Idem vero theatrum, idem et prostibulum, eo quod post ludos exactos meretrices ibi prostrarentur. Idem et lupanar vocatum ab eisdem meretricibus, quae propter vulgati corporis levitatem lupae nuncupabantur: nam lupae meretrices sunt a rapacitate vocatae, quod ad se rapiant miseros et adprehendant. Lupanaria enim a paganis constituta sunt ut pudor mulierum infelicium ibi publicaretur, et ludibrio haberentur tam hi qui facerent quam qui paterentur* (ibid., 18.42).

136. For Isidore's use of Augustine, Lactantius, and Tertullian as sources for the theater as a brothel, see Kelly, *Ideas and Forms,* 49 n. 51; Jones, "Isidore," 10–11.

137. *Spectacula, ut opinor, generaliter nominantur voluptates quae non per semetipsa inquinant, sed per ea quae illic geruntur. Dicta autem spectacula eo quod hominibus publica ibi praebeatur inspectio. Haec et ludicra nuncupata, quod in ludis gerantur aut in cenis* (*Etymologiae* 18.16 *De spectaculis.*).

138. Jones, "Isidore," 18.

139. Ibid., 19.

140. *Simulacra autem a similitudine nuncupata, eo quod manu artificis ex lapide ali-ave materia eorum vultus imitantur in quorum honore finguntur. Ergo simulacra vel pro eo quod sunt similia, vel pro eo quod simulata atque conficta; unde et falsa sunt* (*Etymologiae* 8.11.6, 19–23). For the sources of this passage, see MacFarlane, *Isidore,* 12.

141. See Kelly, *Ideas and Forms,* 40. For the debate over Isidore's references to theater in the imperfect tense and drama in the present, see Marshall, "Theatre," 10; Kelly, *Ideas and Forms,* 47; Jones, "Isidore," 21 n. 17.

142. *Soliloquies* (Gilligan) 2.10 (see Gilligan 401 n. 1). The reference is to Quintus Roscius Gallus, a famous Roman actor.

143. *Soliloquies* (Gilligan) 2.10; cf. 2.16 on the mendacity of performance. Augustine discusses whether to consider male tranvestites false women or false men when they are detected, wicked when they go unnoticed, and in any case true actors. He allows that cross-dressing might be acceptable in certain dire circumstances (e.g., to prevent a wise man's death from freezing) but that determining the edge of the indecency, whether it is willed from necessity or from the desire to deceive, is a serious issue.

144. *Inter 'fallacem' et 'mendacem.' Omnis homo fallax id agit, unde quisque fallatur; non autem omnis vult fallere qui mentitur. Sicut mimi et comoediae, et multa poemata, ubi mendacium delectandi potius studio quam fallendi voluntate scribitur. Nam et omnes fere qui jocantur, mentiuntur* (Isidore *Differentiarum* [Migne *PL* 83.1.210, 31C]). Cf. Jones, "Isidore," 21 n. 21.

145. Augustine *Sermones supposititios* 62 (Migne *PL* 39:1863).

146. *Etymologiae* 10.119–20.

147. See Jones, "Isidore," 15; Kelly, *Ideas and Forms,* 48 n. 45.

148. Marshall suggests face painting: see "Theatre in the Middle Ages: Evidence from Dictionaries and Glosses," *Symposium: A Journal Devoted Foreign Languages and Literatures"* vol. 4, no. 1 (1950): 1–39 esp. 11. That the traditional term *persona* is not used here to describe masks specifically confuses the meaning. Jones ("Isidore," 15) says that Isidore "unquestionably refers to masks," despite the use of *simulacrum* rather than *persona.* Kelly (*Ideas and Forms,* 49 n. 49), who acknowledges that the sermon may not be Augustine's, questions which text is actually the source and points out the minor differences in vocabulary in the two texts.

149. *New Catholic Study Bible,* St. Jerome edition (Nashville: Thomas Nelson Publishers, 1985).

150. *Sed hypocriscorum maculam non habere aut paucorum aut nullorum est. Nam quicumque vult se videri quod non est, hypocrita est. Qui tuba canit faciens eleemosynam, hypocrita est. Qui in synagogis et in platearum angulis orat, ut videatur ab hominibus, hypocrita est. Qui jejunans demolitur faciem, ut ventris inanitatem demonstret in vultu, et hic hypocrita est. Ex quibus omnibus intelligitur hypocritas esse, qui faciunt quodlibet, ut ab hominibus glorificentur* (*Sermones supposititios* 62 [Migne *PL* 39:1863]).

CHAPTER 2

1. There is vast literature on the *Quem quaeritis* trope, its codification with rubrics for performance in the English *Regularis concordia* (965–75), its dissemination, its placement in the Easter liturgies, and the question of its elaboration in *Visitatio sepulchri.* A brief summary, with a caution against reading modern criteria for realism into

such medieval texts, can be found in David Hiley, *Western Plainchant: A Handbook* (Oxford: Clarendon Press, 1993), 252–55. See also Nils Holger Petersen, "Representation in European Devotional Rituals: The Question of the Origin of Medieval Drama in Medieval Liturgy," in *The Origins of Theatre in Ancient Greece and Beyond: From Ritual to Drama*, ed. E. Csapo and M. C. Miller (Cambridge: Cambridge University Press, forthcoming).

2. See William Tydeman et al., eds., *The Medieval European Stage, 500–1500* (Cambridge: Cambridge University Press, 2001), 40–42.

3. See ibid., 19–20.

4. For the transmission of texts, see Giles Brown, "Introduction: The Carolingian Renaissance," in *Carolingian Culture: Emulation and Innovation*, ed. Rosamond McKitterick (Cambridge: Cambridge University Press, 1994), 1–51, esp. 34–44.

5. See Karl Morrison, *I Am You: The Hermeneutics of Empathy in Western Literature, Theology, and Art* (Princeton: Princeton University Press, 1988), 172–73 (following Todorov's semiotics).

6. See ibid., 170.

7. Whether the ritual commemoration of Christ's Passion can be properly understood as dramatic spectacle and can still allow for the sacramental transformation of the mystical body of Christ in the Eucharist is taken up by Hans Urs von Balthasar in part 3, chapter C, section a of *Theo-Drama: Theological Dramatic Theory*, vol. 4, *The Action*, trans. Graham Harrison (San Francisco: Ignatius Press, 1994), esp. 389–94. Von Balthasar (389 n. 2) suggests—in contrast to J. A. Jungmann's assertion that the historical *pascha* of Christ becomes the ongoing, eternal movement of the Church and its people toward God—that the medieval Mass was understood through "top-heavy allegorizing"; the allegorical method construed the Mass as a judicial process, a spiritual battle, and (inappropriately) a kind of theater.

8. For a summary of overlapping performance traditions and pagan survivals, see Marcia L. Colish, *Medieval Foundations of the Western Intellectual Tradition, 400–1400* (New Haven: Yale University Press, 1997), 206–9.

9. John Marenbon, "Carolingian Thought," in *Carolingian Culture: Emulation and Innovation*, ed. Rosamond McKitterick (Cambridge: Cambridge University Press, 1994), 171–92, esp. 172.

10. Colish, *Medieval Foundations*, 68.

11. *De ludo gymnico saltus, cursus, jactus, virtus, atque luctatio* (Rabanus Maurus *De universo* [Migne *PL* 111:548B–C]). Chapters 19–23 of *De universo* describe the games individually.

12. See Jody Enders, *Rhetoric and the Origins of Medieval Drama* (Ithaca: Cornell University Press, 1992), 55 n. 52.

13. *De generibus agonum. Agonum genera fuisse: inmensitas virium, cursui celeritas, sagittandi peritia, standi patientia, ad citharam quoque vel tibias incedendi gestus, de moribus quoque, de forma, de cantandi modulatione, terrestris quoque belli et navalis proelii, perpetiendorumque suppliciorum certamina.* (Isidore *Etymologiarum sive originum* [ed. W. M. Lindsay] 18.26; hereafter, *Etymologiae*).

14. *De agone autem mundano Apostolus sumpsit exemplum ad agonem spiritalem: dicens: "Omnis autem, qui in agone contendit, ab omnibus se abstinet, et illi quidem, ut*

corruptibilem coronam accipiant: nos autem incorruptam . . ." (De universo 20.26 *De generibus agonum* [Migne *PL* 111:549D]).

15. See, for example, 1 Timothy 4:6–10; 2 Timothy 2:5.

16. *A quibus omnibus dixerit, inquiramus, ut possit nobis spiritalis agonis instructio comparatione carnalis acquiri. Illi etenim, qui in hoc agone visibili student legitime decertare, utendi omnibus escis, quas desiderii libido suggesserit, non habent facultatem: sed illis tantummodo, quas eorumdem certaminum statuit disciplina. Et non solum interdictis escis et ebrietate, omnique crapula eos necesse est abstinere: verum etiam cuncta inertia et otio atque desidia, ut quotidianis exercitiis, jugique meditatione virtus eorum possit accrescere: et ita omni sollicitudine ac tristia, negotiisque saecularibus, affectu etiam et opere conjugali efficiuntur alieni: ut praeter exercitium disiplinae nihil aliud noverint, nec ulli mundiali curae penitus implicentur: ab eo tantum, qui certamini praesidet, sperantes quotidiani victus substantiam, et coronae gloriam, condignaque praemia victoriae laude conquirere. Itaque si agonis mundialis intelligimus disciplinam, cujus exemplo beatus apostolus non voluit erudire, docet quanta custodia quid nos conveniat facere: qua puritate oporteat custodire nostri corporis atque animae castitatem, quos necesse est quotidie sacrosanctis agni carnibus vesci. Quod enim illi in corporis puritate cupiunt assequi, nos debemus etiam in cordis conscientia possidere. In qua Dominus arbiter atque agonthea [agonotheta] residens, pugnam cursus atque certaminis nostri jugiter exspectat: ut ea, quae in propatulo horremus admittere, ne intrinsecus quidem concalescere in cauta cogitatione patiamur: et in quibus humana cogitatione confundimur, ne occulta quidem concupiscentia polluamur (De universo* 20.26 [Migne *PL* 111:549D–550A]).

17. For the mnemonic value of the written word, see Mary J. Carruthers, *The Book of Memory: A Study of Memory in Medieval Culture* (Cambridge: Cambridge University Press, 1990), esp. chap. 7, "Memory and the Book."

18. *Proinde nihil esse debet Christiano cum circensi insania, cum impudicitia theatri, cum amphitheatri crudelitate, cum atrocitate arenae, cum luxuria ludi. Deum enim negat, qui talia praesumit, fidei Christianae praevaricator effectus: qui id denuo appetit, quod in lavacro jam pridem renuntiavit, id est, diabolo cum pompis et operibus ejus (De universo* 20.38, *De horoum exsecratione ludorum* [Migne *PL* 111:553D–554A]).

19. *Unde animadvertere debes, Christiane, quod Circum numina inmunda possideant. Quapropter alienus erit tibi locus quem plurimi Satanae spiritus occupaverunt: totum enim illum diabolus et angeli eius repleverunt (Etymologiae* 18.41.5–11).

20. *Equus autem rufus, super quem sedebat ille, qui sumpserat pacem de terra, significat populum sinistrum, ex sessore suo diabolo sanguinolentum, cui semper discordia placet. . . . Diabolus enim et ministri ejus metonymicos mors et infernus dicti sunt: eo quod multis causa mortis et infernorum sunt (De universo* 20.35 [Migne *PL* 111:553B]).

21. *Theatrum est, quo scena includitur, semicirculi figuram habens, in quo stantes omnes inspiciunt. Cujus forma primum rotunda erat sicut amphitheatrum: postea ex medio amphitheatro theatrum factum. Theatrum autem a spectaculo nominatum "apo tes theorias," quod in eo populus stans super atque spectans ludos contemplaretur. Idem vero theatrum, idem et prostibulum, eo quod post ludos exactos meretrices prostarent. Idem et lupanar vocatum ab eisdem meretricibus, quae propter vulgati corporis vilitatem lupae nuncupantur. Nam lupae meretrices sunt a rapacitate vocatae, eo quod ad se rapiant miseros, et apprehendant. Lupanaria enim a paganis constituta sunt, ut pudor mulierum infe-*

licium ibi publicaretur, et ludibrio haberentur tam hi qui facerent, quam qui paterentur (*De universo* 20.36 [Migne *PL* 111:553C–D]). For transmission of the connection between theaters and brothels, see Mary Hatch Marshall, "Theatre in the Middle Ages: Evidence from Dictionaries and Glosses," *Symposium: A Journal Devoted to Modern Foreign Languages and Literatures* 4 (1950): 1–39, esp. 9. See also Henry Ansgar Kelly, *Ideas and Forms of Tragedy from Aristotle to the Middle Ages* (Cambridge: Cambridge University Press, 1993), 49 n. 51, 73.

22. See Marshall, "Theatre," 11; *Etymologiae* 18.42.

23. *Mystice autem theatrum praesentem mundum significare potest: in quo hi, qui luxum hujus saeculi sequuntur, ludibrio habent servos Dei, et eorum poenas spectando laetantur. Unde Apostolus dicit: "Spectaculum sumus facti in hoc mundo angelis et hominibus propter Deum"* (*De universo* 20.36 [Migne *PL* 111:553C–D]).

24. See Marcel Metzger, "The History of the Eucharistic Liturgy in Rome," in *Handbook for Liturgical Studies*, vol. 3, *The Eucharist*, ed. Anscar J. Chupungco (Collegeville, Minn.: Liturgical Press, 1999), 103–32, esp. 103; Anscar J. Chupungco, "History of the Roman Liturgy until the Fifteenth Century," in *Handbook for Liturgical Studies*, vol. 1, *Introduction to the Liturgy*, ed. Anscar J. Chupungco (Collegeville, Minn.: Liturgical Press, 1997), 131–52, esp. 134. Philippe Buc suggests the pervasiveness of graphic rituals in the Frankish territories, which expressed political conflicts, as well as religious beliefs: see *The Dangers of Ritual: Between Early Medieval Texts and Social Scientific Theory* (Princeton: Princeton University Press, 2001), chaps. 1–2, esp. pp. 57–67. Allen Cabaniss, in the introduction to *Liturgy and Literature*, holds that Amalarius of Metz was "almost oblivious" to the battles for land and power, including that between Rome and secular rulers. The liturgist's ritual theories were contested on the very grounds that they proposed disunity and multiple perspectives; in other words, they served imperial ambitions rather than the church. See *Liturgy and Literature: Selected Essays* (University: University of Alabama Press, 1970), 16.

25. See William T. Flynn, *Medieval Music as Medieval Exegesis* (Lanham, Md.: Scarecrow Press, 1999), 117.

26. For Alcuin's Augustinian attitude toward popular performance, see Tydeman et al., *Medieval European Stage*, 28.

27. For the revival of logic in the Alcuin circle and for the application of logic to doctrinal problems, see Marenbon, "Carolingian Thought," 175–77.

28. Allen Cabaniss, *Amalarius of Metz* (Amsterdam: North-Holland, 1954), 14, 31–32.

29. See Cabaniss, *Amalarius*, 42; Rainer Warning, *The Ambivalences of Medieval Religious Drama*, trans. Steven Rendall (Stanford: Stanford University Press, 2001), 32.

30. Flynn (*Medieval Music*, 121) provides an excellent analysis of Amalarius's distinction between the liturgy of the word and the liturgy of the Eucharist. For the relationship between allegory and liturgical practice at this time, see also Josef Jungmann, *The Mass of the Roman Rite*, trans. Francis A. Brunner, vol. 1 (New York: Benziger Brothers, 1951), 89–90.

31. *Si enim gentiles argumentantur ludos aliquos suos allegorice promere, sicut aleatores, qui perhibent tribus tesseris suis tria tempora significari, praesens, praeteritum et futurum, et vias eorum senario numero distinguunt propter sex aetates hominum, quanto magis christianam industriam, orationem sibi a Deo concessam, nullo modo acciderit frus-*

tra aliquid statuere (Amalarius *Epistula Amalarii ad Petrum abbatem nonantulanum* I-B, 5, *Amalarii episcopi opera liturgica omnia* [Hanssens 1:230]). Isidore had also described allegories for ancient dice playing in the *Etymologiae* (18.64).

Moreover certain dice-players seem to themselves to exercise this art physiologically by allegory and invent under a kind of analogy of things. For they say they play with three dice because of the three time periods of the age—present, past, and future—because they don't stand, but run away. But it is argued that even the very paths are separated by six places each because of the ages of men, with three lines each because of the times. Hence also the table, they say, is separated by three lines.

[Quidam autem aleatores sibi videntur physiologice per allegoriam hanc artem exercere, et sub quadam rerum similitudine fingere. Nam tribus tesseris ludere perhibent propter tria saeculi tempora: praesentia, praeterita, et futura; quia non stant, sed decurrunt. Sed et ipsas vias senariis locis distinctas propter aetates hominum ternariis lineis propter tempora argumentantur. Inde et tabulam ternis discriptam dicunt lineis.]

32. Marvin Carlson's survey of dramatic theory and criticism, for example, suggests that Amalarius's allegories emphasized "dramatic elements in the Mass," to which Honorius Augustodunensis applied a specific reference to classical theater in the twelfth century (*Theories of the Theatre: A Historical and Critical Survey, from the Greeks to the Present*, expanded ed. [Ithaca: Cornell University Press, 1993], 36). The arrangement of primary documents dealing with theater from late antiquity to the seventeenth century in *The Medieval European Stage* (Tydeman et al.) classifies Amalarius with Honorius Augustodunensis under the general heading "Symbolic Drama." Studies of medieval theater since the mid-1960s have followed O. B. Hardison, Jr. (*Christian Rite and Christian Drama in the Middle Ages: Essays on the Origin and Early History of Modern Drama* [Baltimore: Johns Hopkins University Press, 1965], 37–79) and constructed a solid foundation for linking ritual with drama and drama's presentation as theater. Tydeman agrees with Hardison that the medieval Mass was "thought of in dramatic terms" and represented "eternal truths by means analogous to those employed in drama" (*The Theatre in the Middle Ages: Western European Stage Conditions, c. 800–1576* [Cambridge: Cambridge University Press, 1978], 187). Glynn Wickham, also following Hardison, reiterates the idea that allegorical interpretations of the Mass opened the way for perceiving "the Church as a theatre for the re-enactment of Christ's triumph over sin and death" (*The Medieval Theatre* [New York: St. Martin's Press, 1974], 12, 33). David M. Bevington reproduces the chapter *De tragoediis* from Honorius's *Gemma animae* as an example of medieval theatricality in *Medieval Drama* (Boston: Houghton Mifflin, 1975), 9. John Wesley Harris maintains the direct link between ritual and theater—with an emphasis on the performance conditions in which the rituals were done—in his chapter "From Ritual to Drama" in *Medieval Theatre in Context: An Introduction* (London: Routledge, 1992), 23–35. Such recent studies as Michal Kobialka's *This Is My Body: Representational Practices in the Early Middle Ages* (Ann Arbor: University of Michigan Press, 1999) have questioned this connection by showing how texts thought to document the history of theater function in other discursive formations and representational practices.

33. Hans Belting has noted that the use of imagery in Christian ceremony was limited not only by carryover from pagan worship but also by Mosaic prohibitions, and the Scriptures (Romans 1:23) accuse the pagans of putting God's incorruptibility in corruptible form. See *Likeness and Presence: A History of the Image before the Era of Art,* trans. Edmund Jephcott (Chicago: University of Chicago Press, 1994), 36–37.

34. *6. Quae aguntur, in caelebratione missae, in sacramento dominicae passionis aguntur, ut ipse praecepit dicens: "Haec quotiescumque feceritis, in mei memoriam facietis." Idcirco presbyter immolans panem et vinum et aquam in sacramento est Christi, panis, vinum et aqua in sacramento carnis Christi et eius sanguinis. 7. Sacramenta debent habere similitudinem aliquam earum rerum quarum sacramenta sunt. Quapropter similis sit sacerdos Christo, sicut panis et liquor similia sunt corpori Christi. Sic est immolatio sacerdotis in altari quodammodo ut Christi immolatio in cruce. Ut similis sit homo Christi resurrectioni, aliquo modo manducat carnem et bibit sanguinem eius* (Amalarius *Liber officialis,* Prooemium [Hanssens 2:14]).

35. Warning, *Ambivalences,* 36.

36. For the position of Hardison's *Christian Rite* in theater scholarship to 1984 and on its literary bias, see Ronald W. Vince, *Ancient and Medieval Theatre: A Historiographical Handbook* (Westport, Conn.: Greenwood Press, 1984), 24–30. For a recent textbook example of the pervasiveness of Hardison's thesis in theater and performance studies (without acknowledgment of the literary bias), see Richard Schechner, *Performance Studies: An Introduction* (London: Routledge, 2002), 25–26.

37. Hardison, *Christian Rite,* 39.

38. Ibid., 44.

39. See, for example, Hardison's explanation of Amalarius's understanding of the *Oremus* and of his placement of the *Secreta* in the *Liber officialis* in the context of his discussion of choreographic symbolism, of the increasing isolation of the celebrant as a central dramatic figure, and of role-playing and the "dramatic quality of the Offertory procession" in the "unfolding drama" of the Mass (Hardison, *Christian Rite,* 59–61). For a helpful discussion of ritual commemoration as cultural memory, see Paul Connerton, *How Societies Remember* (Cambridge: Cambridge University Press, 1989), 41–71.

40. Hardison, *Christian Rite,* 48.

41. Ibid., 64.

42. Ibid., 54–55.

43. Postmodern attitudes toward drama, theater, corporeality, and texts demand reconsideration of an easy shift from ceremonial representation to mimetic reenactment with a narrative structure, though in the case of the allegorical tradition, there has been little direct challenge to the interplay between ceremony and mimesis. The deconstruction of modern drama into postmodern performance and representational practices is evident in the following studies: Elinor Fuchs, *The Death of Character: Perspectives on Theater after Modernism* (Bloomington: Indiana University Press, 1996); Marvin Carlson, ed., *Theatre Semiotics: Signs of Life* (Bloomington: Indiana University Press, 1990); Michal Kobialka, ed., *Of Borders and Thresholds: Theatre History, Practice, and Theory* (Minneapolis: University of Minnesota Press, 1999); Elin Diamond, *Unmaking Mimesis: Essays on Feminism and Theater* (London: Routledge, 1997).

44. For the history of Amalarius's role in the Diocese of Lyons following Louis's

return to the imperial court in 834 and on the question of Amalarius's writings brought before the Council of Kierzy four years later, see Cabaniss, *Amalarius,* 79–93. Warning (*Ambivalences,* 31–39) summarizes the controversy, its theological foundations, and ecclesiastical resistance to allegorization.

45. For the importance of unified ritual to political expression, see, in addition to Buc's *Dangers of Ritual,* Janet L. Nelson's, *The Frankish World, 750–900* (London: Hambledon Press, 1996), 45–46.

46. Warning, *Ambivalences,* 34. See also Cabaniss, *Amalarius,* 87–88. Florus's critique is the *Opuscula adversus Amalarium* 1 (Migne *PL* 119:71–80). On the fraction, see Hardison, *Christian Rite,* 74–76.

47. See Tydeman, *Theatre in the Middle Ages,* 187.

48. *Liber officialis, Prooemium,* 7 (Hanssens 2:14).

49. See *Opuscula adversus Amalarium* 2 (Migne *PL* 119:80C–D, 81B). Florus accuses Amalarius of inventing allegories out of his own imagination and against the proper use of allegory as established by the church fathers. For Amalarius's defense of allegory as an ancient method and for his fidelity to Augustine, see Christine Schnusenberg, *Das Verhältnis von Kirche und Theater: Dargestellt au ausgewählten Schriften der Kirchenväter und liturgischen Texten bis auf Amalarius von Metz* (Bern: Peter Lang, 1981), 156–60.

50. In a letter to another monk (ca. 825), Paschasius Radbertus makes the common complaint that people are less inclined to pursue the mysteries of God's sacraments than they are to attend to poetic tragedies and to praise the performances of mimes. See Tydeman et al., *Medieval European Stage,* 29.

51. See Miri Rubin, "The Eucharist and the Construction of Medieval Identities," in *Culture and History, 1350–1600: Essays on English Communities, Identities, and Writing,* ed. David Aers (Detroit: Wayne State University Press, 1992), 45.

52. The debate over Christ's real or symbolic presence in the Eucharist, carried on in the ninth century by Ratramnus and Paschasius Radbertus of Corbie, would not be resolved doctrinally until 1215 at the Fourth Lateran Council. Michal Kobialka makes a strong case that Honorius Augustodunensis's Paschasian position on the Eucharist in the wake of the Berengarius-Lanfranc controversy in the eleventh century affected allegorical interepretation of the Mass (see chap. 3). For a detailed discussion of the debate at Corbie, its documents, and its repercussions, see Celia Chazelle, *The Crucified God in the Carolingian Era: Theology and Art of Christ's Passion* (Cambridge: Cambridge University Press, 2001), 210–15. For a summary of the debate and its repercussions in the eleventh century, see Colish, *Medieval Foundations,* 73–74, 166–67. See also R. W. Southern, "Lanfranc of Bec and Berengar of Tours," in *Studies in Medieval History Presented to Frederick Maurice Powicke,* ed. R. W. Hunt, W. A. Pantin, and R. W. Southern (Oxford: Clarendon Press, 1948), 27–48. For a summary of explanations for the emergence of the elevation of the Host in the liturgy of the Mass, see Miri Rubin, *Corpus Christi: The Eucharist in Late Medieval Culture* (Cambridge, Cambridge University Press, 1991), 55.

53. Agobard of Lyons, *Liber de correctione antiphonarii* (Migne *PL* 104:334C). See also Cabaniss, *Amalarius,* 86; Hardison, *Christian Rite,* 78. Cf. Wolfgang Steck, *Der liturgiker Amalarius: Eine Quellenkritische Untersuchung zu Leben und Werk eines The-*

ologen der Karolingerzeit, Münchener theologische studien, Historische Abteilung, 1st ser., no. 35 (Ottilien: EOS Verlag Erzabtei, 2000), 161 n. 761. For the reliance on patristic authority in Carolingian theology, see Marenbon, "Carolingian Thought," 180–81.

54. Rainer Warning analyzes the biases in Hardison's approach to the emergence of liturgical drama with respect to ecclesiastical repression and the "common end" of liturgical and vernacular religious drama in the fifteenth century, in "On the Alterity of Medieval Religious Drama," *New Literary History* 10 (1979): 265–70. He also lays out the widely held premise that true mimetic drama was possible only outside the institutional and ceremonial restrictions of the church (269). For the suggestion that there was a common terminus of Catholic drama under Protestant reforms, see Harold C. Gardiner, *Mysteries' End: An Investigation of the Last Days of the Medieval Religious Stage* (New Haven: Yale University Press, 1946; reprint, [Hamden, CT]: Archon Books, 1967). The idea that religious reformation put an end to Catholic drama has been deconstructed by Sarah Beckwith in *Signifying God: Social Relation and Symbolic Act in the York Corpus Christi Plays* (Chicago: University of Chicago Press, 2001).

55. For the imperial Carolingian effort to unify the communities under Carolingian rule with common laws and customs, see Brown, "Introduction," 26–28. Conflicts between the imperial power of Louis the Pious, the territorial claims of his three sons, and the struggle to decentralize power from the baronial class is summarized in Cabaniss, *Amalarius,* 5–8. As Cabaniss points out, even the conciliatory efforts of Gregory IV failed. Conflicts cut across factions—clergy against clergy, clergy against nobility, imperial forces against lay and ecclesiastical barons, clergy against laity, and son against father. For the last years of Louis's reign, including the relative peace from 838 to 840 when the emperor died, and for a persuasive argument for the emperor's centralized influence at the end of this tumultuous period, see Nelson, *Frankish World,* 36–42.

56. See Cabaniss, *Amalarius,* 5. For literature on the "Germanic theology" theory, see Warning, *Ambivalences,* 30.

57. For Amalarius's use of pagan references (e.g., Phoebus and Phoebe for the sun and moon) and of pagan gods (e.g., Mars), see Warning, *Ambivalences,* 35–36. For a summary of the charges at the Council of Kierzy, including the use of classical referents, see Cabaniss, *Amalarius,* 89.

58. *Juxta ordinem orationum et expositionem memoratorum patrum praecatum est in prima oratione missae pro absolutione peccatorum; super mensam vero postulantur bona nobis instar orationis et ymni evangelici, quem Christus cecinit secundum Johannem, commendando discipulos suos Patri ante passionem suam. In ista novissima benedicitur populus. Quid vult ista benedictio? Pugnare vult, utique contra diabolum et eius insidias* (*Liber officialis, Prooemium,* 17 [Hanssens 2:17]).

59. See Hardison, *Christian Rite,* 47–48. Isidore of Seville's definition of the Eucharist, for example, explained the difference between the bread and wine Christ shared with his disciples, the bread and wine taken when the Eucharist was celebrated, and the actual body and blood of Christ, which was sacrificed on the cross. These were distinct registers of Christian knowledge and experience, each with its own temporal and physical properties, which were reconciled in the mystery of the ceremony. Allegory blurred distinctions between history, spiritual meaning, and ceremonial representation, which were otherwise assumed. The difference in approaches is evident in the following

passage from Isidore, in comparison with the passage from the *Prooemium* just quoted (n. 59), in which the physical enactment of the Mass conflates the three registers into an experience in real time.

"Panis" enim "quem frangimus" corpus Christi est qui dixit: "Ego sum panis vivus qui de caelo discendi," vinum autem sanguis eius est, et hoc est quod scriptum est: "Ego sum vitis." Sed panis quia corpus confirmat ideo corpus Christi nuncupatur; vinum autem, quia sanguinem operatur in carne, ideo ad sanguinem Christi refertur. Haec autem dum sunt visibilia, sanctificata tamen per spiritum sanctum in sacramentum divini corporis transeunt. (Isidore De sacrificio 1:18 [Sancti Isidori episcopi hispalensis: De ecclesiasticis officiis, ed. Christopher M. Lawson (Turnhout: Brepols, 1989), CCSL *113:20]).*

["Bread," indeed, "which we break" is the body of Christ, who says, "I am the bread of life that came down from the sky": the wine is also his blood, and this is what the Scripture means by "I am life." So for that reason the bread confirms that the body would be called Christ's body; the wine also for that reason is said to be the blood of Christ that labors in the flesh. These things are visible, sanctified also by the Holy Spirit in the sacrament of the translation of the divine body.]

60. Warning, *Ambivalences*, 36.

61. *Christus resurrexit a mortuis et iam non moritur. Per corpus Christi quod manducat homo digne, anima, resurrectione accepta per baptismum sive per penitentiam, vivit, usque dum adimpleatur plena resurrectio in octava die (Liber officialis, Prooemium, 7* [Hanssens 2:14–15]).

62. *... quod ad solum sacerdotem pertinet, id est immolatio panis et vini, secreto agitur. Quantum enim victima praestabat in veteri testamento ad Domini sacrificium, postquam ducta erat ad hostium tabernaculi, tantum praestat sacrificium in prima positione altaris; non potest iam mutari neque in melius neque in deterius (Liber officialis, De secreta,* 20.2 [Hanssens 2:323]).

63. 2. *Praesens officium illud tempus nobis ad memoriam reducit, quando Christus in caena ascendit in cenaculum magnum stratum, et ibi locutus est multa cum discipulis, et ymnum retulit Deo Patri, quem Johannes commemorat, usque dum exiret in montem Oliveti. Ibi gratias egit Deo, ibi ymnum cantavit, in quo precatus est Patrem, ut servaret discipulos suos a malo, dicendo: "Non rogo ut tollas eos de mundo, sed ut serves eos a malo"; et ut sancti permaneant, subiungit: "Sanctifica eos in veritate"; et iterum: "Et pro eis sanctifico meipsum, ut sint et ipsi sanctificati in veritate;" et, ut in caelum transeant, dicit in sequentibus: "Pater, quos dedisti mihi, volo ut ubi ego sum, et illi sint mecum, ut videant claritatem meam, quam dedisti mihi". 3. Juxta nunc sensum, altare est mensa Domini, in qua convivabatur cum discipulis; corporale, linteum quo erat ipse praecinctus; sudarium labor de Juda proditore (Liber officialis, De ymno ante Passionem Domini sive praeparatione,* 21.2–3 [Hanssens 2:324]).

64. See Cabaniss, *Amalarius,* 55.

65. *Liber officialis* 3.26.10 (Hanssens 2:346 ff.). Trans. Cabaniss, *Amalarius,* 62–64. The biblical account is at 1 Timothy 3:8–13.

66. Cabaniss, *Amalarius,* 64–65.

67. For the *artes memorativae* in the ninth century, see Carruthers, *Book of Memory*, 144–45.

68. *Asserit itaque doctor praefatus, inter alia, corpus Christi triforme et tripartitum esse, imo tria esse Christi corpora. Corpus Christi quod in sacramento a fidelibus sumitur, vel in coelum invisibiliter recipi, vel in corporibus sumentium manere usque in diem sepulturae, vel ex incisione venarum cum sanguine fluere, vel in secessum labi opinatur. Diaconos, altari cum assistunt inclines, asserit signifcare apostolos in passione Domini metuentes atque latitantes; subdiaconos, mulieres cruci intrepide assistentes; presbyterum, Joseph ab Arimathia; archidiaconum, Nicodemum; calicem, sepulcrum; oblationem Dominici corporis dicit crucifixionem; lignum ipsum designare dicit doctores; lignum unde pendet, crucem; funem quo attrahitur, fidem; tintinnabulum quo resonat, linguam; manum trahentis cum levatur, vitam contemplativam; cum deponitur, activam. Exorcismos catechumenorum, ad spiritalem emundationis affectum simpliciter depromendos, ad quinque sensus corporeos nimia carnalitate convertit* (*Opuscula adversus Amalarium* 2.5 (Migne *PL* 119:81B). Elsewhere, Florus suggests that Amalarius's allegories gave the Scriptures an inappropriately visual, sensual, and tangible dimension.

> *Docet praeceptor ipse Amalarius egregius, ita corpus Christi esse triforme et tripartitum, ut tria Christi corpora: primum quod ipse suscepit, secundum in nobis, qui super terram ambulamus; tertium in illis qui sepulti jacent. Asserit in mysterio sacrificii hac de causa tres debere fieri partes: unam calicis pro Christo, alteram in patena pro vivis, tertiam in altari pro mortuis. Dicit panem illum esse carnem Christi, sanguinem animam, ut sit totus Christus. Haesitandum dicit, utrum corpus Christi de altari sumptum, in corpore nostro maneat usque in diem sepulturae, an recipiatur invisibiliter in coelum, an quando venam incidimus, cum sanguine profluat, an cum caeteris quae in os intrant, in secessum labatur. . . . Calicem Domini vocat sepulcrum, presbyterum Joseph ab Arimathia, archidiaconum Nicodemum tanquam sepultores Christi; diaconos retro acclines apostolos, se in passione Domini velut contrahentes et occultare volentes; subdiaconos ad faciem erectos, mulieres libere astantes. Aliam partem mysticae orationis, qua corpus Domini consecratur, Christo tribuit oranti in monte Oliveti; aliam in cruce pendenti, et post nescio quas fatuas divisiones, aliam morienti.* (*Opuscula adversus Amalarium* 1.4 [Migne *PL* 119:74C–D]).

For a clear, detailed analysis of the Eucharistic debate in this period, with attention to the problems of Christ's "triform" body and the ritual repetition of an event conceived theologically as unique in human history, see Chazelle, *Crucified God*, chap. 6, pp. 209–38.

69. For the issue of Christ's real or symbolic presence initiated by Pascasius Radbertus of Corbie's *De corpore et sanguine Domini* and for the status of the Eucharistic elements in the celebration of the Mass in the ninth century, see Rubin, "Eucharist," esp. 44.

70. For a catalog of allegorical writings by Amalarius and others, see Hanssens 1:83–91.

71. . . . *ut Amalarium de fidei ratione consulerent, qui et verbis, et libris suis mendaciis, et erroribus, et phantasticis atque haereticis disputationibus plenis omnes pene apud Franciam ecclesias, et nonnullas etiam aliarum regionum quantum in se fuit infecit, atque*

corrupit: ut non tam ipse de fide interrogari, quam omnia scripta ejus saltem post mortem ipsius debuerint igne consumi, ne simpliciores quique, qui eos multum diligere, et legendo frequentare dicuntur.... (Remigius [attributed] *De tribus epistolis liber 40, De Amalario; de scriptis Joannis Scoti* [Migne *PL* 121:1054C–D]). See Hardison, *Christian Rite,* 38; Cabaniss, *Amalarius,* 93.

72. The relationship between the Eucharist and the body of Christ has been a central concern in late twentieth-century re-thinkings of medieval representational practices and performance along the axis of the human body. Miri Rubin, Sarah Beckwith, Caroline Walker Bynum, and Michal Kobialka, as well as numerous other scholars, have addressed the "medieval body" with concern for the complex and uniquely Christian relationship between the historical and spiritual body of Christ and its representation in the Eucharist. See Rubin, *Corpus Christi;* Sarah Beckwith, *Christ's Body: Identity, Culture and Society in Late Medieval Writings* (London: Routledge, 1993); Caroline Walker Bynum, *The Resurrection of the Body in Western Christianity, 200–1336* (New York: Columbia University Press, 1995); Kobialka, *This Is My Body.* Current discussions of mimesis and the Eucharist have also taken up postmodern literary theories and considered the signifying potential of the contemporary Eucharist. See, for example, John D. Caputo and Michael J. Scanlon, *God, the Gift, and Postmodernism* (Bloomington: Indiana University Press, 1999); John Milbank, *The Word Made Strange: Theology, Language, Culture* (Cambridge: Blackwell Publishers, 1997); Catherine Pickstock, *After Writing: On the Liturgical Consummation of Philosophy* (Oxford: Blackwell Publishers, 1997); Kevin Hart, *The Trespass of the Sign: Deconstruction, Theology, and Philosophy,* 2d ed. (New York: Fordham University Press, 2000).

73. A. Hardison, *Christian Rite,* 43.

74. *annon videmus quibus et quam sordidis animalibus sive locis fusus pateat sanguis humanus? absint ab animo fideli de mysterio salutari atque coelesti tam ineptae et sordidae cogitationes! Prorsus panis ille sacrosanctae oblationis corpus est Christi, non materie vel specie visibili, sed virtute et potentia spirituali. Neque enim in agro nobis corpus Christi gignitur, aut in vinea sanguis ejus exoritur, vel torculari exprimitur. Simplex e frugibus panis conficitur, simplex e botris vinum liquatur, accedit ad haec offerentis Ecclesiae fides, accedit mysticae precis consecratio, accedit divinae virtutis infusio; sicque, miro et ineffabili modo, quod est naturaliter ex germine terreno panis et vinum, efficitur spiritualiter corpus Christi, id est vitae et salutis nostrae mysterium, in quo aliud oculis corporis, aliud fidei videmus obtentu; nec id tantum quod ore percipimus, sed quod mente credimus, libamus (Opuscula adversus Amalarium* 1.9 [Migne *PL* 119:77C–D]).

75. *Christus enim Dei virtus, et Dei sapientia in eo sumitur; quae sapientia, ut Scriptura testatur, candorem lucis aeternae, et emanatio quaedam claritatis Dei sinceris, et ideo nihil inquinatum in illam incurrit, attingit autem ubique suam munditiam. Corpus igitur Christi, ut praedictum est, non est in specie visibili, sed in virtute spirituali, nec inquinari potest faece corporea, quod et animarum et corporum vitia mundare consuevit (Opuscula adversus Amalarium* 1.9 [Migne *PL* 119:78B]).

76. *Haec igitur in sacris rite improbata jure videntur esse punita, utpote quibus tantum mysterium impie violatur (Opuscula adversus Amalarium* 1.10 [Migne *PL* 119:78D]).

77. *Praecessit enim in praefata nuper Ecclesia per praelatum ejus Amalarium error insanus et vanus, fidei et veritatis inimicus, religioni et saluti contrarius, quem primum quidem, aggregata presbyterorum synodo, circumsedentibus omnibus, et velut praeceptorem*

audientibus, viva voce conatus est serere, imo tota intentione et studio per totum triduum proponendo, exponendo, exigendo, omnibus inculcavit et tradidit, quasi Novi Testamenti minister tabulis cordis carnalibus cuncta quae asserebat, indelebiliter vellet imprimere. Deinde etiam magnum quemdam codicem quatuor voluminibus diffusum, a se compositum atque digestum, legendum transcribendumque tradidit, asserens eum Officialem nuncupari, tanquam de sacris officiis prudentissime et sufficientissime disputantem, qui tantis vesaniis et erroribus confertus est, ut quibuslibet etiam imperitis palam ridendus conspuendusque videatur (*Opuscula adversus Amalarium* 1.2 [Migne *PL* 119:73C–D]).

78. See Peter Jeffery, *Re-envisioning Past Musical Cultures: Ethnomusicology in the Study of Gregorian Chant* (Chicago: University of Chicago Press, 1992), 66–67.

79. See Cabaniss, *Amalarius*, 86.

80. See ibid., 85. For a recent argument that Agobard's goal in the *Liber de correctione antiphonarii* was to remove from the Antiphonal all texts not of biblical origin, not to attack Amalarius specifically (Agobard's work does not mention Amalarius by name but has been interpreted as a criticism of the latter's *Liber de ordine antiphonarii*), and for questions of the authorship of *De divina psalmodia* and *Contra libros quattour Amalarii abbatis*, see Steck, *Der liturgiker Amalarius*, 161 n. 761. For the comparison of texts, see Agobard of Lyons, *Agobardi Lugdunensis Opera Omnia*, ed. L. van Acker (Turnhout: Brepols, 1981), *CCCM* 52:335–51, 353–67; Migne *PL* 104:325C–330A.

81. Agobard *De correctione antiphonarii* (Migne *PL* 104:329–340, esp. 334C). See Cabaniss, *Amalarius*, 85.

82. *Beatus Hieronymus cum exponeret praeceptum Apostoli, ubi ait:* "*Implemini Spiritu loquentes vobismetipsis in psalmis et hymnis et canticis spiritalibus, cantantes et psallentes in cordibus vestris Domino,*" *non tacuit quod in cantoribus Ecclesiae reprehendendum videbat. Canere igitur, ait, et psallere et laudare Dominum magis animo quam voce debemus. Hoc est quippe quod dicitur:* "*Cantantes et psallentes in cordibus vestris Domino.*" *Audiant haec adolescentuli, audiant hi quibus psallendi in Ecclesia officium est, Deo non voce, sed corde cantandum; nec in tragoedorum modum guttur et fauces dulci medicamine colliniendae sunt, ut in Ecclesia theatrales moduli audiantur et cantica; sed in timore, in opere, in scientia Scripturarum. Quamvis sit aliquis, ut solent illi appellare,* "*cacophonos,*" *si bona opera habuerit, dulcis apud Deum cantor est. Sic cantet servus Christi, ut non vox canentis, sed verba placeant quae leguntur; ut spiritus malus qui erat in Saule, ejiciatur ab his qui ab eo similiter possidentur, et non introducatur in eos qui de domo Dei scenam fecere populorum. In quibus verbis magnopere pensandum est, quod eos qui in morem psallentis David cum timore et gravitate spiritali canunt, malignum spiritum etiam ab auditoribus suis excludere posse confirmat; eos vero qui theatralibus sonis et scenicis modulationibus, et quamvis in divinis verbis, vocis dulcedine intemperantius delectantur, eum non solum ab aliis non excludere, sed, quod est terribile, in seipsos introducere testatur* (*De correctione antiphonarii* 12 [Migne *PL* 104:334B–C]; see also *Collectio canonum libri V, CCCM* 6:192).

83. For a summary of the variance in technical details in early medieval descriptions of ancient theaters, see Marshall, "Theatre," 1–39.

84. See Kelly, *Ideas and Forms*, 50–51.

85. *Apud enim antiquos mos fuit histrionum, ut in theatris hominibus quibuscumque vellent nuda facie illuderent, sed hoc cum displicuisset, adhibitae sunt larvae, in quibus et maior sonus propter concavitatem ederetur et nulli aperte illuderetur. Hae ergo larvae per-*

sonae dictae sunt, eo quod histriones in his singulorum hominum substantias repraesenta-
bant. Unde et personae quasi per se sonantes sunt dictae. Et sciendum, quia quorum sub-
stantias repraesentabant, eorum dictis et factis fabulis et gesticulatione corporis illudebant.
Ab his itaque personis, id est larvis, translatum est, ut omnium hominum substantiae indi-
viduae personae vocarentur (Edward Kennard Rand, ed., "Der Kommentar des Johannes
Scottus zu den Opuscula Sacra des Boethius," in *Quellen und Untersuchungen*
zur lateinischen Philologie des Mittelalters, 3.22–24, ed. Ludwig Traube [Munich:
C. H. Beck'sche, Verlagbuchhandlung, 1906], 63). See Kelly, *Ideas and Forms,* 50 n. 57; for
the attribution to Remigius and for a portion of the Latin text, see ibid., 51 n. 58. Mary
Hatch Marshall traces the idea and use of "persona" from Boethius's "De duabus naturis
et una persona Jesu Christi, contra Eutychen et Nestorium" to Thomas Aquinas. See Mary
Hatch Marshall, "Boethius' Definition of 'Persona' and the Medaeval Understanding of
Roman Theater" (*Speculum: A Journal of Medieval Studies* 25, no. 4 [1950]: 471–82.

86. Kelly, *Ideas and Forms,* 51.

87. Remigius described scenes as theatrical poetry performed under a "shade" *(in*
scenis id est in theatris) (Commentum in Martianum Capellam 2.51.19 [Lutz 2:163]).

88. *. . . scenicas meretriculas vocat ipsas Musas quasi deceptrices, quia scena, ut*
quidam dicunt, est unguentum quo perungebantur meretrices ut suis amatoribus gratum
praestarent odorem sicque eos ad suam voluptatem inflectere possent (Remigius of Auxerre, *Saeculi noni auctoris in Boetii Consolationem Philosophiae commentarius,* ed.
Edmund Taite Silk, Papers and Monographs of the American Academy in Rome, vol. 9
[[Rome]: American Academy in Rome, 1935], 316). For Isidore's use of Augustine, Lactantius, and Tertullian as sources for the theater as a brothel, see Kelly, *Ideas and Forms,*
49 n. 51; Joseph R. Jones, "Isidore and the Theatre," *Drama in the Middle Ages: Compar-*
ative and Critical Essays, ed. Clifford Davidson and John H. Stroupe, AMS Studies in the
Middle Ages, no. 18 (New York: AMS Press, 1991), 10–11.

89. See Marenbon, *Early Medieval Philosophy (480–1150): An Introduction* (London: Routledge & Kegan Paul, 1983), 78; Kelly, *Ideas and Forms,* 50.

90. See Kelly, *Ideas and Forms,* 53. Marshall pointed out in 1950 that by the eighth
century, a diversion from the historical effort of Isidore's *Etymologiae* is evident in the
Liber glossarum and in numerous Anglo-Saxon and Old High German glossaries. She
points out that the glossaries and dictionaries of the seventh, eighth, and ninth centuries
treated theater and theatrical terms as "ideas without reality" or "folk-superstition."
Her brief but thorough survey of more marginal manuscript glosses suggests that theater referred to indigenous folk traditions as well as to the Greco-Roman heritage. In
either case, theater was identified with non-Christian practices, based on its deceptive-
ness and its appearance in non-Christian cultures (which made theater not only deceptive but grounded in untrue beliefs). In summary, regarding Anglo-Saxon compilers of
the eighth century and extended to Germanic compilers as well, a dominant meaning of
scena had nothing to do with the theater as such but, rather, with masking and folk
belief in evil spirits, apparently taking *scena* in the sense of "appearance," "false appearance," or "disguise." See Marshall, "Theatre," 13.

91. *SCENICAS theatrales. HAS SCENICAS MERETRICULAS appellat Musas quia*
earum carmina in scenis recitabantur. Est autem scena locus ubi exercebantur ludi et
carmina recitabantur vel scenicas meretriculas vocat ipsas Musas quasi deceptrices, quia
scena, ut quidam dicunt, est unguentum quo perungebantur meretrices ut suis amatoribus

gratum praestarent odorem sicque eos ad suam voluptatem inflectere possent. Ita ergo carmina poetarum se legentes ad sui amorem pertrahunt et quodam modo sibi intendere faciunt. (*Consolationem commentarius* [Silk, 316]).
Derivations of Remigius's terms can be found in his discussion on meter.

> The praise of Philosophy concerning meters and songs. "Buskin-wearing songs," that is tragic, and high-sounding. "Bring forth," that is, sing, "On Stage," that is, in theatres. "Skia" is Greek for "shade," hence the stage is an "arbor" *(umbraculum)* where poets used to recite. "And accustomed to wear the comic sock." The "sock" is a kind of shoe that the comic poets used. The "buskin" is a tragic shoe or hunting shoe suited to either foot. "And accustomed to echo the songs which we bore," that is, which we, the Muses, carried. "Your care," that is, through your care or for your care. "Favoring" us, that is, applauding, "which rhythmic song," that is, with sweet song.

> *Laus Philologiae de metris et carminibus. COTURNATOS CANTUS id est tragicos et altisonos, DEPROMERE id est canere, IN SCENIS id est in theatris. Scea Grece umbra, hinc scena umbraculum ubi poetae recitabant. ET SUETA FERRE SOC-CUM COMICUM Soccus genus est calciamenti quo comici poetae utebantur. Coturnus calciamentum tragicum vel venatorium utrique pedi aptum. ET SUETA REBOARE CARMINA QUAE TULIMUS id est portavimus nos Musae, TUA CURA id est per tuam curam, vel pro tua cura, FAVENTE id est applaudente, nobis RITHMICO MELO id est dulci carmine.* (*Commentum in Martianum Capellam* 2.51.19 [Lutz 2:163])

92. *Haec est in libro consequentia: AN TU IN HANC VITAE SCAENAM. Ideo pro amissis non debes dolere, quia non SUBITUS sed praemeditatus nec HOSPES, id est nouus, sed consuetus VENISTI IN HANC SCAENAM, id est in hoc umbraculum vitae. Scaena per varietatem sui mundum significat. Erat enim versilis et ductilis, quae ideo vertebatur, ut, sicut diversae tragoediae in ea recitabantur, ita diversae figurae oculis residentium anteponerentur et ita varietate "figurum" sicut diversitate tragoediarum delectarentur. Quae etiam constabat duplicibus tabulis. Ubi vero ducta fuisset in circuitu subducebantur priores tabulae ut figuris quoque interioris ibi residentes delectarentur; vel ideo agebatur, ut diversis personis a comicis ibi repraesentatis ipsae figurae concurrerent. ULLAMNE HUMANIS: Probat a maiori quod non sit mirum si humanis rebus non sit vera firmitas, quia nec etiam ipse homo perdurat diu sed cito dissoluitur. Probat item quod Fortuna mutatur, quia, licet non discedat in vita hominis, discedet tamen cum homo ipse morietur* (*Consolationem commentarius* [Silk], 76–77).

93. *Commentum in Martianum Capellam* 2.51.19 (Lutz 2:163).

94. See Kelly, *Ideas and Forms*, 52.

95. *Opus naturae est duplex: vel quando aliquid surgit ex iactis seminibus, sicut homo ex homine et arbores ex arboribus, vel per se surgit, sicut quaedam arbores per se surgunt absque iacto semine. Opus vero artificis imitantis naturam est sicut statua alicuius. Sensilis igitur mundus est opus Dei factus ex illa materia quae ὕλη appellabatur, id est ex confusione elementorum, quae olim chaos dicebatur, et ex forma idea, scilicet quae erat in mente divina, id est ex figura proveniente ab imagine et conceptione mentis divinae. Ecce habes cuius opus sit iste mundus et unde sit factus et qualiter* (*Consolationem commentarius* [Silk], 157).

CHAPTER 3

1. See William Tydeman et al., eds., *The Medieval European Stage, 500–1500* (Cambridge: Cambridge University Press, 2001), 45. Abelard himself drew on the demonic theater of *The City of God* to inveigh against debauched performances in Christian festivals, which he compared to ancient theater: "people invite jesters, dancers, singers, and magicians to the table instead of dedicating themselves to praising God; paying performers at festivals is akin to sacrificing to demons; it is the work of the devil to bring shameful scenes into churches. People have been led into evil, temples are dedicated to devils, and under the guise of worship and prayer, people celebrate vigils to Venus" (Peter Abelard, *Opera theologica II*, ed. E. M. Buytaert, [Turnhout: Brepols, 1969], *CCCM* 12:129, 192–93).

2. See Sabina Flanagan, "The *Speculum virginum* and Traditions of Medieval Dialogue," in *Listen Daughter: The "Speculum virginum" and the Formation of Religious Women in the Middle Ages*, ed. Constant J. Mews (New York: Palgrave, 2001), 181–200. The dialogue form was used frequently by twelfth-century writers, including Aelred of Rievaulx, Peter Abelard, St. Anselm, and Peter Alfonsi. Flanagan points out that Conrad of Hirsau's *Speculum virginum*, in which Theodora responds to her spiritual advisor Peregrinus, is unusual in the genre for its suggestion of a method for writing in dialogue form. As Flanagan notes, the *Speculum virginum* is also one of few twelfth-century dialogues in which all the voices are in third person (183) and the mode is realistic rather than allegorical (188). Flanagan agrees that the *Speculum virginum* may have been used as a guide for priests instructing women religious (191). In the dialogue, Theodora also accuses Peregrinus of representing her as if she were Geta, merely a character from a play, and of ignoring the power of her inner spiritual life. The comparison highlights the spectral quality of stage or literary characters as personae in comparison with their living, flesh-and-blood referents. See Conrad of Hirsau attr., *Speculum virginum*, ed. Jutta Seyfarth (Turnhout: Brepols, 1990), *CCCM* 5:56, 423. Seyfarth proposes Hugh of Fouilly as the author of the Speculum virginum.

3. Constant J. Mews, *The Lost Love Letters of Heloise and Abelard: Perceptions of Dialogue in Twelfth-Century France* (New York: St. Martin's Press, 1999), 19, 45h.

4. Setting aside modern debates about the line between ritual and drama and exactly what constiutes dramatic representation (e.g., text, costume, rubrics, degree of impersonation, etc.), the genre of liturgical drama is generally traced to liturgical ceremonies in which participants act out biblical events either within the liturgy or in additional ceremonies (see chap. 2 in the present book). An excellent assessment of the relationship between liturgy and dramatization—including a detailed discussion of the assumptions and terminology in fields of modern scholarship and a section on Byzantine theater, drama, and liturgy—can be found in Nils Holger Petersen, "Representation in European Devotional Rituals: The Question of the Origin of Medieval Drama in Medieval Liturgy," in *The Origins of Theatre in Ancient Greece and Beyond: From Ritual to Drama*, ed. E. Csapo and M. C. Miller (Cambridge: Cambridge University Press, forthcoming). (Professor Petersen generously sent me this paper prior to its publication.) The twelfth century also saw the rise of mimesis as a hermeneutic, devotional, and pedagogical strategy within ceremonial observances. The Palm Sunday procession from the *Ecclesiastica officia*, for example, describes the ritual distribution of palm branches to

monks, novices, lay brothers, and others present, followed by a procession around the cloister in imitation of the biblical Palm Sunday procession (Daniele Choisselet and Placide Vernet, eds., *Les ecclesiastica officia Cisterciens du XIIeme siècle* [Reiningue France: La Documentation Cistercienne: 1989], 22, 96–98). Between 1100 and 1160, elaborate dramatizations of biblical events were done in the major Benedictine monasteries at Limoges, Fleury, St. Gall, Richenau, and Ripoll during the Easter and Christmas seasons. The Benediktbeuren Passion play (1120), Hilarius's *History of Daniel* (1140), and the Montecassino Passion play (1150) accompanied official ceremonies. Tydeman, et al. (*Medieval European Stage,* 45 n. 2) notes that the later Beauvais *Play of Daniel* (ca. 1175) might have been influenced by the revival of interest in classical plays in the twelfth century. The *Ordo virtutum* of Hildegard von Bingen (1098–1179), written ca. 1151, is unusual in that it depicts not a biblical event corresponding to the liturgy or cycle of Scripture readings but an allegory of the battle between the Virtues (singing roles) and the Devil (a speaking role) over human souls (singing roles). Its structure is similar to that of the *Psychomachia* of Prudentius (348–ca. 404) rather than the episodic liturgical dramas. See Peter Dronke, *Poetic Individuality in the Middle Ages: New Departures in Poetry, 1000–1150* (Oxford: Clarendon Press, 1970), 152. For concise summaries of theatrical practice in the twelfth century, see William Tydeman's chapter "Classic and Christian," in *The Theatre in the Middle Ages: Western European Stage Conditions, c. 800–1576* (Cambridge: Cambridge University Press, 1978), 22–45; David Wiles's essay "Theatre in Roman and Christian Europe," in *The Oxford Illustrated History of Theatre,* ed. John Russell Brown (Oxford: Oxford University Press, 1995), 49–92. For the relationship between the texts of the Fleury *Playbook* and liturgy, as well as for the argument that the *Visitatio* offices should be interpreted as ritual rather than drama, see C. Clifford Flanigan, "The Fleury *Playbook,* the Traditions of Medieval Latin Drama, and Modern Scholarship," in *The Fleury "Playbook": Essays and Studies,* ed. Thomas P. Campbell and Clifford Davidson (Kalamazoo: Medieval Institute Publications, Western Michigan University, 1985), 1–25, esp. 3–5. For the effects of the Council of Trent on the tendency to isolate drama from liturgy and music, see Andrew Hughes, "Liturgical Drama: Falling Between the Disciplines," in *The Theatre of Medieval Europe: New Research in Early Drama,* ed. Eckehard Simon (Cambridge: Cambridge University Press, 1991), 42–62.

5. See, for example, the complaint of Gerhoh of Reichersberg (1093–1169) in *De investigatione Antichristi* 3, written ca. 1161 (Migne *PL* 194:1443–80). The conventions of biblical dramas—imitating figures such as Herod or the Antichrist, transfiguring oneself with a demon mask, representing what one is not by creating false imagery, and pretending in liturgical plays—might compromise the character of an individual and obscure the "true face" of the church. For translated excerpts given as an example of the church's negative attitude toward theater, see Tydeman et al., *Medieval European Stage,* 113–14; Karl Young, *The Drama of the Medieval Church* (Oxford: Clarendon Press, 1933), 2:524–25.

6. See Nancy van Deusen, *The Harp and the Soul: Essays in Medieval Music* (Lewiston, N.Y.: Edwin Mellen Press, 1989), 81, 85, 87.

7. See Marcia L. Colish's presentation of the twelfth-century Renaissance in *Medieval Foundations of the Western Intellectual Tradition, 400–1400* (New Haven: Yale University Press, 1997), 176, 181.

8. R. W. Southern, *Scholastic Humanism and the Unification of Europe*, vol. 1, *Foundations* (Oxford: Blackwell Publishers, 1995), 18.

9. See ibid., 17–28. Cf. C. Stephen Jaeger, *The Envy of Angels: Cathedral Schools and Social Ideals in Medieval Europe, 950–1200* (Philadelphia: University of Pennsylvania Press, 1994), 278–80. Jaeger is skeptical of twelfth-century humanism as a "renaissance" and exposes its roots in the eleventh-century schools.

10. See Southern, *Scholastic Humanism*, 22, 27.

11. See M. W. F. Stone, "Augustine and Medieval Philosophy," *The Cambridge Companion to Augustine*, ed. Eleonore Stump and Norman Kretzmann (Cambridge: Cambridge University Press, 2001), 253–66, esp. 254.

12. See Valerie I. J. Flint, "Honorius Augustodunensis of Regensburg," in *Authors of the Middle Ages, Historical and Religious Writers of the Latin West*, vol. 2, no. 6, ed. Patrick J. Geary (London: Variorum, Ashgate, 1995) 1–183. Honorius's materialist orientation is summarized by M. D. Chenu in *Nature, Man, and Society in the Twelfth Century: Essays on New Theological Perspectives in the Latin West*, ed. and trans. Jerome Taylor and Lester K. Little (Chicago: University of Chicago Press, 1968), 26.

> For Honorius, creation comes to fulfillment in a universe in which natures of diverse character insure an over-all harmony; it is in the integration existing among these that the greatness of God's plan lies. . . . Matter has significance in the Christian universe, and it is man that gives it that significance.

Honorius's emphasis on the centrality of humanness to Christian salvation, a strong theme in the *Inevitabile sive dialogus de libero arbitrio* and the *Elucidarius,* likely reflects study under Anselm. See John Marenbon, *Early Medieval Philosophy (480–1150): An Introduction* (London: Routledge & Kegan Paul, 1983), 171–92; Peter Dronke, ed., *A History of Twelfth-Century Western Philosophy* (Cambridge: Cambridge University Press, 1988), 450. For the influence of Anselm's thinking on the *Elucidarius,* which also illustrates Honorius's tendency to simplify complex theological ideas in service of accessibility, see Valerie I. J. Flint, "The *Elucidarius* of Honorius Augustodunensis and Reform in Late Eleventh-Century England," in *Ideas in the Medieval West: Texts and Their Contexts* (London: Variorum Reprints, 1988), 178–89, esp. 180–83. Flint discusses the range of Honorius's texts and argues that Honorius's work, especially the *Elucidarius* and including the *Eucharistion* and *Gemma animae,* were largely devoted to pastoral application. See, in the same volume, Flint, "The Place and Purpose of the Works of Honorius Augustodunensis," 97–119. Most of Honorius's writing was done at Regensburg after 1125, following a tenure at Canterbury, and the *Gemma animae* was most likely begun in England. The crudity of Honorius's Eucharistic theology and the penchant for biblical exegesis that drove his expositions, as well his affection for *Cur Deus homo* and the *Monologion,* is well documented in Flint, "*Elucidarius.*"

13. Caroline Walker Bynum, *The Resurrection of the Body in Western Christianity, 200–1336* (New York: Columbia University Press, 1995), 147–48. Bynum also presents criticism of the *Elucidarium* and *Clavis physicae* on the issue of Christ's corporeality and the transformation of matter and spirit drawn from John Scotus Eriugena. The concern for Honorius's presentation of the theology did not apparently extend to the liturgical allegories. See ibid., 150–51. That Honorius Augustodunensis's writings were prolific and eclectic has been well noted. See Flint, "Honorius."

14. Much work remains to be done on liturgical allegory as a genre and on changes in twelfth-century worship, such as the increasing use of polyphonic settings, episodic reenactments of biblical events, scriptural exegesis, reform efforts, and efforts to communicate with laypeople, as well as the continuities and differences between Amalarius and Honorius. For the purposes of this study, I focus on one allegory as a marker of intellectual change. For the relationship between Scripture readings and narrative continuity in the celebration of daily liturgies beginning in the eleventh century, see William T. Flynn, *Medieval Music as Medieval Exegesis* (Lanham, Md.: Scarecrow Press, 1999), 107–38, esp. 107–16.

15. *Sciendum quod hi qui tragoedias in theatris recitabant, actus pugnantium gestibus populo repraesentabant. Sic tragicus noster pugnam Christi populo Christiano in theatro Ecclesiae gestibus suis repraesentat, eique victoriam redemptionis suae inculcat. Itaque cum presbyter "Orate" dicit, Christum pro nobis in agonia positum exprimit, cum apostolos orare monuit. Per secretum silentium, significat Christum velut agnum sine voce ad victimam ductum. Per manuum expansionem, designat Christi in cruce extensionem. Per cantum praefationis, exprimit clamorem Christi in cruce pendentis. Decem namque psalmos, scilicet a "Deus meus respice" usque "In manus tuas commendo spiritum meum" cantavit, et sic exspiravit. Per Canonis secretum innuit Sabbati silentium. Per pacem, et communicationem designat pacem datam post. Christi resurrectionem et gaudii communicationem. Confecto sacramento, pax et communio populo a sacerdote datur, quia accusatore nostro ab agonotheta nostro per duellum prostrato, pax a judice populo denuntiatur, ad convivium invitatur. Deinde ad propria redire cum gaudio per "Ite missa est" imperatur. Qui gratias Deo jubilat et gaudens domum remeat* (*Gemma animae* 1.83, *De tragoediis* (Migne *PL* 172:570B–C).

16. Rabanus Maurus *De universo* 20.26 (Migne *PL* 111:549D). See, in the present book, chap. 2 n. 16.

17. For a rich discussion of liturgy as exegesis, a discussion that clarifies the tradition from which Honorius departs in *De tragoediis*, see Marie Anne Mayeski, "Reading the Word in a Eucharistic Context: The Shape and Methods of Early Medieval Exegesis," in *Medieval Liturgy: A Book of Essays*, ed. Lizette Larson-Miller (New York: Garland, 1997), 61–84, esp. 63–64.

18. On the practice of scriptural allegory, with attention to the details of written script as well as to the noncontingent status of the Scriptures as God's word in Hugh of St. Victor, see A. J. Minnis and A. Brian Scott with David Wallace, eds. *Medieval Literary Theory and Criticism, c. 1100–c. 1375: The Commentary Tradition* (Oxford: Clarendon Press, 1988), 65–73.

19. O. B. Hardison, Jr., *Christian Rite and Christian Drama in the Middle Ages: Essays on the Origin and Early History of Modern Drama* (Baltimore: Johns Hopkins University Press, 1965), 291.

20. Ibid., 40.

21. See Flint, "Honorius," 138; *Gemma Animae* (Migne *PL* 172:543).

22. *Missa quoque imitatur cujusdam pugnae conflictum, et victoriae triumphum, qua hostis noster Amalech prosternitur, et via nobis ad patriam per Jesum panditur, Jesus quippe imperator noster cum diabolo pugnavit, et coelestem rempublicam ab hostibus destructam hominibus reparavit: qui cum posset producere duodecim legiones angelorum . . .* (*Gemma animae* 1.72, *De pugna Christianorum spirituali* [Migne *PL* 172:566C–D]).

23. van Deusen, *The Harp and the Soul*, 78–85. For the Aristotelian relation of part to whole during and after the twelfth century, cf. Karl Frederick Morrison, *The Mimetic Tradition of Reform in the West* (Princeton: Princeton University Press, 1982), 175–76.

24. The scholarship on the emergence and development of "liturgical drama" is vast. For a summary discussion of the *Quem quaeritis* trope, its codification in the English *Regularis concordia*, its dissemination, its placement in the liturgy of the Night Office or Mass, and the question of its elaboration as the more "dramatic" *Visitatio sepulchri* (with a caution against reading modern criteria for realism into such medieval liturgical texts), see David Hiley, *Western Plainchant: A Handbook* (Oxford: Clarendon Press, 1993), 252–55.

25. Hardison, *Christian Rite*, 78.

26. Michal Kobialka, *This Is My Body: Representational Practices in the Early Middle Ages* (Ann Arbor: University of Michigan Press, 1999).

27. Ibid., 68, 147. For alternative and contrasting readings of the transubstantiation controversy and for its relevance to liturgical practice, see R. W. Southern, "Lanfranc of Bec and Berengar of Tours," in *Studies in Medieval History Presented to Frederick Maurice Powicke*, ed. R. W. Hunt, W. A. Pantin, and R. W. Southern (Oxford: Clarendon Press, 1948); Marcia L. Colish, *The Mirror of Language: A Study in the Medieval Theory of Knowledge* (New Haven: Yale University Press, 1968), 72–74.

28. Kobialka, *This Is My Body*, 150–51.

29. *Fertur quod olim sacerdotes e singulis domibus vel familiis farinam accipiebant. Quod adhuc Graeci servant, et inde Dominicum panem faciebant, quem pro populo offerebant, et hunc consecratum eis distribuebant. Nam singuli farinam offerentium missae interfuerunt, et pro his in Canone dicebatur "Omnium circumstantium qui tibi hoc sacrificium laudis offerunt." Postquam autem Ecclesia numero quidem augebatur, sed sanctitate minuebatur propter carnales, statutum est ut qui possent singulis Dominicis, vel tertia Dominica, vel summis festivitatibus, vel ter in anno communicarent, ne ante confessionem et poenitentiam pro aliquo crimine judicium sibi sumerent. Et quia, populo non communicante, non erat necesse panem tam magnum fieri, statutum est eum in modum denarii formari vel fieri, et ut populus pro oblatione farinae denarios offerrent, pro quibus traditum Dominum cognoscerent, qui tamen denarii in usum pauperum, qui membra sunt Christi, cederent, vel in aliquid quod ad hoc sacrificium pertineret* (*Gemma animae* 1.66, *De Dominico pane* [Migne *PL* 172:564D–565A]). The translation in the text is by Warren Smith, University of New Mexico at Albuquerque.

30. *Ideo autem hoc sacramentum de vino fit, quia Christus se vitem dixit, et Scriptura eum vinum jucunditatis asseruit. Uva autem, in praelo duobus lignis expressa, in vinum liquatur, et Christus duobus lignis crucis pressus, sanguis ejus in potum fidelibus fundebatur. Ideo et sanguis Christi de vino conficitur, quod de multis acinis exprimitur quia per illum corpus Christi Ecclesia recreatur, quae de multis justis congregatur. Haec pressuris mundi, quasi in torculari, calcatur, et Christo per passiones incorporatur* (*Gemma animae* 1.33, *De sacrificio vini* [Migne *PL* 172:554D]).

31. Marenbon, *Early Medieval Philosophy* 99.

32. For a discussion of St. Anselm's *Cur Deus homo* and the emphasis on the human body in eleventh- and twelfth-century thought as it affected theatrical representation, see Michal Kobialka, "Historical Time, Mythical Time, and Mimetic Time: The

Impact of the Humanist Philosophy of Saint Anselm on Early Medieval Drama,"
Medieval Perspectives 3 (Spring 1988): 172–90.

33. See Stephen G. Nichols, "The New Medievalism: Tradition and Discontinuity
in Medieval Culture," in *The New Medievalism*, ed. Marina S. Brownlee, Kevin Brownlee, and Stephen G. Nichols (Baltimore: Johns Hopkins University Press, 1991), 1–26,
esp. 1–2.

34. Hardison draws on the allegorical tradition, beginning with Amalarius's *Eclogae de officio missae* (814) and its elaboration in the *Liber officialis* (821, 835). Evidence for
Kobialka's emphasis on Honorius's Paschasian Eucharistic theology comes from the
widely read *Elucidarium* (ca. 1100) and its short, derivative treatise on the body of
Christ, the *Eucharistion* (ca. 1120).

35. See Chenu, *Nature*, 26.

36. For the continuation of theater in the mechanical arts tradition, see Glending
Olson, "The Medieval Fortunes of *Theatrica*," *Traditio: Studies in Ancient and Medieval
History, Thought, and Religion* 42 (1986): 265–86.

37. See Mary Hatch Marshall, "Boethius' Definition of Persona and Mediaeval
Understanding of the Roman Theater," *Speculum: A Journal of Mediaeval Studies* 25, no.
4 (1950): 471–82, esp. 474.

38. *Laquearium picturae sunt exempla justorum, quae Ecclesiae repraesentant orna-
mentum morum. Ob tres autem causas fit pictura: primo, quia est laicorum litteratura;
secundo, ut domus tali decore ornetur; tertio, ut priorum vita in memoriam revocetur*
(*Gemma animae* 1.132, *De pictura* [Migne *PL* 172:586]).

39. For eleventh-century "living iconography" and its importance to emotional
experience in private devotion, see Hans Belting, *Likeness and Presence: A History of the
Image before the Era of Art*, trans. Edmund Jephcott (Chicago: University of Chicago
Press, 1994), 260–61.

40. *"Lumina," quae circa capita sanctorum in ecclesia in modum circuli depingun-
tur, designant quod lumine aeterni splendoris coronati fruuntur. Idcirco vero secundum
formam rotundi scuti pinguntur, quia divina protectione ut scuto nunc muniuntur. . . .
Usus enim candelabri et thuribuli a lege coepit.* (*Gemma animae* 1.133, *De corona in ecclesia* [Migne *PL* 172:586C–D]).

41. *Lectores et cantores sunt Domini negotiatores* (*Gemma animae* 1.14, *De subdia-
cono* [Migne PL 172:548D]); *Cantores qui choros regunt, sunt apostoli qui Ecclesias laudes
Dei instruxerunt. Hi qui "Graduale" cantant, significant eos qui in activa vita Christo
serviunt. . . . Qui "Alleluia" cantant, designant eos qui in contemplativa vita Christum lau-
dant. Hi cantantes altius consistunt; quia tales in celsitudine virtutum coelestia contemp-
lando scandunt. Sequentiam chori alternatim jubilabunt, quia frequentiae angelorum et
hominum in domo Dei Dominum in saeculum saeculi laudabunt* (*Gemma animae* 1.16, *De
cantoribus* [Migne *PL* 172:549B–C]).

42. *Per episcopum, repraesentatur nobis Christus; per diaconum, ordo apostolicus.
Diaconus qui legit, est Petrus qui pro omnibus respondet. Episcopus lecturum diaconum
benedicit; quia Christus convocatis apostolis, benedictione eos replevit, dum eis potestatem
super omnia daemonia dedit, et eos regnum Dei praedicare misit. . . . In hoc quippe loco,
altare Hierusalem designat, in qua apostoli verbum praedicationis a Domino acceperunt, et
exeuntes per totam terram praedicaverunt. Diaconus in sinistro brachio librum portat, quia
sinistra praesentem vitam significat. Et in hac vita tantum praedicari Evangelium debet;*

quia in futura vita nullus doctrina eget, nam omnes a minimo usque ad maximum Dominum cognoscent (*Gemma animae* 1.20, *De diacono* [Migne *PL* 172:550D–551A]).

43. See Belting, *Likeness and Presence*, 161.

44. *Schola, dicitur vocatio, in qua si quis adhuc surdis auribus cordis torpescat, cantor cum excelsa tuba sonat in aurem ejus dulcedinem melodiae, ut excitetur. Cantores qui respondent primo canenti, vox est auditorum quasi evigilantium et Dominum laudantium. Versus, est arans servus per dulcedinem modulationis corda carnalium, quae se aperiunt more sulci confessione vocis et lacrymarum. Arant qui aratro compunctionis corda scindunt, in lectione pascitur auditor quasi quodammodo bos. Bos ad hoc pascitur, ut in eo opus agriculturae exerceatur. Bos est praedicator, cantor, quodammodo bubulcus, qui jubilat bobus, ut hilarius aratrum trahant, scilicet instigat canentes ut laetius canant* (*Gemma animae* 1.17, *De servo arante* [Migne *PL* 172:549D]).

45. See Jerome Taylor, introduction to *The "Didascalicon" of Hugh of St. Victor*, ed. and trans. Jerome Taylor (New York: Columbia University Press, 1961), 4; Chenu, *Nature*, 153.

46. Jaeger, *Envy of Angels*, 258.

47. See Taylor, introduction to *The "Didascalicon,"* 11.

48. Ibid., 9. On labor and the soul, see George Ovitt, Jr., *The Restoration of Perfection: Labor and Technology in Medieval Culture* (New Brunswick: Rutgers University Press, 1987). For a discussion of the term *mechanicae* and its use in sources on which Hugh may have drawn, see Elspeth Whitney, *Paradise Restored: The Mechanical Arts from Antiquity through the Thirteenth Century*, Transactions of the American Philosophical Society, vol. 80, no. 1 (Philadelphia: American Philosophical Society, 1990), 67–69. For the modern debate over the value of the mechanical arts in Christian theology and for the rifts between sociological and historical methods, see ibid., 7–8. For a survey of positions held by Jacques Le Goff, Lynn White, George Ovitt, Jr., and Olaf Pederson, see ibid., 12–15. The philosophical context for the lower status of mechanics against contemplation and reason is discussed by Franco Alessio, "La filosofia e le 'artes mechanicae' nel secolo XII," *Studi Medievali*, 2d ser., anno 6 (1965): 71–161.

49. Taylor, The "Didascalicon," 2.20. See Taylor, introduction to *The "Didascalicon,"* 75.

50. See Jaeger, *Envy of Angels*, 259–61.

51. *Didascalicon* 2.27. See Taylor, introduction to *The "Didascalicon,"* 79.

52. Honorius *De animae exsilio et patria* (Migne *PL* 172:1245B–C).

53. For Honorius's enthusiasm for Benedictines' rights to administer pastoral care and for his propensity for encouraging their ministry to the poor and disenfranchised, see Flint, "Honorius," 1–183.

54. See Flint, "Honorius," 138.

55. Gerhoh's complaints are akin to those of John of Salisbury and Aelred of Rievaulx about the excesses of vocal music and polyphony in worship. Gerhoh complains that priests are not properly dedicated to the church's ministry but "turn the churches themselves, the houses of prayers, into theaters and fill them with feigned spectacles of plays" (see Tydeman et al., *Medieval European Stage*, 113). Unlike Honorius, who invokes Greco-Roman theater positively in *De tragoediis*, Gerhoh is concerned about the effects of mimetic dramatizations on congregants. The complaint is similar to

John's in the concern that repeated behavior, even in jest, will eventually transform the character of a person. See, in the present chapter, n. 5.

56. For John's use of classical authors and the Old Testament, his use of exempla, and the textual background to the *Policraticus,* see Cary J. Nederman, introduction to *Policraticus: Of the Frivolities of Courtiers and the Footprints of Philosophers,* by John of Salisbury, ed. and trans. Cary J. Nederman (Cambridge: Cambridge University Press, 1990), xv–xx. Chapters 7 and 8 of book 3 are not included in Nederman's translation.

57. Cary J. Nederman, *John of Salisbury* (Tempe: Medieval and Renaissance Texts and Studies, forthcoming, 2005). Nederman's biography provides details of John's shift from scholarly inquiry to administration, the political machinations that led to the continuation of the poetic *Entheticus maior* in the *Policraticus,* and a sequence of its composition in conjunction with the *Metalogicon.*

58. See Nederman, *John of Salisbury;* Jaeger, *Envy of Angels,* 279.

59. As Nederman notes in a brief discussion of John's support of Henry against King Stephen, as well as his support of Thomas à Becket against Henry, John's career was marked by a rigorous skepticism of the policies imposed and actions taken by men in high offices. Nederman, introduction to *Policraticus,* xvii.

60. See Jaeger, *Envy of Angels,* 265; Hans Liebeschütz, *Mediaeval Humanism in the Life and Writings of John of Salisbury* (London: Warburg Institute, University of London, 1950), 27.

61. See Marshall, "Boethius' Definition," 471. For a more recent consideration of John's understanding of Roman drama, focusing on what John did or did not know about theater from ancient and contemporary sources, see Henry Ansgar Kelly, *Ideas and Forms of Tragedy from Aristotle to the Middle Ages* (Cambridge: Cambridge University Press, 1993), 78–79. Kelly (78) also suggests that new interpretations of classic texts in the twelfth century did not significantly alter medieval understandings of tragedy and comedy. Though the basic understanding of ancient drama and theatrical performance remained fairly constant, the treatment and use of that understanding expanded significantly in the twelfth century. Scholars disagree about the depth of John's knowledge of the sources he cites. Cf. Nederman, introduction to *Policraticus,* xx, for the observation that John's references are frequently from florilegia rather than full texts. Rodney Thomson also asserts that John's use of classical sources as authorities for his own ideas outstripped an in-depth familiarity with them; see "John of Salisbury and William of Malmesbury: Currents in Twelfth-Century Humanism," in *The World of John of Salisbury,* ed. Michael Wilks (Oxford: Published for the Ecclesiastical History Society by Basil Blackwell, 1984), 117–25; esp. 118.

62. *Ioannis Saresberiensis, Policraticus I–IV,* ed. K. S. B. Keats-Rohan (Turnhout: Brepols, 1993), CCCM 118:190. Keats-Rohan's edition refers to Clement C. J. Webb's edition, *Ioannis Saresberiensis episcopi Carnotensis Policratici* (Oxford: Clarendon Press, 1909; reprint, New York: Arno Press, 1979). In Tydeman et al., *Medieval European Stage,* 43–44, as evidence of a humanist turn in the medieval treatment of Roman theater, portions of chapters 7 and 8 from Joseph B. Pike's translation (*Frivolities of Courtiers and Footprints of Philosophers, Being a Translation of the First, Second, and Third Books and Selections from the Seventh and Eighth Books of the "Policraticus" of John of Salisbury* [Minneapolis: University of Minnesota Press, 1938], 169–77) are reproduced with the relevant passage from Hugh of St. Victor's *Didascalicon.*

63. *Policraticus* 3.8.1–3, 5–7 (Keats-Rohan 190, 191). See Pike, *Frivolities*, 171, 172.

64. . . . *fere totus mundus ex Arbitri nostri sententia mimum videtur implere, ad comediam suam quodammodo respiciens. Et quod deterius est, eo usque comediae suae insistunt ut in se cum opus fuerit redire non possint* (*Policraticus* 3.8.25–8 [Keats-Rohan 191]; see Pike, *Frivolities*, 172).

65. *Magnorum proinde virorum sensus saecularis haec expugnat comedia. Varia figura temporum actuum quaedam varietas est. Porro actibus personae deserviunt, dum in eis fortunae iocantis ludus impletur* (*Policraticus* 3.8.34–37 [Keats-Rohan 192]; see Pike, *Frivolities*, 172).

66. *In eoque vita hominum tragediae quam comediae videtur esse similior quod omnium fere tristis est exitus, dum omnia mundi dulcia quantacumque fuerint amarescunt et extrema gaudii luctus occupat* (*Policraticus* 3.8.45–48 [Keats-Rohan 192]; see Pike, *Frivolities*, 173). John cites Job 21:7–13.

67. See Kate L. Forhan, "The Not-So-Divided Self: Reading Augustine in the Twelfth Century," *Augustiniana* 42 (1992): 95–110.

68. *Huius itaque tam immensae tam mirabilis et inenarrabilis tragediae vel comediae theatrum quo peragi possit, ei mirabiliter coaequatur. Tanta est area eius quantus et orbis* (*Policraticus* 3.8.119–21 [Keats-Rohan 195]; Pike, *Frivolities*, 176).

69. *Illa tamen aetas, ut sic interim dicam, honestiores habuit histriones, si tamen aliquo modo honestum est quod omni homine libero comprobatur indignum* (*Policraticus* 1.8.6–8 [Keats-Rohan 53]; see Pike, *Frivolities*, 36).

70. *Verumtamen quid in singulis prosit vel deceat, animus sapientis aduertit, nec apologos refugit aut narrationes aut quaecumque spectacula, dum virtutis aut honestae utilitatis habeant instrumentum* (*Policraticus* 1.8.71–4 [Keats-Rohan 55]; see Pike, *Frivolities*, 38).

71. *Policraticus* 1.8.49–50 (Keats-Rohan 53, 54); Pike, *Frivolities*, 36, 37, 38.

72. John takes up the proper use and performance of liturgical music in *Policraticus* 1.6 (Keats-Rohan 46–51; Pike, *Frivolities*, 30–34). Unlike the *Anticlaudianus* of Alan of Lille, which praises the complexities of polyphony in an extended metaphor on learning and the senses that lead to knowledge of God and man's perfection, John of Salisbury disdains the false emotions stirred by virtuosic performances, excessive harmonies and phrase repetitions, and musical affect beyond natural harmonics (in particular, the lascivious Phrygian mode). Cf. Alan of Lille, *Anticlaudianus; or the Good and Perfect Man*, trans. James J. Sheridan (Toronto: Pontifical Institute of Mediaeval Studies, 1973), 111–12 (3.423–24), 35 (Sheridan's commentary). For John of Salisbury's concern that polyphony and singers' elaborations dull the judgment of both mind and soul, potentially producing more "arousal in the loins than devotion in the mind," see Timothy J. McGee, *The Sound of Medieval Song: Ornamentation and Vocal Style according to the Treatises*, Latin trans. Randall A. Rosenfeld (Oxford: Clarendon Press, 1998), 23.

73. *Policraticus* 1.8.55–56 (Keats-Rohan 54); Pike, *Frivolities*, 38.

74. Southern, *Scholastic Humanism*, 22.

75. Cf. Gilbert of Poitiers, *De Trinitate liber primus: The Commentaries on Boethius*, ed. Nikolaus M. Häring (Toronto: Pontifical Institute of Mediaeval Studies, 1966), 66 (16.10–14): *Neque enim excitamur ad aliquid optime faciendum iactacione fame et inanibus clamoribus vulgi: hac scilicet causa ut fama nostra ad exteros transeat et inter nostros, sicut solet facere, comicos et ceteros, qui delectare volunt, poetas scenicus nos et theatralis applausus extollat. Sensus: non exteriori favore sed conscientie secreto delector.*

76. Slightly more than half a century later, Aelred of Rievaulx would chastise liturgical singers given to "imitating the agonies of the dying and the terror of those enduring eternal torment." These singers, he observes, use techniques associated with actors: "sometimes the entire body is agitated in actors' gestures: the lips twist, the eyes roll, the shoulders heave, and at every note the fingers are flexed to match." Aelred of Rievaulx, like John of Salisbury in his critique of the poor quality of twelfth-century entertainments, refers not to ancient theater but to that of his own day. His concern, like Augustine's, is that live performance seduces people by producing false emotions. Congregations "watch, not without derisive laughter, the lustful gesticulations of the singers, the harlot-like alternations and subdivisions of the voices, so that you would think they had assembled not at an oratory but at a theatre, not for praying but for watching." See Aelred of Rievaulx, *Speculum charitatis*, 2.23 (Migne *PL* 195:571). The English translation and Latin text are in McGee, *The Sound of Medieval Song*, 24, 156.

Aelred of Rievaulx's distinction between watching theater and experiencing ritual is very much akin to that made by C. Clifford Flanigan. Theater and ritual are both communal activities. Rituals are entirely participatory and require no audiences or spectators, whereas theater, in the domain of "the arts," requires a division between those who perform and those who watch. See C. Clifford Flanigan, "Medieval Liturgy and the Arts: *Visitatio Sepulchri* as Paradigm," in *Liturgy and the Arts in the Middle Ages: Studies in Honour of C. Clifford Flanigan*, ed. Eva Louise Lillie and Nils Holger Petersen (Copenhagen: Museum Tucsulanum Press, University of Copenhagen, 1996), 9–35, esp. 10. Honorius's use of classical theater as an analogy to the Mass allows him to avoid entirely any such associations with contemporary entertainment. Like John of Salisbury, Honorius idealizes the theater of the past as a separate practice from liturgical "dramas" or "theatrical" performances of polyphony.

77. Amalarius *Liber officialis, Prooemium*, 17 (Hanssens 2:17).

78. See Marcel Metzger, "A Eucharistic Lexicon," in *Handbook for Liturgical Studies*, vol. 3, *The Eucharist*, ed. Anscar J. Chupungco (Collegeville, Minn: Liturgical Press, 2000), 1–8, esp. 3; Honorius *Gemma animae* 1.3, *De Agnus Dei* (Migne *PL* 172:581); Amalarius *Eclogae de ordine Romano* 32 (Hanssens 3:263–64).

CHAPTER 4

1. For the argument that Aristotelian ideas had infused European thought in the twelfth century much earlier than the texts themselves were made available, see Cary J. Nederman, "Aristotelian Ethics before the *Nichomachean Ethics*: Alternate Sources of Aristotle's Concept of Virtue in the Twelfth Century," in *Medieval Aristotelianism and Its Limits: Classical Traditions in Moral and Political Philosophy, 12th–15th Centuries* (Aldershot: Variorum/Ashgate, 1997), 55–75. The first three essays in this collection trace virtue, the science of politics, nature, ethics, and *habitus* in twelfth-century thought, which Nederman suggests are Aristotelian concepts derived from subterranean sources.

2. For the evolution, however erratic, of a systematic classification of knowledge in the liberal arts curriculum of the thirteenth century and for the position of poetry as logic, see Palémon Glorieux, *La faculté des arts et ses maitres au XIIIe siècle* (Paris: J. Vrin,

1971), 13–32. For an example of how available knowledge was compiled and organized into systematic forms of study (manuals, examinations, syllabi) at Paris that supports the argument that the Aristotelian *Poetics* was categorically separated both from ancient theatrical presentations and from direct application to lyric and dramatic performance, see P. Osmund Lewry, "Thirteenth-Century Examination Compendia from the Faculty of Arts," in *Les genres littéraires dans les sources théologiques et philosophiques médiévales: Definition, critique et exploitation* (Louvain: Université Catholique de Louvain, 1982), 5:101–16.

3. Henry Ansgar Kelly, "Aristotle-Averroes-Alemannus on Tragedy: The Influence of the *Poetics* on the Latin Middle Ages," *Viator: Medieval and Renaissance Studies* 10 (1979): 161.

4. John Wesley Harris, *Medieval Theatre in Context: An Introduction* (London: Routledge, 1992), 8.

5. Aristotle, [*Aristotilis de Arte*] *Poetica*, trans. William of Moerbeke, *AL* 1–37, here 12.29–30; hereafter, *AL* (Moerbeke).

6. Ibid., 11.24–25.

7. Ibid., 9.7

8. Ibid., 14.10–11.

9. See O. B. Hardison, Jr., *Christian Rite and Christian Drama in the Middle Ages: Essays on the Origin and Early History of Modern Drama* (Baltimore: Johns Hopkins University Press, 1965), 39–40.

10. Modern expectations for theatrical representation draw on Renaissance concepts of imitation as verisimilitude (representation of truth) and similitude (precise physical likeness) rather than the more general medieval senses of probability and similarity. As a recent example of modern dramaturgy applied to medieval texts, see Dunbar H. Ogden, *The Staging of Drama in the Medieval Church* (Newark: University of Delaware Press, 2002).

11. Brian Vickers, "Rhetoric and Poetics," in *The Cambridge History of Renaissance Philosophy*, ed. Charles B. Schmitt, Quentin Skinner, and Eckhard Kessler (Cambridge: Cambridge University Press, 1988), 718.

12. See Harris, *Medieval Theatre*, 19.

13. For inadequacies of Herman the German's translation on these aspects of dramatic plotting, see E. N. Tigerstedt, "Observations on the Reception of the Aristotelian *Poetics* in the Latin West," *Studies in the Renaissance* 15 (1968): 8–9.

14. See, for example, Oscar Brockett, *History of the Theatre*, 8th ed. (Boston: Allyn and Bacon, 1999), 125–27.

15. Marvin A. Carlson, *Theories of the Theatre: A Historical and Critical Survey, from the Greeks to the Present*, expanded ed. (Ithaca: Cornell University Press, 1993), 37.

16. Nils Holger Petersen, "Music, Dramatic Extroversion, and Contemplative Introspection: Hildegard of Bingen's *Ordo virtutum*," in *Ritual, Performance, Culture: Papers by C. Clifford Flanigan, His Students, and Colleagues*, ed. Robert Clark (Auckland: Wim Husken, forthcoming).

17. For the issue of medieval subjectivity and mimesis, see David Aers, "A Whisper in the Ear of Early Modernists; or, Reflections on Literary Critics Writing the 'History of the Subject,' " in *Culture and History 1350–1600: Essays on English Communities, Identi-*

ties, and Writing, ed. David Aers (Detroit: Wayne State University Press, 1992), 177–202, esp. 178–80.

18. G. Dahan, "Notes et textes sur la poétique au moyen âge," *Archives d'histoire doctrinale et littéraire du moyen âge* 47 (1980): 177.

19. For the placement of poetics in the trivium, see ibid., 175– 78. For the mechanical arts tradition, see Glending Olson, "The Medieval Fortunes of *Theatrica*," *Traditio: Studies in Ancient and Medieval History, Thought, and Religion* 42 (1986): 265–86.

20. See Gundisalvi *De logica* 16–18 (Baur 71). Henri Hugonnard-Roche shows how the classifications of knowledge in *De divisione philosophiae* combine Alexandrine, Latin, Arabic, and Jewish traditions, and he also reveals the dominance of the Arabic tradition, especially from Avicenna, in Gundisalvi's schema. See "La classification des sciences de Gundissalinus et l'influence d'Avicenne," in *Etudes sur Avicenne*, ed. Jean Jolivet and Roshdi Rashed (Paris: Société d'édition Les Belles Lettres, 1984), 41–75.

21. *De logica* 3–4 (Baur 74).

22. *Iste ergo sunt species sillogismorum et arcium sillogisticarum et species locucionum, quibus utuntur homines ad verificandum alliquid in rebus omnibus, set hee quinque hiis etiam nominibus appellari possunt: certificativa, putativa, errativa, sufficiens, ymaginativa* (*De logica* 12–16 [Baur 74]).

23. *De logica* 20–25 (Baur 81); see Hugonnard-Roche, "Classification," 47.

24. *De logica* 20, 21 (Baur 81).

25. *Set quia grammatica docet recte loqui, poetica delectare, rethorica persuadere, thopica fidem facere, demonstratio certificare, ideo ist ordo est naturalis scientiarum eloquentie* (*De logica* 20–23 [Baur 81]).

26. *De logica* 16–18 (Baur 74); see Hugonnard-Roche, "Classification," 58.

27. Gundisalvi does not confirm that he has access to or knows of an Aristotelian treatise on poetics, though he is aware of several texts outside the Greek-Arabic *Organon*. In *De partibus pratica philosophie* (8–9 [Baur 136]), he makes specific reference to Aristotle's *Politics* and *Ethics* as sources for his discussions of truth, goodness, and universal moral behavior in civic and domestic life: *Et hec quidem sciencia continentur in libro Aristotelis, qui politica dicitur, et est pars ethice*. Baur's notes to *De poetica* cite secondary Latin sources for Gundisalvi's discussion of poetics, including Isidore's *Etymologies*, Donatus's *Ars grammatica*, Horace's *Ars poetica*, Bede's *Ars metrica*, and Virgil's *Aeneid*. Immediately following the paragraph on poetics and mental imagery in *De logica*, Gundisalvi makes specific reference to the *Posterior Analytics* (22 [Baur 74]), the *Prior Analytics* (5 [Baur 75]), and the *Perihermenias* (9 [Baur 75]).

28. A tabular summary of the classification of knowledge conceived by Ralph of Longchamps, as well as a narrative summary of the *Anticlaudianus*, is in Martin Grabmann, *Die Geschichte der Scholastischen Methode* (Freiburg im Breisgau: Herdersche Verlagshandlung, 1911), 48–54; see esp. 49. See also Jan Sulowski, ed., *Radulphus de Longo Campo: In Anticlaudianum Alani Commentum* (Warsaw: Zakad Narodowy Imienia Ossoliskich Wydawnictwo Polskiej Akademii Nauk, 1972).

29. The *Anticlaudianus* has been translated with commentary by James J. Sheridan in *Anticlaudianus; or the Good and Perfect Man* (Toronto: Pontifical Institute of Mediaeval Studies, 1973). Alan of Lille (d. 1202) wrote the *Anticlaudianus* between 1182 and 1184, most likely in Paris or Montpellier. His writing shows the influences of Gilbert of Poitiers and, in its Platonism, the school of Thierry of Chartres.

There a new painter, with a new art, an imitator of reality, displays the battle of the elenchi and the duel of logic. He shows how the power of logic flashes its two-edged sword and when the face of truth has been maimed, cuts down the false, refusing to allow falsehood to be hidden beneath the appearance of truth; why the pseudo-logician, thief and corrupter of art, liar and hypocrite, clandestine plunderer and sophist, imitates the outer aspect of logic and relying on certain stunts, tries to sell falsehood packaged as truth. (3.28–44; trans. Sheridan 92)

30. Rita Copeland, *Rhetoric, Hermeneutics, and Translation in the Middle Ages: Academic Traditions and Vernacular Texts* (Cambridge: Cambridge University Press, 1991), 260 n. 23. See also Kelly, "Aristotle-Averroes-Alemannus," 175. For a tabulation of fourteenth-century references to the *Middle Commentary,* including the *Summa theologiae,* see William F. Boggess, "Arisotle's *Poetics* in the Fourteenth Century," *Studies in Philology* 67 (1970): 284–94.

31. See Dahan, "Notes et texts," 179. For Roger Bacon and Jean Buridan on poetics, see ibid., 181–82; on Roger Bacon, see Kelly, "Aristotle-Averroes-Alemanus," 172–73.

32. See Claude Lafleur, "Logique et théorie de l'argumentation dans le 'Guide de l'étudiant' (c. 1230–1240) du ms. Ripoll 109," *Dialogue: Canadian Philosophical Review* 29 (1990): 336.

33. The translation of the *Organon* from the Neoplatonic Alexandrine school commentator Simplicius (fl. 533 C.E.)—first into Syriac, then into Arabic, and from Arabic to Latin—gave the Scholastics the *Categories (Categoriae), On Interpretation (De interpretatione),* the *Prior Analytics (Analytica Priora),* the *Posterior Analytics (Analytica Posteriora),* the *Topics (Topica),* the *Sophistical Refutations (Sophisticis elenchis),* and the *Rhetoric* and *Poetics*—the last two defined as studies of the sciences of language. Though the modern *Organon* consists of the six main treatises, with the *Poetics* set apart as literary criticism, medieval European scholars would have assumed the *Rhetoric* and *Poetics* to be part of the *Organon* and thus a scientific inquiry into the general principles of language. For the Arabic transmission, see Ismail M. Dahiyat, *Avicenna's Commentary on the "Poetics" of Aristotle: A Critical Study with an Annotated Translation of the Text* (Leiden: E. J. Brill, 1974), 12; Salim Kemal, *The "Poetics" of Alfarabi and Avicenna* (Leiden: E. J. Brill, 1991), 2. Deborah Black analyzes the context theory of the placement of the *Poetics* with logic, in *Logic and Aristotle's "Rhetoric" and "Poetics" in Medieval Arabic Philosophy* (Leiden: E. J. Brill, 1990), 1–3. The Latin translations of Aristotle's treatises are tabulated in Norman Kretzmann, Anthony Kenny, and Jan Pinborg, eds., *The Cambridge History of Later Medieval Philosophy: From the Rediscovery of Aristotle to the Disintegration of Scholasticism, 1100–1600,* (Cambridge: Cambridge University Press, 1982), 74–79.

34. The extant manuscripts relating to the Arabic *Middle Commentary* (twenty-four of Herman the German's translations and the 1307 *Brevis expositio supra Poeticam Aristoteles* of Bartholemew of Bruges) suggest at least some interest in poetics as a discipline of logic in the thirteenth and fourteenth centuries. For references to Herman the German's translation and for thirteenth-century florilegium preserving twenty-six excerpts from the *Middle Commentary,* see William F. Boggess, "Aristotle's *Poetics.*"

35. William of Moerbeke's *[Aristotilis de Arte] Poetica* was written and copied at the papal court in Viterbo. Two copies were made in—and apparently stayed in—Italy.

Kelly traces later citations of Moerbeke's *Poetics* to Albertino Mussato in his *Vita Senece* and possibly to Petrarch in his *Invective contra medicum*. See Henry Ansgar Kelly, *Ideas and Forms of Tragedy from Aristotle to the Middle Ages* (Cambridge: Cambridge University Press, 1993), 118.

36. With regard to the history of European theater, Marvin Carlson (*Theories*, 34) notes that the Latin *Poetics* "created no stir whatever." Boggess ("Aristotle's *Poetics*," 278) states that William's translation "does not seem to have been used at all." Kelly ("Aristotle-Averroes-Alemannus," 161) remarks that the Latin translation of the Greek "received almost no notice until the twentieth century." Tigerstedt ("Observations," 9), who distrusts the foundation of the negative attitude toward Moerbeke's *Poetics* by *argumentum e silentio*, still concludes that there are "no certain traces" of the study of Aristotle's *Poetics* as such in the Latin Middle Ages. Kretzmann, Kenny, and Pinborg's *Cambridge History of Later Medieval Philosophy* (45) concludes that Moerbeke's *Poetics* "remained unknown" in the European Middle Ages.

37. See O. B. Hardison, Jr. introduction and translation of "The *Middle Commentary* on the *Poetics* of Aristotle," in *Medieval Literary Criticism: Translations and Interpretations*, ed. O. B. Hardison, Jr., Alex Preminger, and Kevin Kerrane, (New York: Frederick Ungar, 1974), 81–122. Hardison's exhaustive analyses of the Latin version of the *Middle Commentary* deal with the Arabic text's misinterpretation of Aristotle and with Herman the German's misinterpretations of Averroës, as well as with the placement of the *Poetics* with logic in the Middle Ages. See also in A. J. Minnis and A. Brian Scott with David Wallace, eds., "Placing the *Poetics*: Hermann the German; an Anonymous Question on the Nature of Poetry," in *Medieval Literary Theory and Criticism, c. 1100–c. 1375: The Commentary Tradition* (Oxford: Clarendon Press, 1988), 277–88. See Vickers, "Rhetoric and Poetics," 715, for the application of poetics and rhetoric to ethics in the liberal arts curriculum of the Renaissance.

38. Black, *Logic*, 4. Black's treatment of the medieval *Poetics* opposes studies, such as Hardison's, that approach the *Middle Commentary* as literary criticism.

39. Here I am primarily concerned with the presentation of the *Poetics* in European Scholasticism and its reception. Herman the German's translation and its interpretation of the Arabic text, as well as the Arabic interpretation of the Syriac translation from the Greek, has been well studied. Averroës (Ibn Rushd, 1126–98) wrote two commentaries on the *Poetics*, one short and the other "middle-sized" (he apparently did not write a long commentary on this particular treatise). The *Middle* (middle-sized) *Commentary* (ca. 1175) shifted Aristotle's highly theoretical analysis of the properties of poetry in an effort to "redirect Arabic poetry itself, to turn it away from frivolous, irresponsible, even voluptuous and dissolute concerns and to make it serve moral goals," as well as to identify the rules of poetry that apply universally over time. See Charles E. Butterworth, trans., *Averroes' "Middle Commentary" on Aristotle's "Poetics"* (Princeton: Princeton University Press, 1986), xi, xii, 49. Averroës replaced Aristotle's specific references to Attic poetry with Arabic songs and poetry. In translating Averroës's *Middle Commentary*, Herman the German either omitted the Arabic references, substituted Latin or more familiar Arabic equivalents for Averroës's examples, or translated the Arabic examples into Latin verse or prose. A summary of Herman the German's adaptations is provided by William F. Boggess in "Hermannus Alemannus' Latin Anthology of Arabic Poetry," *Journal of the American Oriental Society* 88 (1969): 657–70. See Her-

mannus Alemannus [Herman the German], *Poetria Ibinrosdin, AL* 39–74; hereafter, *AL* (Herman the German). Herman the German's references do overlap with Averroës's scriptural references, as in the following example.

You often find examples [of things represented in tragedies without arousing pity or fear] in the historical writings of Scripture, as songs of praise of the virtues are not discovered in the Arabic poems, and not discovered in our time except in scriptural writings.

[Et tu reperies multa ad modum omnium istorum in scripturis legalibus, cum carmina laudativa virtutum non inveniantur in poematibus Arabum, et non inveniuntur in hoc nostro tempore nisi in legibus scriptis.] (*AL* [Herman the German], 56)

Scriptural references are used in both texts to illustrate eulogy (Arabic) or tragedy (Latin) poems. For example, the scriptural story relating God's command that the patriarch Abraham sacrifice his son illustrates imitation that arouses sadness, compassion, and fear. In Herman the German's translation, the scriptural account of Joseph and his brothers illustrates virtue. For an English translation of Herman the German's *Middle Commentary*, see Hardison, "The *Middle Commentary*," in *Medieval Literary Criticism*, 89–122.

40. See Black, *Logic*, 3; Minnis and Scott, *Medieval Literary Theory*, 279–80; Butterworth, *Averroes' "Middle Commentary*," 49. Averroës (1126–98) lived and wrote primarily in Córdoba and drew on Avicenna's 1020 commentary on the *Poetics*. For the Arabic interpretation of Aristotle, see Dahiyat, *Avicenna's Commentary;* Kemal, *The "Poetics" of Alfarabi*. The Arabic tradition, as Black points out, assumed poetics to be a form of syllogistic reasoning. However, none of the three main Arabic commentators—Avicenna, al-Farabi, and Averroës—explained exactly how poetry functioned syllogistically. For a discussion of the ambiguities in the Arabic understanding of poetics as logic, see Black, *Logic*, 209–25.

41. *Suscipiant igitur, si placet, et huius editionis Poetrie translationem viri studiosi, et gaudeant se cum hac adeptos logici negotii Aristotilis complementum* (*AL* [Herman the German], 41).

42. For a helpful discussion of the intellectual context for Arabic translations, see F. E. Peters, *Aristotle and the Arabs: The Aristotelian Tradition in Islam* (New York: New York University Press, 1968), 69–78. Remnants of theatrical performances in the Greco-Roman tradition in the Middle East are documented by Shmuel Moreh in *Live Theatre and Dramatic Literature in the Medieval Arab World* (Edinburgh: Edinburgh University Press, 1991).

43. *AL* (Herman the German), 41.

44. *Et ista est ars logicalis de qua est consideratio in isto libro* (ibid., 43).

45. The Arabic tradition gave value to the responses poetry elicited. While poetry might be a less effective cognitive tool than objective reasoning by assertion, syllogism, or demonstrative argumentation as proposed in the first six parts of the Arabic and Latin *Organon*, the hearing and analysis of poetry nevertheless could lead to conviction. Poetry thus constituted a form of reasoning. Subjective, emotional, or aesthetic responses to poetry could also be used to promote social unity and to convince subjects

of limited ability to reason. See Kemal, *The "Poetics" of Alfarabi,* 2–3. The Islamic tradition, as Black points out (*Logic,* 52), provided "a fully developed account of what sort of discipline logic must be if it is to encompass the arts of rhetoric and poetics" through the use of conception and assent.

46. *Et quemadmodum quidam hominum naturaliter coimaginantur quibusdam et representant ipsos in actionibus, ut est representatio quorumdam ipsorum ad quosdam in coloribus et in figuris et in vocibus. Et hoc aut est ex arte aut ex habitu reperto in ipsis representatoribus aut ex parte consuetundinis quam iam diu habuerunt in hoc; sic reperitur in ipsis representatio per sermones naturaliter* (*AL* [Herman the German], 42; see also 44–45 on the natural human tendency to make likenesses).

47. See Nicolette Zeeman, "The Schools Give a License to Poets," in *Criticism and Dissent in the Middle Ages,* ed. Rita Copeland (Cambridge: Cambridge University Press, 1996), 153; Marcia L. Colish, *The Mirror of Language: A Study in the Medieval Theory of Knowledge* (New Haven: Yale University Press, 1968), 156–57; Copeland, *Rhetoric,* 159.

48. *Et pars tertia tragedie est credulitas; et hec est potentia representandi rem sic esse aut sic non esse. Et hoc est simile ei quod conatur rethorica in declaratione quod res existat aut non existat, nisi quod rethorica conatur ad hoc per sermonem persuasivum, et poetria per sermonem representativum* (*AL* [Herman the German], 49).

49. "It is not the job of a poet to represent things other than those that exist or can exist" (ibid., 51).

50. Cf. songs of praise or tragedies, which must represent things that exist in nature, not fictions with invented names: "Praise songs have as their intent the movement of acts of the will" *[Carmina namque laudativa intentionem habent promovendi actiones voluntarias]* (ibid., 52). L. M. de Rijk makes the case that after 1250, medieval logicians "shifted their attention from explaining the variations of the truth-value of a proposition over time to justifying predication regarding non-existent individuals and empty classes" ("The Origins of the Theory of the Properties of Terms," in *The Cambridge History of Later Medieval Philosophy: From the Rediscovery of Aristotle to the Disintegration of Scholasticism, 1100–1600,* ed. Norman Kretzmann, Anthony Kenny, and Jan Pinborg [Cambridge: Cambridge University Press, 1982], 161–73, 187). Herman the German's translation, which dealt explicitly with discerning the truth-value in representations, could be seen as part of this shift in focus.

51. *Et ex quo representatores et assimilatores per hoc intendunt instigare ad quasdam actiones que circa voluntaria consistunt et retrahere a quibusdam, erunt necessario ea que intendunt per suas representationes virtutes aut vitia* (*AL* [Herman the German], 43).

52. *Oportet denique ut in omni assimilatione inveniantur iste due differentie, scilicet approbatio decentis et detestatio turpis; non inveniuntur autem due hee differentie nisi in assimilatione et representatione que fiunt per sermonem, non in representationae que fit per metrum neque in representatione que fit per consonantiam* (ibid., 43–44).

53. *Et pars sexta est consideratio, scilicet argumentatio seu probatio rectitudinis credulitatis aut operationis non per sermonem persuasivum (hoc enim non pertinet huic arti neque est conveniens ei), sed per sermonem representativum; ars nempe poetrie non est consistens in argumentationibus neque in speculatione considerativa et proprie tragedia. Ideoque non utitut carmen laudativum arte gesticulationis neque vultuum acceptione sicut utitur hiis rethorica* (ibid., 49).

54. See Kelly, "Aristotle-Averroes-Alemannus," 167.

55. *Omnis enim representatio aut imperat sibi locum per representationem sui contrarii, et post permutatur ad suam intentionem (et est modus qui dicitur apud eos circulatio), aut rem ipsam non faciens mentionem aliquam sui contrarii (et hoc est quod ipsi vocabant significationem)* (*AL* [Herman the German], 48).

56. *Et directio humana et circulatio non usitantur nisi in inquisitione et refutatione; et hec species directionis est que movet animam quandoque ad miserendum et quandoque ad timendum* (ibid., 54).

57. *Quod enim non crediderit quis non movebit eum neque ad timendum neque ad miserendum* (ibid., 56).

58. *Homines enim naturaliter moventur altero duorum sermonum: aut sermone demonstrativo aut sermone non demonstrativo* (ibid.).

59. *Et ars scientalis que monstrat sive docet ex quibus et qualiter componuntur poemata principalior et perfectior est quam ipsa operatio poematum. Omnis enim ars instruens et continens quod sub ipsa de operativis sui operis, dignior est eis que sub ipsa sunt* (ibid., 49).

60. For analysis of how Herman the German adapted the Arabic into Latin Christian terms, see B. L. Ullman, "Hermann the German's Translation of Aristotle's *Poetics*," *Estudis Romanics* 8 (1961): 43–48. For a detailed comparison of Herman's editing of Arabic songs, see Boggess, "Latin Anthology." The Arabic text is translated in Butterworth, *Averroes' Middle Commentary*.

61. For a detailed study of medieval concepts of tragedy from Roman sources through Remigius, Isidore of Seville, and Boethius to the theologians and philosophers of the twelfth and thirteenth centuries (William of Conches, Gilbert of Poitiers, Peter Abelard, John of Salisbury, John of Garland, and Thierry of Chartres), see Kelly, *Ideas and Forms*. The scope of Kelly's meticulous study acknowledges that while tragic performances were used as a metaphor by John of Salisbury (1159) and Honorius Augustodunensis (1100), medieval tragedy as a genre consisted primarily of poetry in elegiac meters, based on Roman models; tragic narrative was generally conceived as a "joy to sorrow" movement based on the content of the story. The significant exception to the tradition is the *Ysagoge in theologiam* (ca. 1150), which was included with the treatises of the *Organon*.

62. Moerbeke wrote:

> Now to imitate is a natural inclination of man from childhood, and this distinguishes man from other animals; he is the most imitative and makes imitations because all delight in imitations. . . . for to learn is not only a philosopher's delight but similarly for all men who share in it a little time.]
>
> *[Nam imitari connatum hominibus est ex pueris, et hoc differunt ab aliis animalibus, quia maxime imitativum est et imitationes facit et propter gaudere imitaminibus omnes. . . . quia addiscere non solum philosophis delectabilissimum, sed et aliis similiter omnibus ad breve communicantibus ipso.]* (*AL* [Moerbeke], 6)

The parallel passage in Herman the German's *Middle Commentary* focused on comparative reasoning.

At first, from the moment of his birth, man naturally compares one thing to another and represents one thing for another; the act of comparing and representing was revealed in infancy and is that which is particular to man with respect to other animals . . .

[Prima quidem quoniam in homine existit naturaliter a prima sua nativitate assimilatio rei ad rem et representatio rei per rem; scilicet hic assimilandi et representandi actus etiam in infantibus reperitur, et istud proprium est homini respectu ceterorum animalium . . .] (AL [Herman the German], 44–45)

63. "What we would otherwise see as harsh, in the hour it is formed in imagery we take pleasure in contemplating, for example, forms of base beasts and of the dead" *[Que enim ipsa tristabiliter videmus, horum ymagines que maxime expresse considerantes gaudemus, puta bestiolarum formas vilissimarum et mortuorum] (AL* [Moerbeke], 6); "It is pleasurable, and we are pleased by representations of things that to the sense are not pleasurable" *[est quod delectamur et gaudemus in representatione aliquarum rerum in quarum sensu non delectamuri] (AL* [Herman the German], 45).

64. *AL* (Moerbeke), 6.

65. *De poetica ipsaque et speciebus ipsius, quam virtutem habet, et quomodo oportet constituere fabulas si debeat bene habere poesis, adhuc autem ex quot et qualibus est partibus, similiter autem et de aliis quecumque sunt eiusdem methodi, dicamus incipientes secundum naturam primo a primis. Epopoiia itaque et que tragodie poesis, adhuc autem komodia et que dithyrambopoetica . . . (AL* [Moerbeke], 3).

66. Ibid.

67. *Nichil autem commune est Homero et Empedocli preter metrum, propter quod hunc quidem poetam iustum vocare, hunc autem fysiologum magis quam poetam* (ibid., 4).

68. *Et multotiens non invenitur in sermonibus, qui nominantur "poemata" quedam de intentione poetica, preter quam metrum tantum, ut sunt sermones Socratis metrici et sermones Empedoclis in naturalibus, secundum diversum eius quod est in poematibus Homeri (AL* [Herman the German], 43).

69. For the literary character of classical plays in Latin, including the tenth-century plays of Hrotswitha and twelfth-century *commedia,* see Ronald W. Vince, *Ancient and Medieval Theatre: A Historiographical Handbook* (Westport, Conn.: Greenwood Press, 1984), 131.

70. *AL* (Herman the German), 41.

71. *AL* (Moerbeke), 3.

72. Ibid., 6.

73. ". . . and poetry itself was called '*dran*' (that is, to act), the Athenians also called it '*pratten*' (that is, to do)" (ibid., 5).

74. *AL* (Herman the German), 54.

75. *AL* (Moerbeke), 15.

76. *Et imitatio simplex est in qua usitatur aliqua duarum specierum ymaginationis, scilicet aut species que nominatur circulatio, aut species que nominatur directio (AL* [Herman the German], 53).

77. "From what has been said about what are the intentions of poetic words, representations that come about by the invention of false figures are not the work of poets.

These are things called proverbs and parables, as are in the books of Aesop and similar to the fables written. Indeed, a poet speaks only what pertains to things that are or are possible to be; because these are what desire or refute or what is an agreeable comparison following what is said in the headings on imitation" *[Et patet etiam ex hiis que dicta sunt de intentione sermonem poeticorum, quoniam representationes que fiunt per figmenta mendosa adinventitia non sunt de opere poete. Et sunt ea que nominantur proverbia et exempla, ut ea que sunt in libro Esopi et consimilibus fabulosis conscriptionibus. Ideo poete non pertinet loqui nisi in rebus que sunt aut quas possibile est esse; talia quippe sunt que appetenda sunt aut refutanda aut quarum conveniens est assimilatio secundum quod dictum est in capitulis representationum]* (AL [Herman the German], 51).

78. AL (Moerbeke), 14.

79. *Dico autem simplicem quidem actionem qua existente, ut determinatum continua et una sine peripetia et anagnorismo transitio fit, complexa autem locutio cum anagnorismo aut peripetia aut ambobus transitio est. Hec autem oportet fieri ex ipsa consistentia fabule, quare ex pregestis accidit aut ex necessitate aut secundum verisimile fieri hec; differt enim multum fieri hec propter hec aut post hec. Est autem peripetia quidem que ad contrarium eorum que aguntur transmutatio, sicut dictum est, et hoc autem sicut dicebamus secundum verisimile aut necessarium* (ibid.).

80. For a brief and comprehensive summary of writers, texts, and trends in thought on poetry and rhetoric from the late classical period through Scholasticism, see Colish, *Mirror*, 156–62.

81. *Et oportet ut tragedie, id est artis laudandi, sex partes sint: scilicet sermones fabulares representativi, et consuetudines, et metrum seu pondus, et credulitates, et consideratio, et tonus* (AL [Herman the German], 48).

82. *Oportet ergo ut habitudo sermonis recitantis et representantis in tragedia sit habitudo et figura certi et non dubii, et dicentis seriosa, non iocosa, ut sunt sermones virorum summe honestatis in moribus et opinionibus et actionibus . . .* (AL [Herman the German], 47). Cf. Hardison, "The *Middle Commentary*," 95.

83. *Est igitur tragodia imitatio actionis studiose et perfecte, magnitudinem habentis, delectante sermone seorsum unaquaque specierum in partibus, actitantium et non per enuntiationem, per misericordiam et timorem concludens talium mathematum purificationem. . . . Quoniam autem agentes faciunt imitationem, primo quidem ex necessitate utique erit aliqua pars tragodie visus ornatus* (AL [Moerbeke], 8–9).

84. *Omne itaque poema et omnis oratio poetica aut est vituperatio aut est laudatio* (AL [Herman the German], 41).

85. *Ideoque non utitut carmen laudativum arte gesticulationis neque vultuum acceptione sicut utitur hiis rethorica* (ibid., 49).

86. *Quarum una est habitudo significans morem et consuetudinem, ut qui loquitur sermonem intelligentis aut sermonem iracundi; et altera est habitudo significans hominis credulitatem seu opinionem; non est enim habitudo eius qui loquitur certus existens de re, habitudo eius qui loquitur dubius existens* (ibid., 47).

87. "[Aristotle] refers to what lawyers frequently do, as in extending their voices saying 'no, no, no'; and similarly extending their voices when saying 'this is not so' and making them larger. Oppositional responses are like half verses, having tone and meter" *[. . . hoc quod frequenter faciunt litigantes, ut cum dicunt "non, non, non," extendentes per hoc vocem suam; et, cum dicunt "non sic est hoc," similiter et per hoc extendentes vocem*

suam et spaciosam eam facientes; huiusmodi namque responsive resistentie sunt, quasi semiversus habentes tonum et metrum] (ibid., 46).

88. *Quare hac quidem idem utique erit imitator Homero Sophocles, imitantur enim ambo studiosos; hac autem Aristofani, agentes enim imitantur et actitantes ambo. Unde et dramata (idest actitamina) vocari ipsa quidam aiunt quia imitantur actitantes* (AL [Moerbeke], 5).

89. *Principium quidem igitur et velut anima tragodie fabula, secundum autem mores. . . . Estque imitatio actionis et propter hanc maxime agentium. Tertium autem rati-ocinatio, scilicet posse dicere inentia et que congruunt, quod quidem in sermonibus politice et rethorice opus est* (ibid., 10).

90. Butterworth, *Averroes' Middle Commentary*, 86.

91. Kelly, "Aristotle-Averroes-Alemannus," 167.

92. For the history of theatrical entertainments as civic and social practice in the Arab world from the late classical to the medieval period, see Moreh, *Live Theatre*.

93. *Neque etiam indiget poeta peritus seu perfectus ut compleat representationem suam per ea que extrinsecus sunt, ut est in gestibus theatralibus et vultuum dispositionibu. . . . Adiutorium ergo fit ad earum imitationem per ea que extrinsecus sunt, et proprie quando intenditur imitatio credulitatem* (AL [Herman the German], 52–53).

94. Ibid., 7.

95. Cf. "Even dancing, flute playing, and lyre playing can make such distinctions [in diversity of human character]" *[Et enim in saltatione et fystulatione et chytharizatione est fieri has dissimiltudines]* (AL [Moerbeke], 5).

96. "Considering, therefore, whether or not tragedy has evolved sufficiently in its species judging by its own qualities and in the theater is another issue" *[Superintendendi quidem igitur si habet iam tragodia speciebus sufficienter aut non, sique ipsumque secundum se iudicatur esse et ad theatra, alia ratio]* (ibid., 7).

97. *Oportet enim fabulas consistere et locutione cooperari quam maxime pre oculis positum (sic enim utique efficacissime videns sicut apud ipsa gesta presens inveniet decens et minime utique latebunt que subcontraria; signum autem huius quod increpat Karkino; nam Amphiaraus ex sacro utique erat, quod non videntem inspectorem latebat, in skene autem decidit aspernantibus hoc inspectoribus), quecumque autem possibile et scematibus cooperantem* (ibid., 21).

98. For developments in logic in late Scholasticism and the reassessment of Aristotle, especially the terminists' emphasis on full propositions as the only grammatical context in which logical arguments could be made, see Marcia L. Colish, *Medieval Foundations of the Western Intellectual Tradition, 400–1400* (New Haven: Yale University Press, 1997), 302–15, esp. 302 on the post-Aristotelianism of Henry of Ghent, John Duns Scotus, and William of Ockham.

99. See Dahan, "Notes et texts," 185.

100. For a comparison of Bartholomew's *Brevis expositio* with Bacon and Buridan, see ibid., 186.

101. Bartholomew of Bruges, *Brevis expositio supra poetriam*, MS 16089, Bibliothèque Nationale, Paris, fols. 146r–151r. See A. Patton, "Bartolomaeus van Brugge Vlaams Wijsgeer en Geneesheer," *Tijdschrift voor Filosofie* 30 (1968): 118–50. References are to Dahan's transcription in "Notes et texts," 171–239.

102. For the argument for a thirteenth-century recension, see Boggess, "Aristotle's *Poetics*"; Kelly, "Aristotle-Averroes-Alemannus."

103. Tigerstedt ("Observations," 10) points out that many of the ideas in the Aristotelian *Poetics*—for example, musical catharsis—were already available in other texts. For the theory of an "underground" Aristotelianism that made key Aristotelian concepts available apart from their primary documents, see Nederman, "Aristotelian Ethics," 75.

104. See Boggess, "Aristotle's *Poetics*," 282; Kelly, "Aristotle-Averroes-Alemannus," 175.

105. "*Anima rationalis est sicut tabula rasa in qua nihil scriptum.*" Verum: sicut tabula est in potentia ad omnes picturas, sic et anima rationalis est in potentia ad omnem cognoscientiam et cognitionem* (Dahan, "Notes et texts," 223).

106. *Ideo opus est arte et scientia que huiusmodi instrumentorum tradat veram cognitionem. . . . Hanc autem eruditionem tradit logica: docet enim verum a falso discernere in speculativis et bonum a malo in practicis* (ibid.).

107. Ibid., 224.

108. Ibid., 188.

109. Ibid., 225.

110. Ermolao Barbaro would make this distinction clearly when, in his humanist lectures in Padua, he privileged the knowledge of the Greeks over that of the Arabs who had provided translations. See Tigerstedt, "Observations," 12.

111. *Similiter autem, quia in omnibus huiusmodi processibus contingit obliquiri a processu rationis, ideo opus fuit quadam scientia que doceret vitare huiusmodi obliquitates et causas a cavillatore factas dissolvere. Et sic completur scientia de modo sciendi vel de instrumento sciendi, quod idem est, ut alias patuit* (Dahan, "Notes et texts," 224).

112. *. . . propinqua et intrinseca causa est cognitio perfecta dicti instrumenti, vel dicte contextionis; causa finalis remota est cognitio perfecta instrumentorum sciendi et universaliter completio philosophie* (ibid., 225).

113. Ibid., 224.

114. Ibid., 227.

115. *Item nota quod dicit sermones poeticos esse assimilativos, eo quod non directe exprimunt rem, sed in suo simili vel proportionali, vel quia utuntur similibus et proportionibus, e contrario sermonibus demonstrativis, qui directe exprimunt rem. Vel dicit hoc quia procedunt ex assimilationibus, ut patet in littera. Item dicit eos ymaginativos, vel quia exprimunt rem in sua ymagine, id est simulitudine, vel quia non semper procedunt ex hiis que sunt, sed que sunt possibilia ymaginari . . .* (ibid.).

116. *Item nota quod habitus consuetudinis videtur mihi idem cum experimento, et est in cogitaciam sicut in subjecto, et differt iste habitus ab arte, quia ars est universalium et iste non, sed singularium. Etiam ars cognoscit rem operalem ex suis principiis, sed iste non, et maxime universalibus principiis, quia per talia principia videtur omne operans cognitione noscere; aliter enim non posset operari* (ibid., 228).

117. Ibid., 227.

118. Ibid., 229.

119. Boggess, "Hermannus Alemannus and Catharsis in the Mediaeval Latin *Poetics*," *Classical World* 62, no. 6 (1969): 212–14. Hardison's emphasis on the catharsis in the

narrative structure of the Mass as suggested in Honorius Augustodunensis's allegory is part of this twentieth-century interest in cathartic release of emotions.

120. *Et oportet ut sit fabularis adinventio pavorosa dolorosa inventio quasi ante oculos constituta, que quasi ex visu fidem habeat. Quando enim fabularis narratio ambigua fuerit et adinventa adinventione dubitabili, non aget actionem que per ipsam intenta fuerat. Quod enim non crediderit quis non movebit eum neque ad timendum neque ad admiserendum* (*AL* [Herman the German], 56).

121. *Et oportet ut sit fabularum, in qua ostendit qualia timorosa et dolorosa debent accipi in instigationibus. . . . Pavorosa, idest incutiens pavorem. Que quasi ex visu fidem habeat: ita quod fabula ex duobus movet, scilicet ex evidentia ipsius et dispositione componentis* (Dahan, "Notes et texts," 236).

122. *Et oportet ut sit fabularum, ex quibus passionalibus debet componi, hic tertio ostendit ex quibus et qualibus virtuosis, quia ex virtuosis formaliter que sunt ex scientia et voluntate, et non ex virtuosis naturaliter, que possunt esse preter scientiam vel voluntatem ut patet 3 et 4 ethicorum de iustitia . . .* (ibid.).

123. *Et oportet ut sit fabularum quia ibi ostendit ex quibis et qualibus virtuosis et passionibus fit tragedia; vel posset dici quod, cum multiplices sint actiones hominis, quod hic ostendit ex quibus actionibus eius laus est, quia ex voluntariis et scienticis que bone sunt* (ibid., 237).

124. See Kelly, "Aristotle-Averroes-Alemannus," 183–84.

Bibliography

MANUSCRIPT COLLECTIONS

Bartholomew of Bruges. *Brevis expositio supra Poetriam*. MS 16089. Bibliothèque Nationale, Paris.

ARTICLES IN JOURNALS

Alessio, Franco. "La filosofia e le 'artes mechanicae' nel secolo XII." *Studi Medievali*, 2d ser., anno 6 (1965): 71–161.

Boggess, William F. "Aristotle's *Poetics* in the Fourteenth Century." *Studies in Philology* 67 (1970): 278–94.

———. "Hermannus Alemannus and Catharsis in the Mediaeval Latin *Poetics*." *Classical World* 62, no. 6 (1969): 212–14.

———. "Hermannus Alemannus' Latin Anthology of Arabic Poetry." *Journal of the American Oriental Society* 88 (1969): 657–70.

Dahan, G. "Notes et texts sur la Poétique au moyen âge." *Archives d'histoire doctrinale et littéraire du moyen âge* 47 (1980): 171–239.

Forhan, Kate L. "The Not-So-Divided Self: Reading Augustine in the Twelfth Century." *Augustiniana* 42 (1992): 95–110.

Kelly, Henry Ansgar. "Aristotle-Averroes-Alemannus on Tragedy: The Influence of the *Poetics* on the Latin Middle Ages." *Viator: Medieval and Renaissance Studies* 10 (1979): 161–209.

Kobialka, Michal. "Historical Time, Mythical Time, and Mimetic Time: The Impact of the Humanistic Philosophy of Saint Anselm on Early Medieval Drama." *Medieval Perspectives* 3 (Spring 1988): 172–90.

LaFleur, Claude. "Logique et théorie de l'argumentation dans le 'Guide de l'étudiant' (c. 1230–1240) du ms. Ripoll 109." *Dialogue: Canadian Philosophical Review* 29 (1990): 335–55.

Marshall, Mary Hatch. "Boethius' Definition of Persona and Mediaeval Understanding of the Roman Theater." *Speculum: A Journal of Mediaeval Studies* 25, no. 4 (1950): 471–82.

———. "Theatre in the Middle Ages: Evidence from Dictionaries and Glosses." *Symposium: A Journal Devoted to Modern Foreign Languages and Literatures* 4 (1950): 1–39.

Olson, Glending. "The Medieval Fortunes of *Theatrica.*" *Traditio: Studies in Ancient and Medieval History, Thought, and Religion* 42 (1986): 265–86.

Patton, A. "Bartolomaeus van Brugge Vlaams Wijsgeer en Geneesheer." *Tijdschrift voor Filosofie* 30 (1968): 118–50.

Tigerstedt, E. N. "Observations on the Reception of the Aristotelian *Poetics* in the Latin West." *Studies in the Renaissance* 15 (1968): 7–24.

Ullman, B. L. "Hermann the German's Translation of Aristotle's *Poetics.*" *Estudis Romanics* 8 (1961): 43–48.

Warning, Rainer. "On the Alterity of Medieval Religious Drama." *New Literary History* 10 (1979): 265–92.

ARTICLES IN BOOKS

Aers, David. "A Whisper in the Ear of Early Modernists; or, Reflections on Literary Critics Writing the 'History of the Subject.' " In *Culture and History, 1350–1600: Essays on English Communities, Identities, and Writing,* edited by David Aers, 177–202. Detroit: Wayne State University Press, 1992.

Armstrong, A. Hilary. "St. Augustine and Christian Platonism." In *Augustine: A Collection of Critical Essays,* edited by Robert A. Markus, 3–37. Garden City: Anchor Books, 1972.

Brown, Giles. "Introduction: The Carolingian Renaissance." In *Carolingian Culture: Emulation and Innovation,* edited by Rosamond McKitterick, 1–51. Cambridge: Cambridge University Press, 1994.

Chupungco, Anscar J. "History of the Roman Liturgy until the Fifteenth Century." In *Handbook for Liturgical Studies,* vol. 1, *Introduction to the Liturgy,* edited by Anscar J. Chupungco, 131–52. Collegeville, Minn.: Liturgical Press, 1997.

Cranz, F. Edward. "*De Civitate Dei,* XV, 2, and Augustine's Idea of the Christian Society." In *Augustine: A Collection of Critical Essays,* edited by Robert A. Markus, 404–21. Garden City: Anchor Books, 1972.

de Rijk, L. M. "The Origins of the Theory of the Properties of Terms." In *The Cambridge History of Later Medieval Philosophy: From the Rediscovery of Aristotle to the Disintegration of Scholasticism, 1100–1600,* edited by Norman Kretzmann, Anthony Kenny, and Jan Pinborg, 161–73. Cambridge: Cambridge University Press, 1982.

Flanagan, Sabina. "The *Speculum virginum* and Traditions of Medieval Dialogue." In *Listen Daughter: The "Speculum virginum" and the Formation of Religious Women in the Middle Ages,* edited by Constant J. Mews, 181–200. New York: Palgrave, 2001.

Flanigan, C. Clifford. "The Fleury *Playbook,* the Traditions of Medieval Latin Drama, and Modern Scholarship." In *The Fleury "Playbook": Essays and Studies,* edited by Thomas P. Campbell and Clifford Davidson, 1–25. Kalamazoo: Medieval Institute Publications, Western Michigan University, 1985.

————. "Medieval Liturgy and the Arts: *Visitatio sepulchri* as Paradigm." In *Liturgy and the Arts in the Middle Ages: Studies in Honour of C. Clifford Flanigan,* edited by Eva Louise Lillie and Nils Holger Petersen, 9–35. Copenhagen: Museum Tusculanum Press, University of Copenhagen, 1996.

Flint, Valerie I. J. "The *Elucidarius* of Honorius Augustodunensis and Reform in Late Eleventh-Century England." In *Ideas in the Medieval West: Texts and Their Contexts,* ed. Valerie I. J. Flint, 178–89. London: Variorum Reprints, 1988.

————. "Honorius Augustodunensis of Regensburg." In *Authors of the Middle Ages, Historical and Religious Writers of the Latin West,* vol. 2, no. 6, edited by Patrick J. Geary, 1–183. London: Variorum, Ashgate, 1995.

————. "The Place and the Purpose of the Works of Honorius Augustodunensis." In *Ideas in the Medieval West: Texts and Their Contexts,* ed. Valerie I. J. Flint, 97–127. London: Variorum Reprints, 1988.

Geary, Patrick J. "Oblivion Between Orality and Textuality in the Tenth Century." In *Medieval Concepts of the Past: Ritual, Memory, Historiography,* edited by Gerd Althoff, Johannes Fried, and Patrick J. Geary, 111–22. Cambridge: Cambridge University Press, 2002.

Hardison, O. B., Jr. Introduction to and translation of the *"Middle Commentary" of Averroes in Medieval Literary Criticism: Translations and Interpretations,* edited by O. B. Hardison, Jr., et al., 81–122. New York: Frederick Ungar, 1974.

Hardison, O. B., Jr. "Placing the *Poetics:* Hermann the German; an Anonymous Question on the Nature of Poetry." In A. J. Minnis and A. Brian Scott with David Wallace eds. *Medieval Literary Theory and Criticism, c. 1100–c. 1375: The Commentary Tradition* (Oxford: Clarendon Press, 1988) 277–88.

Hill, Edmund. Introduction and notes to *Teaching Christianity: "De doctrina Christiana,"* The Works of St. Augustine: A Translation for the 21st Century, vol. 11, edited by John E. Rotelle. Hyde Park, N.Y.: New City Press, 1990.

Hughes, Andrew. "Liturgical Drama: Falling Between the Disciplines." In *The Theatre of Medieval Europe: New Research in Early Drama,* edited by Eckehard Simon, 42–62. Cambridge: Cambridge University Press, 1991.

Hugonnard-Roche, Henri. "La classification des sciences de Gundissalinus et l'influence d'Avicenne." In *Etudes sur Avicenne,* edited by Jean Jolivet and Roshdi Rashed, 41–75. Paris: Société d'édition Les Belles Lettres, 1984.

Jones, Joseph R. "Isidore and the Theatre." In *Drama in the Middle Ages: Comparative and Critical Essays,* edited by Clifford Davidson and John H. Stroupe, 1–23. AMS Studies in the Middle Ages, no. 18. New York: AMS Press, 1991.

Kirwan, Christopher. "Augustine's Philosophy of Language." In *The Cambridge Companion to Augustine,* edited by Eleonore Stump and Norman Kretzmann, 186–204. Cambridge: Cambridge University Press, 2001.

Lewry, P. Osmund. "Thirteenth-Century Examination Compendia from the Faculty of Arts." In *Les genres littéraires dans les sources théologiques et philosophiques médiévales: Definition, critique et exploitation,* 5:101–16. Louvain: Université Catholique de Louvain, 1982.

Marenbon, John. "Carolingian Thought." In *Carolingian Culture: Emulation and Innovation,* edited by Rosamond McKitterick, 171–92. Cambridge: Cambridge University Press, 1994.

Markus, Robert A. "Signs, Communication, and Communities in Augustine's *De doctrina Christiana*." In *"De doctrina Christiana": A Classic of Western Culture*, edited by Duane W. H. Arnold and Pamela Bright, 97–108. Notre Dame: University of Notre Dame Press, 1995.

Mayeski, Marie Anne. "Reading the Word in a Eucharistic Context: The Shape and Methods of Early Medieval Exegesis." In *Medieval Liturgy: A Book of Essays*, edited by Lizette Larson-Miller, 61–84. New York: Garland, 1997.

McGinn, Bernard. "The Religious World of the Twelfth Century: Introduction." In *Christian Spirituality: Origins to the Twelfth Century*, edited by Bernard McGinn and John Meyendorff with Jean Leclercq, 194–95. New York: Crossroad, 1985.

Metzger, Marcel. "A Eucharistic Lexicon." In *Handbook for Liturgical Studies*, vol. 3, *The Eucharist*, edited by Anscar J. Chupungco, 1–8. Collegeville, Minn.: Liturgical Press, 2000.

———. "The History of the Eucharistic Liturgy in Rome." In *Handbook for Liturgical Studies*, vol. 3, *The Eucharist*, edited by Anscar J. Chupungco, 103–32. Collegeville, Minn.: Liturgical Press, 1999.

Nederman, Cary J. "Aristotelian Ethics before the *Nichomachean Ethics*: Alternate Sources of Aristotle's Concept of Virtue in the Twelfth Century." In *Medieval Aristotelianism and Its Limits: Classical Traditions in Moral and Political Philosophy, 12th–15th Centuries*, 55–75. Aldershot: Variorum/Ashgate, 1997.

———. Introduction to *Policraticus: Of the Frivolities of Courtiers and the Footprints of Philosophers*, by John of Salisbury. Edited and translated by Cary J. Nederman. Cambridge: Cambridge University Press, 1990.

Nichols, Stephen G. "The New Medievalism: Tradition and Discontinuity in Medieval Culture." In *The New Medievalism*, edited by Marina S. Brownlee, Kevin Brownlee, and Stephen G. Nichols, 1–26. Baltimore: Johns Hopkins University Press, 1991.

Petersen, Nils Holger. "Music, Dramatic Extroversion, and Contemplative Introspection: Hildegard of Bingen's *Ordo virtutum*." In *Ritual, Performance, Culture: Papers by C. Clifford Flanigan, His Students, and Colleagues*, edited by Robert Clark. Auckland: Wim Husken, forthcoming.

———. "Representation in European Devotional Rituals: The Question of the Origin of Medieval Drama in Medieval Liturgy." In *The Origins of Theatre in Ancient Greece and Beyond: From Ritual to Drama*, edited by E. Csapo and M. C. Miller. Cambridge: Cambridge University Press, forthcoming.

Rand, Edward Kennard. "Der Kommentar des Johannes Scottus zu den Opuscula Sacra de Boethius." In *Quellen und Untersuchungen zur lateinischen Philologie des Mittelalters*, edited by Ludwig Traube. Munich: C. H. Beck, 1906.

Rubin, Miri. "The Eucharist and the Construction of Medieval Identities." In *Culture and History, 1350–1600: Essays on English Communities, Identities, and Writing*, edited by David Aers, 43–63. Detroit: Wayne State University Press, 1992.

Schäublin, Christoph. "*De doctrina Christiana*: A Classic of Western Culture?" In *"De doctrina Christiana": A Classic of Western Culture*, edited by Duane W. H. Arnold and Pamela Bright, 47–67. Notre Dame: University of Notre Dame Press, 1995.

Southern, R. W. "Lanfranc of Bec and Berengar of Tours." In *Studies in Medieval His-*

tory Presented to Frederick Maurice Powicke, edited by R. W. Hunt, W. A. Pantin, and R. W. Southern, 27–48. Oxford: Clarendon Press, 1948.

Stone, M. W. F. "Augustine and Medieval Philosophy." In *The Cambridge Companion to Augustine,* edited by Eleonore Stump and Norman Kretzmann, 253–66. Cambridge: Cambridge University Press, 2001.

Taylor, Jerome. Introduction to *The "Didascalicon" of Hugh St. Victor: A Medieval Guide to the Arts.* Edited and translated by Jerome Taylor. New York: Columbia University Press, 1961.

Thomson, Rodney. "John of Salisbury and William of Malmesbury: Currents in Twelfth-Century Humanism." In *The World of John of Salisbury,* edited by Michael Wilks, 117–25. Oxford: Published for the Ecclesiastical History Society by Basil Blackwell, 1984.

Van Fleteren, Frederick. "*De Civitate Dei:* Miscellaneous Observations." In *The City of God: A Collection of Critical Essays,* edited by Dorothy F. Donnelly, 415–29. New York: Peter Lang, 1995.

Vickers, Brian. "Rhetoric and Poetics." In *The Cambridge History of Renaissance Philosophy,* edited by Charles B. Schmitt, Quentin Skinner, and Eckhard Kessler, 715–45. Cambridge: Cambridge University Press, 1988.

Wiles, David. "Theatre in Roman and Christian Europe." In *The Oxford Illustrated History of Theatre,* edited by John Russell Brown, 49–92. Oxford: Oxford University Press, 1995.

Zeeman, Nicolette. "The Schools Give a License to Poets." In *Criticism and Dissent in the Middle Ages,* edited by Rita Copeland, 151–80. Cambridge: Cambridge University Press, 1996.

BOOKS

Aers, David, ed. *Culture and History, 1350–1600: Essays on English Communities, Identities, and Writing.* Detroit: Wayne State University Press, 1992.

Abelard, Peter. *Opera theologica II.* Edited by E. M. Buytaert. Vol. 12 of *Corpus Christianorum Continuatio Mediaevalis.* Turnhout: Brepols, 1969.

Agobard of Lyons. *Liber de correctione antiphonarii.* In *Patrologiae Latinae,* edited by J.-P. Migne, 104:329–40. Paris: Apud Garnier Fratres, 1895.

———. *Agobardi Lugdunensis Opera Omnia.* Edited by L. van Acker. Vol. 52 of *Corpus Christianorum Continuatio Mediaevalis.* Turnhout: Brepols, 1981.

Aelred of Rievaulx. *Speculum charitatis.* In *Patrologiae Latinae,* edited by J.-P. Migne, 195:501–620. Paris: Apud Garnier Fratres, 1895.

———. *Speculum charitatis.* Translated by Randall A. Rosenfeld. In *The Sound of Medieval Song: Ornamentation and Vocal Style according to the Treatises,* by Timothy J. McGee, 23–24. Oxford: Clarendon Press, 1998.

Alan of Lille. *Anticlaudianus; or the Good and Perfect Man.* Translated by James J. Sheridan. Toronto: Pontifical Institute of Mediaeval Studies, 1973.

Althoff, Gerd, Johannes Fried, and Patrick J. Geary, eds. *Medieval Concepts of the Past: Ritual, Memory, Historiography.* Cambridge: Cambridge University Press, 2002.

Amalarius of Metz. *Epistula Amalarii ad Petrum abbatem nonantulanum: Amalarii epis-copie opera liturgica omnia*. Edited by Johannes Michael Hanssens. 3 vols. Vatican City: Biblioteca Apostolica Vaticana, 1950.

————. *Liber officialis, Amalarii episcopie opera liturgical omnia*. Edited by Johannes Michael Hanssens. 3 vols. Vatican City: Biblioteca Apostolica Vaticana, 1950.

Aristotle. [*Aristotilis de Arte*] *Poetica*. Translated by William of Moerbeke. In *Aristoteles Latinus*, vol. 33, edited by Laurentius Minio-Paluello. Brussels: Desclée de Brouwer, 1968.

Arnold, Duane W. H., and Pamela Bright, eds. *De doctrina Christiana: A Classic of Western Culture*. Notre Dame: University of Notre Dame Press, 1995.

Augustine. *The City of God against the Pagans*. Edited and translated by R. W. Dyson. Cambridge: Cambridge University Press, 1998.

————. *Concerning the Teacher*. Translated by George C. Leckie. Appleton-Century Philosophy Source-Books. New York: D. Appleton-Century Company, 1938.

————. *Confessions*. Translated by Vernon J. Bourke. Vol. 5 of *Fathers of the Church: A New Translation*. Washington, D.C.: Catholic University of America Press, 1966.

————. *De doctrina Christiana*. Edited and translated by R. P. H. Green. Oxford Early Christian Texts. Oxford: Clarendon Press, 1995.

————. *Sermones supposititios*. In *Patrologiae Latinae*, edited by J.-P. Migne, 39:1735–2354. Paris: Apud Garnier Fratres, 1895.

————. *Soliloquies*. Translated by Thomas F. Gilligan. In *Writings of Saint Augustine*, vol. 1 of *Fathers of the Church: A New Translation*. New York: Cima Publishing, 1948.

Barish, Jonas. *The Antitheatrical Prejudice*. Berkeley and Los Angeles: University of California Press, 1981.

Beacham, Richard C. *The Roman Theatre and Its Audience*. Cambridge: Harvard University Press, 1992.

Beare, William. *The Roman Stage: A Short History of Latin Drama in the Time of the Republic*. 3d ed. London: Methuen, 1964.

Beckwith, Sarah. *Christ's Body: Identity, Culture, and Society in Late Medieval Writings*. London: Routledge, 1993.

————. *Signifying God: Social Relation and Symbolic Act in the York Corpus Christi Plays*. Chicago: University of Chicago Press, 2001.

Belting, Hans. *Likeness and Presence: A History of the Image before the Era of Art*. Translated by Edmund Jephcott. Chicago: University of Chicago Press, 1994.

Bevington, David M. *Medieval Drama*. Boston: Houghton Mifflin, 1975.

Bieber, Margarete. *The History of Greek and Roman Theatre*, 2d ed. Princeton: Princeton University Press, 1961.

Black, Deborah L. *Logic and Aristotle's "Rhetoric" and "Poetics" in Medieval Arabic Philosophy*. Leiden: E. J. Brill, 1990.

Brams, J., and W. Vanhamel, eds. *Guillaume de Moerbeke: Recueil d'études à l'occasion du 700e Anniversaire de sa mort (1286)*. Ancient and Medieval Philosophy, 1st ser., vol. 7. Leuven: Leuven University Press, 1989.

Brehaut, Ernest. *An Encyclopedist of the Dark Ages: Isidore of Seville*. New York: Columbia University; Longman, Green, and Company, 1912.

Brockett, Oscar G. *History of the Theatre*. 8th ed. Boston: Allyn and Bacon, 1999.

Brownlee, Marina Scordilis, Kevin Brownlee, and Stephen G. Nichols, eds. *The New Medievalism.* Baltimore: Johns Hopkins University Press, 1991.

Buc, Philippe. *The Dangers of Ritual: Between Early Medieval Texts and Social Scientific Theory.* Princeton: Princeton University Press, 2001.

Butterworth, Charles E., trans. *Averroes' "Middle Commentary" on Aristotle's "Poetics."* Princeton: Princeton University Press, 1986.

Bynum, Caroline Walker. *The Resurrection of the Body in Western Christianity, 200–1336.* New York: Columbia University Press, 1995.

Cabaniss, Allen. *Amalarius of Metz.* Amsterdam: North-Holland, 1954.

———. *Liturgy and Literature: Selected Essays.* University: University of Alabama Press, 1970.

Campbell, Thomas P., and Clifford Davidson, eds. *The Fleury "Playbook": Essays and Studies.* Kalamazoo: Medieval Institute Publications, Western Michigan University, 1985.

Caputo, John D., and Michael J. Scanlon. *God, the Gift, and Postmodernism.* Bloomington: Indiana University Press, 1999.

Carlson, Marvin A. ed. *Theatre Semiotics: Signs of Life.* Bloomington: Indiana University Press, 1990.

———. *Theories of the Theatre: A Historical and Critical Survey, from the Greeks to the Present.* Expanded ed. Ithaca: Cornell University Press, 1993.

Carruthers, Mary J. *The Book of Memory: A Study of Memory in Medieval Culture.* Cambridge: Cambridge University Press, 1990.

Chazelle, Celia. *The Crucified God in the Carolingian Era: Theology and Art of Christ's Passion.* Cambridge: Cambridge University Press, 2001.

Chenu, M. D. *Nature, Man, and Society in the Twelfth Century: Essays on New Theological Perspectives in the Latin West.* Edited and translated by Jerome Taylor and Lester K. Little. Chicago: University of Chicago Press, 1968.

Choisselet, Daniele, and Placide Vernet, eds. *Les ecclesiastica officia Cisterciens du XXIIeme siècle la documentation Cistercienne.* Reiningue: France: La Documentacion Cistercienne, 1989.

Chupungco, Anscar J., ed. *Handbook for Liturgical Studies.* Vol. 3, *The Eucharist.* Collegeville, Minn.: Liturgical Press, 1999.

———, ed. *Handbook for Liturgical Studies.* Vol. 1, *Introduction to the Liturgy.* Collegeville, Minn.: Liturgical Press, 1997.

Clark, Robert, ed. *Ritual, Performance, Culture: Papers by C. Clifford Flanigan, His Students, and Colleagues.* Auckland: Wim Husken, forthcoming.

Colish, Marcia L. *Medieval Foundations of the Western Intellectual Tradition, 400–1400.* New Haven: Yale University Press, 1997.

———. *The Mirror of Language: A Study in the Medieval Theory of Knowledge.* New Haven: Yale University Press, 1968.

Connerton, Paul. *How Societies Remember.* Cambridge: Cambridge University Press, 1989.

Conrad of Hirsau. *Speculum virginum.* Edited by Jutta Seyfarth. Vol. 5 of *Corpus Christianorum Continuatio Mediaevalis.* Turnhout: Brepols, 1990.

Copeland, Rita. *Rhetoric, Hermeneutics, and Translation in the Middle Ages: Academic Traditions and Vernacular Texts.* Cambridge: Cambridge University Press, 1991.

————, ed. *Criticism and Dissent in the Middle Ages.* Cambridge: Cambridge University Press, 1996.

Csapo, Eric, and Miller, Margaret C., eds. *The Origins of Theatre in Ancient Greece and Beyond: From Ritual to Drama.* Cambridge: Cambridge University Press, forthcoming.

Curtius, Ernst Robert. *European Literature and the Latin Middle Ages.* Translated by Willard R. Trask. New York: Pantheon Books, 1953.

Dahiyat, Ismail M. *Avicenna's Commentary on the "Poetics" of Aristotle: A Critical Study with an Annotated Translation of the Text.* Leiden: E. J. Brill, 1974.

Davidson, Clifford, ed. *Gesture in Medieval Drama and Art.* Kalamazoo: Medieval Institute Publications, Western Michigan University, 2001.

Davidson, Clifford, and John H. Stroupe, eds. *Drama in the Middle Ages: Comparative and Critical Essays.* AMS Studies in the Middle Ages, no. 18. New York: AMS Press, 1991.

Deacon Florus of Lyons. *Opuscula adversus Amalarium.* In *Patrologiae Latinae,* edited by J.-P. Migne, 119:71–94. Paris: Apud Garnier Fratres, 1895.

Diamond, Elin. *Unmaking Mimesis: Essays on Feminism and Theater.* London: Routledge, 1997.

Donnelly, Dorothy F., ed. *The City of God: A Collection of Critical Essays.* New York: Peter Lang, 1995.

Dronke, Peter. *Poetic Individuality in the Middle Ages: New Departures in Poetry, 1000–1150.* Oxford: Clarendon Press, 1970.

————, ed. *A History of Twelfth-Century Western Philosophy.* Cambridge: Cambridge University Press, 1988.

Enders, Jody. *The Medieval Theater of Cruelty: Rhetoric, Memory, Violence.* Ithaca: Cornell University Press, 1999.

————. *Rhetoric and the Origins of Medieval Drama.* Ithaca: Cornell University Press, 1992.

Flint, Valerie I. J., ed. *Ideas in the Medieval West: Texts and Their Contexts.* London: Variorum Reprints, 1988.

Florus. *Opuscula adversus Amalarium I and II.* In *Patrologiae Latinae,* edited by J.-P. Migne, 119:71–80. Paris: Apud Garnier Fratres, 1895.

Flynn, William T. *Medieval Music as Medieval Exegesis.* Lanham, Md.: Scarecrow Press, 1999.

Fontaine, Jacques. *Isidore de Séville: Genèse et originalité de la culture hispanique au temps de Wisigoths.* Turnhout: Brepols, 2000.

French, Dorothea. "Christian Emperors and Pagan Spectacles: The Secularization of the 'Ludi,' A.D. 382–525." Ph.D. diss., University of California, Berkeley, 1985.

Fuchs, Elinor. *The Death of Character: Perspectives on Theater after Modernism.* Bloomington: Indiana University Press, 1996.

Gardiner, Harold C. *Mysteries' End: An Investigation of the Last Days of the Medieval Religious Stage.* New Haven: Yale University Press, 1946. Reprint, [Hamden, Conn.]: Archon Books, 1967.

Geary, Patrick J., ed. *Authors of the Middle Ages.* Vol. 2, nos. 5–6, *Historical and Religious Writers of the Latin West.* Aldershot: Variorum, Ashgate, 1995.

Gerhoh of Reichersberg. *De Spectaculis Theatricis in Ecclesia Dei Exhibitis.* In *The*

Medieval European Stage, 500–1550, edited by William Tydeman, et al. Cambridge: Cambridge University Press, 2001.

Gibson, Gail McMurray. *The Theater of Devotion: East Anglian Drama and Society in the Late Middle Ages.* Chicago: University of Chicago Press, 1989.

Gilbert of Poitiers. *De Trinitate liber primus: The Commentaries on Boethius.* Edited by Nikolaus M. Häring. Toronto: Pontifical Institute of Mediaeval Studies, 1966.

Glorieux, Palémon. *La faculté des arts et ses maitres au XIIIe siècle.* Paris: J. Vrin, 1971.

Grabmann, Martin. *Die Geschichte der Scholastischen Methode.* Freiburg im Breisgau: Herdersche Verlagshandlung, 1911.

Gundisalvi, Domingo. *Dominicus Gundissalinus: De divisione philosophiae.* Edited by Ludwig Baur. Beiträge zur Geschichte der Philosophie und Theologie des Mittelalters, vol. 4, nos. 2–3. Münster: Aschendorffschen Buchhandlung, 1903.

Hardison, O. B., Jr. *Christian Rite and Christian Drama in the Middle Ages: Essays on the Origin and Early History of Modern Drama.* Baltimore: Johns Hopkins University Press, 1965.

Hardison, O. B., Jr., Alex Preminger, and Kevin Kerrane, eds. *Medieval Literary Criticism: Translations and Interpretations.* New York: Frederick Ungar, 1987.

Harris, John Wesley. *Medieval Theatre in Context: An Introduction.* London: Routledge, 1992.

Hart, Kevin. *The Trespass of the Sign: Deconstruction, Theology, and Philosophy.* 2d ed. New York: Fordham University Press, 2000.

Hermannus Alemannus [Herman the German]. *Poetria Ibinrosdin.* In *Aristoteles Latinus,* vol. 33, edited by Laurentius Minio-Paluello and Gérard Verbeke. Bruges: Desclée de Brouwer, 1953–.

Hiley, David. *Western Plainchant: A Handbook.* Oxford: Clarendon Press, 1993.

Holsinger, Bruce W. *Music, Body, and Desire in Medieval Culture: Hildegard of Bingen to Chaucer.* Stanford: Stanford University Press, 2001.

Honorius Augustodunensis. *De animae exsilio et patria.* In *Patrologiae Latinae,* edited by J.-P. Migne, 172:1241–46. Paris: Apud Garnier Fratres, 1895.

———. *Gemma animae.* In *Patrologiae Latinae,* edited by J.-P. Migne, 172:541–738. Paris: Apud Garnier Fratres, 1895.

Hugh of St. Victor. *The "Didascalicon" of Hugh St. Victor: A Medieval Guide to the Arts.* Edited and translated by Jerome Taylor. New York: Columbia University Press, 1961.

Hunt, R. W., W. A. Pantin, and R. W. Southern, eds. *Studies in Medieval History Presented to Frederick Maurice Powicke.* Oxford: Clarendon Press, 1948.

Isidore of Seville. *Differentiarum.* In *Patrologiae Latinae,* edited by J.-P. Migne, 83:1–98. Paris: Apud Garnier Fratres, 1895.

———. *Etymologiarum sive originum.* Edited by W. M. Lindsay. 2 vols. Oxford: Clarendon Press, 1911.

———. *Sancti Isidori episcopi hispalensis: De ecclesiasticis officiis.* Edited by Christopher M. Lawson. Vol. 113 of *Corpus Christianorum Series Latina.* Turnhout: Brepols, 1989.

Jaeger, C. Stephen. *The Envy of Angels: Cathedral Schools and Social Ideals in Medieval Europe, 950–1200.* Philadelphia: University of Pennsylvania Press, 1994.

Jeffery, Peter. *Re-envisioning Past Musical Cultures: Ethnomusicology in the Study of Gregorian Chant.* Chicago: University of Chicago Press, 1992.

John of Salisbury. *Ioannis Saresberiensis: Policraticus I–IV.* Edited by K. S. B. Keats-Rohan. Vol. 118 of *Corpus Christianorum Continuatio Mediaevalis.* Turnhout: Brepols, 1993.

Jolivet, Jean, and Roshdi Rashed, eds. *Etudes sur Avicenne.* Paris: Société d'édition Les Belles Lettres, 1984.

Jungmann, Josef. *The Mass of the Roman Rite.* Translated by Francis A. Brunner. 2 vols. New York: Benziger Brothers, 1951–55.

Kelly, Henry Ansgar. *Ideas and Forms of Tragedy from Aristotle to the Middle Ages.* Cambridge: Cambridge University Press, 1993.

Kemal, Salim. *The "Poetics" of Alfarabi and Avicenna.* Leiden: E. J. Brill, 1991.

Kitto, H. D. F. *Greek Tragedy.* 2d ed. London: Methuen, 1950.

Kobialka, Michal. *This Is My Body: Representational Practices in the Early Middle Ages.* Ann Arbor: University of Michigan Press, 1999.

———, ed. *Of Borders and Thresholds: Theatre History, Practice, and Theory.* Minneapolis: University of Minnesota Press, 1999.

Kretzmann, Norman, Anthony Kenny, and Jan Pinborg, eds. *The Cambridge History of Later Medieval Philosophy: From the Rediscovery of Aristotle to the Disintegration of Scholasticism, 1100–1600.* Cambridge: Cambridge University Press, 1982.

Lakoff, George. *Women, Fire, and Dangerous Things: What Categories Reveal about the Mind.* Chicago: University of Chicago Press, 1987.

Larson-Miller, Lizette, ed. *Medieval Liturgy: A Book of Essays.* New York: Garland, 1997.

Leyerle, Blake. *Theatrical Shows and Ascetic Lives: John Chrysostom's Attack on Spiritual Marriage.* Berkeley and Los Angeles: University of California Press, 2001.

Liebeschütz, Hans. *Mediaeval Humanism in the Life and Writings of John of Salisbury.* London: Warburg Institute University of London, 1950.

Lillie, Eva Louise, and Nils Holger Petersen, eds. *Liturgy and the Arts in the Middle Ages: Studies in Honour of C. Clifford Flanigan.* Copenhagen: Museum Tusculanum Press, University of Copenhagen, 1996.

MacFarlane, Katherine Nell. *Isidore of Seville on the Pagan Gods ("Origines" VIII.11).* Transactions of the American Philosophical Society, vol. 70, no. 3. Philadelphia: American Philosophical Society, 1980.

MacMullen, Ramsay. *Christianity and Paganism in the Fourth to Eighth Centuries.* New Haven: Yale University Press, 1997.

Marenbon, John. *Early Medieval Philosophy (480–1150): An Introduction.* London: Routledg & Kegan Paul, 1983.

Markus, Robert A., ed. *Augustine: A Collection of Critical Essays.* Garden City: Anchor Books, 1972.

Maurus, Rabanus. *De universo.* In *Patrologiae Latinae,* edited by J.-P. Migne, 111:1–614. Paris: Apud Garnier Fratres, 1895.

McGee, Timothy J. *The Sound of Medieval Song: Ornamentation and Vocal Style according to the Treatises.* Translations from Latin by Randall A. Rosenfeld. Oxford: Clarendon Press, 1998.

McGinn, Bernard, and John Meyendorff, with Jean Leclercq, eds. *Christian Spirituality: Origins to the Twelfth Century.* New York: Crossroad, 1985.

McKinnon, James W. *The Advent Project: The Later-Seventh-Century Creation of the Roman Mass Proper.* Berkeley and Los Angeles: University of California Press, 2000.

McKitterick, Rosamond, ed. *Carolingian Culture: Emulation and Innovation.* Cambridge: Cambridge University Press, 1994.

Mews, Constant J. *The Lost Love Letters of Heloise and Abelard: Perceptions of Dialogue in Twelfth-Century France.* New York: St. Martin's Press, 1999.

———, ed. *Listen Daughter: The "Speculum virginum" and the Formation of Religious Women in the Middle Ages.* New York: Palgrave, 2001.

Milbank, John. *The Word Made Strange: Theology, Language, Culture.* Cambridge: Blackwell Publishers, 1997.

Minnis, A. J., and A. Brian Scott, with David Wallace, eds. *Medieval Literary Theory and Criticism, c. 1100–c. 1375: The Commentary Tradition.* Oxford: Clarendon Press, 1988.

Moreh, Shmuel. *Live Theatre and Dramatic Literature in the Medieval Arab World.* New York: New York University Press, 1992.

Morrison, Karl Frederick. *I Am You: The Hermeneutics of Empathy in Western Literature, Theology, and Art.* Princeton: Princeton University Press, 1988.

———. *The Mimetic Tradition of Reform in the West.* Princeton: Princeton University Press, 1982.

Nederman, Cary J. *John of Salisbury.* Tempe: Medieval and Renaissance Texts and Studies, forthcoming 2005.

———. *Medieval Aristotelianism and Its Limits: Classical Traditions in Moral and Political Philosophy, 12th–15th Centuries.* Aldershot: Variorum, Ashgate, 1997.

———, ed. and trans. *Policraticus: Of the Frivolities of Courtiers and the Footprints of Philosophers,* by John of Salisbury. Cambridge: Cambridge University Press, 1990.

Nelson, Janet L. *The Frankish World, 750–900.* London: Hambledon Press, 1996.

New Catholic Study Bible. St. Jerome edition. Nashville: Thomas Nelson Publishers, 1985.

Nicoll, Allardyce. *Masks, Mimes, and Miracles: Studies in the Popular Theatre.* London: G. C. Harrap, 1931.

O'Connell, Robert J. *St. Augustine's "Confessions": The Odyssey of the Soul.* 2d ed. New York: Fordham University Press, 1989.

Ogden, Dunbar H. *The Staging of Drama in the Medieval Church.* Newark: University of Delaware Press, 2002.

Ovitt, George, Jr. *The Restoration of Perfection: Labor and Technology in Medieval Culture.* New Brunswick: Rutgers University Press, 1987.

Peters, F. E. *Aristotle and the Arabs: The Aristotelian Tradition in Islam.* New York: New York University Press, 1968.

Pickard-Cambridge, Arthur Wallace. *Dithyramb, Tragedy, and Comedy.* 2d ed., revised by T. B. L. Webster. Oxford: Clarendon Press, 1962.

———. *The Dramatic Festivals of Athens.* 2d ed., revised by John Gould and D. M. Lewis. London: Oxford University Press, 1968.

Pickstock, Catherine. *After Writing: On the Liturgical Consummation of Philosophy.* Oxford: Blackwell Publishers, 1997.

Pike, Joseph Brown, trans. *Frivolities of Courtiers and Footprints of Philosophers, Being a Translation of the First, Second, and Third Books and Selections from the Seventh and Eighth Books of the "Policraticus" of John of Salisbury.* Minneapolis: University of Minnesota Press, 1938.

Radulphus de Longo Campo. In *Anticlaudianum Alani Commentum.* Edited by Jan

Sulowski. Warsaw: Zakad Narodowy Imienia Ossoliskich Wydawnictwo Polskiej Akademii Nauk, 1972.

Remigius of Auxerre. *De tribus epistolis liber.* In *Patrologiae Latinae,* edited by J.-P. Migne, 121:985–1068. Paris: Apud Garnier Fratres, 1895.

———. *Commentum in Martianum Capellam. Libri I and II.* vol. 1. Edited with an introduction by Cora E. Lutz. Leiden: E. J. Brill, 1962–65.

———. *Saeculi noni auctoris in Boetii Consolationem Philosophiae commentarius.* Edited by Edmund Taite Silk. Papers and Monographs of the American Academy in Rome, vol. 9. Rome: American Academy in Rome, 1935.

Rubin, Miri. *Corpus Christi: The Eucharist in Late Medieval Culture.* Cambridge: Cambridge University Press, 1991.

Schechner, Richard. *Performance Studies: An Introduction.* London: Routledge, 2002.

Scherb, Victor I. *Staging Faith: East Anglian Drama in the Later Middle Ages.* Madison: Fairleigh Dickinson University Press, 2001.

Schnusenberg, Christine. *Das Verhältnis von Kirche und Theater: Dargestellt au ausgewählten Schriften der Kirchenväter und liturgischen Texten bis auf Amalarius von Metz.* Bern: Peter Lang, 1981.

Schmitt, Charles B., Quentin Skinner, and Eckhard Kessler, eds. *The Cambridge History of Renaissance Philosophy.* Cambridge: Cambridge University Press, 1988.

Scodel, Ruth. *Theater and Society in the Classical World.* Ann Arbor: University of Michigan Press, 1993.

Simon, Eckehard, ed. *The Theatre of Medieval Europe: New Research in Early Drama.* Cambridge: Cambridge University Press, 1991.

Slater, William J., ed. *Roman Theater and Society.* Ann Arbor: University of Michigan Press, 1995.

Southern, R. W. *Scholastic Humanism and the Unification of Europe.* Vol. 1, *Foundations.* Oxford: Blackwell Publishers, 1995.

Sponsler, Claire. *Drama and Resistance: Bodies, Goods, and Theatricality in Late Medieval England.* Minneapolis: University of Minnesota Press, 1997.

Steck, Wolfgang. *Der liturgiker Amalarius: Eine Quellenkritische Untersuchung zu Leben und Werk eines Theologen der Karolingerzeit.* Münchener theologische studien, Historische Abteilung, 1st ser., no. 35. Ottilien: EOS Verlag Erzabtei, 2000.

Stump, Eleonore, and Norman Kretzmann, eds. *The Cambridge Companion to Augustine.* Cambridge: Cambridge University Press, 2001.

Traube, Ludwig, ed. *Quellen und Untersuchungen zur lateinischen Philologie des Mittelalters.* Vol. 1. Munich: C. H. Beck'sche Verlagbuchhandlung, 1906.

Tydeman, William. *The Theatre in the Middle Ages: Western European Stage Conditions, c. 800–1576.* Cambridge: Cambridge University Press, 1978.

Tydeman, William, et al., eds. *The Medieval European Stage, 500–1500.* Cambridge: Cambridge University Press, 2001.

van Deusen, Nancy. *The Harp and the Soul: Essays in Medieval Music.* Lewiston, N.Y.: Edwin Mellen Press, 1989.

Vince, Ronald W. *Ancient and Medieval Theatre: A Historiographical Handbook.* Westport, Conn.: Greenwood Press, 1984.

von Balthasar, Hans Urs. *Theo-Drama: Theological Dramatic Theory.* Vol. 4, *The Action.* Translated by Graham Harrison. San Francisco: Ignatius Press, 1994.

Warning, Rainer. *The Ambivalences of Medieval Religious Drama*. Translated by Steven Rendall. Stanford: Stanford University Press, 2001.

Webb, Clement Charles Julian. *Ioannis Saresberiensis episcopi Carnotensis Policratici*. Oxford: Clarendon Press, 1909. Reprint, New York: Arno Press, 1979.

Whitney, Elspeth. *Paradise Restored: The Mechanical Arts from Antiquity through the Thirteenth Century*. Transactions of the American Philosophical Society, vol. 80, no. 1. Philadelphia: American Philosophical Society, 1990.

Wickham, Glynne William Gladstone. *The Medieval Theatre*. New York: St. Martin's Press, 1974.

Wilks, Michael, ed. *The World of John of Salisbury*. Oxford: Published for the Ecclesiastical History Society by Basil Blackwell, 1984.

Winkler, John J., and Froma I. Zietlin, eds. *Nothing to Do with Dionysus? Athenian Drama in Its Social Context*. Princeton: Princeton University Press, 1990.

Young, Karl. *The Drama of the Medieval Church*. 2 vols. Oxford: Clarendon Press, 1933.

Index